JOSHUA- VICTORIOUS BY FAITH

JOSHUA-
VICTORIOUS
BY FAITH

By Theodore H. Epp

Founder and Director
of Back to the Bible Broadcast

$1.50 each

order from

BACK TO THE BIBLE BROADCAST

Box 233   Lincoln, Nebraska 68501

25,000 printed to date—1968
(8469—15M—118)

Printed in the United States of America

Foreword

By today's standards Joshua should have long been on the retirement list when he was appointed Israel's leader. He was 85 years of age at the time but, like Moses at 80, was of unusual vigor of mind, body and spirit.

In addition to his administrative tasks Joshua was general of the army. Six years of rigorous campaigns followed his appointment as leader until the land was subdued from Mount Seir in the south to Mount Hermon in the north. He continued to serve Israel until his death at the age of 110 (Josh. 24:29).

The course of Joshua's life is quite fully disclosed in the Bible, and it shows his conduct was not marred by some special sin as were some of Israel's other leaders. He had weaknesses, but he lived on a high spiritual level. It is very evident that the principle he stated at the end of his life was one that he had followed most of his days. He said, "As for me and my house, we will serve the Lord." Thus Joshua's record is that of a man who actively sought God's control for his life and willingly followed wherever God led.

The studies in this book were originally given as messages over the special international radio network of the Back to the Bible Broadcast. Incidents from Joshua's life and his experiences with Israel serve as illustrations and guides with regard to the life of victory in Christ, the kind of life that Joshua so well exemplified.

—John I. Paton
Literature Editor

CONTENTS

Chapter One

JOSHUA'S INTRODUCTION TO FAITH

In some ways there is more to be learned of practical Christian living from the lives of individuals in the Bible than from any other source. This has been true in my own case. After learning the teaching and principles of the Word of God from the great doctrinal sections, I have found how these work out in a practical way by studying the experiences of Bible characters. We sometimes get the feeling that the men and women of the Bible were superbeings who reached levels of spiritual living to which we cannot aspire. But such is not the case. They were human as we are human, perhaps the only difference being that they believed God and followed Him in such a way that He was able to reveal His strength in and through them.

The man whose life we will now study is Joshua, a person of faith and courage. These two characteristics made him a man of action. He was submissive to God, obedient to the Word of God and faithful in meeting the obligations and responsibilities placed upon him. I must add here, however, that these studies are concerned with Joshua only in part. The major portion of them are related to Joshua and Israel in their conquest of Canaan. This second aspect comes into focus when we take up the spiritual lessons found in the Book of Joshua.

Joshua, in an outstanding way, exhibits many of the things that will help us in our own spiritual lives. We often consider the matter of the victorious Christian life and wonder how we can attain it. Joshua's life furnishes us with many fine illustrations of how this can be done.

The great work for which Joshua is especially remembered was his leadership of Israel in their conquering

9

the land of Canaan. There were, however, preliminary stages in his life which laid the foundation for his able leadership after Moses died.

The life of Joshua can be divided into three stages. The first stage, covering some 40 years, he spent as a slave in Egypt. At the same time the foundation of his spiritual life was laid, for though he was a slave to Pharaoh, he was also the servant of God. When the Israelites left Egypt under the leadership of Moses, Joshua became his minister or understudy. This was the second stage of Joshua's life and it lasted another 40 years. The third stage, in which he was leader of the children of Israel, possibly covered some 25 more years. In all these phases of his life we find him to be a victorious believer, one who though not perfect, had a high degree of success as a spiritual warrior. He had his failures and these will help us see why we sometimes fail. We will also find out the secret of his consistently high quality of spiritual life.

In the earliest stage of Joshua's life, as we have seen, he was a slave in Egypt. He was born in slavery. It was in this capacity that he learned obedience and submission to a hard taskmaster. This illustrates a spiritual situation that we ourselves were in when we were slaves to the world and to the flesh and to the Devil. At that time we, too, were under a hard taskmaster. Satan is never so pleased as when he can impress on human beings some of the hardness of his own rule.

When he was about the age of 40, Joshua experienced glorious deliverance from Egypt. We do not have a great deal of information concerning his life at this period, but what follows seems to be a safe conclusion. According to I Chronicles 7:27 Joshua was the eldest son in his family. This is significant, for the final plague that God sent against Egypt was the death of the firstborn. The Israelites were not exempted from this judgment save only as they obeyed God's requirement and slew a lamb and sprinkled the blood on the doorposts of their houses. This could have brought some anxious moments to Joshua since he was the oldest in the family; and this could well have been one of the great tests of his faith in God. We must remember also that this whole episode of the passover symbolizes for us our being spared from the judgment of sin upon us because God's Son died in our place.

War With Amalek

So far we have been left largely to conjecture with regard to Joshua. The first time he comes into clear focus in the Bible is in Exodus 17:9. The incident related in this portion took place possibly within the first year after the Israelites had left the land of Egypt. They found themselves opposed by Amalek, a ruthless and relentless foe of Israel.

The record is: "Then came Amalek, and fought with Israel in Rephidim. And Moses said unto Joshua, Choose us out men, and go out, fight with Amalek: tomorrow I will stand on the top of the hill with the rod of God in mine hand" (Ex. 17:8,9). This as we have said is the first mention of Joshua, and there is always something interesting about the first mention of a person or thing or object in the Bible. Invariably in that first mention there is supplied to us the key to the person's life, or if it is an object, the key to its significance.

Such is the case with Joshua here. He had learned to obey and was thus qualified now to command. This is a very important principle. There are persons who would like to have authority; they like to supervise others, but they themselves have never learned to take orders.

This is one thing Joshua had learned apparently while he was a slave. Then he further learned it as God's minister under Moses. Joshua's information and his orders came personally through Moses. It is as a warrior that Joshua first appears to us, a man of war. This first battle he fought was no ordinary one and illustrates the kind of warfare he faced all through his life. It was not only a physical battle, but a spiritual battle also. It was not fought and won by mere physical effort, but on the basis of faith. This forms a unique background for us to study spiritual warfare as illustrated both in the life of Joshua and in the Book of Joshua.

As we have already remarked, Amalek was Israel's enemy at this time. It got its name from Amalek, the grandson of Esau. Those who are familiar with the Old Testament know that Esau was the twin brother of Jacob, and that Esau was the older of the two. Thus, according to the usual customs of inheritance, Esau was heir to the family birthright. Now, the birthright was not necessarily confined to material or physical property plus headship of the family. In the case of Isaac's family it included priesthood so that there was a strong spiritual aspect to it. For any person to assume such a role, however, required that he himself be of a spiritual mind and nature. Esau was far from this and despised his birthright. He was more interested in things for his body and his flesh nature than he was for the things of God. He sold his birthright to his brother Jacob for a serving of boiled lentils.

With this background we can understand how Amalek becomes in this incident a type of the old self-life, the flesh life. Israel in turn is a type of the spiritual Christ-life, and the battle therefore represents a spiritual battle, fought and won on a spiritual basis.

Joshua did as he was instructed and led the armies of Israel against Amalek. He as leader went out into the front lines to fight the enemy. Moses, on the other hand, entered into a spiritual warfare on behalf of Israel. It is clear from the history given us that Moses' intercession was essential to Joshua gaining the victory. This is true with regard to our own lives. If we are to be victorious in the spiritual warfare we are engaged in, we must recognize our dependence upon the One who makes intercession for us.

Joshua obeyed Moses and fought with the armies of Israel against Amalek. "And Moses, Aaron, and Hur went up to the top of the hill. And it came to pass, when Moses held up his hand, that Israel prevailed: and when he let down his hand, Amalek prevailed. But Moses' hands were heavy; and they took a stone, and put it under him, and he sat thereon; and Aaron and Hur stayed up his hands, the one on the one side, and the other on the other side; and his hands were steady until the going down of the sun. And Joshua discomfited Amalek and his people with the edge of the sword" (Ex. 17:10-13). Joshua fought the physical battle in the valley, but the spiritual battle was fought on the mountaintop in the place of intercession. Joshua obeyed, Moses interceded, so by prayer and faith and physical combat, the battle was won.

Our Spiritual Heritage

We, too, have a spiritual heritage. We read in Hebrews 7:25: "Wherefore he [the Lord Jesus Christ] is able also to save them to the uttermost that come unto God by him, seeing he ever liveth to make intercession for them." This saving to the uttermost does not merely mean saving from condemnation. That is only one part of salvation. It also includes saving daily from the enemy—the world, the flesh and the Devil—as our Saviour makes intercession for us.

In his Letter to the Ephesians the Apostle Paul described for us the exceeding greatness of God's power to us, a power which was wrought in Christ when He was raised from the dead. Then He ascended to the right hand of the Father. To Christ was given a Name above all principalities and powers and might and dominion This means He was given authority over all these principalities and powers when He was seated in the heavenlies. He is also the Head of the Body, the Church of which you and I as believers in Him are members.

Then we are told in chapter 2 of Ephesians that we have been raised together with Christ to sit with Him in the heavenly places. Furthermore, He has blessed us with all spiritual blessings in these same heavenly places. This is our position in Him. So, as Joshua was fighting the battle in the valley, Moses was making intercession to the Father. As Moses continued to pray, the battle was finally won. This pictures what is taking place now on our behalf. The Lord Jesus is at the right hand of the Father today praying for us that we might be victorious. Potential victory is ever held out as long as we trust Him and go forth saying "no" to self, to the flesh and to the Devil.

Israel's victory over Amalek required two things: the aggressive warfare of Israel led by Joshua and the faithful intercession of Moses. The one without the other was not sufficient. So it is in our spiritual warfare. We have the assurance of the intercession of our Saviour; our responsibility is to walk in faith and obedience to the Word under the control of the Holy Spirit and fight the fight of faith. With this combination victory is certain.

A Threefold Enemy

We have already pointed out that the Bible teaches the Christian's enemy is a threefold one: the flesh, the world and the Devil. The flesh is the old self-life, the fallen nature in each one of us. The world is the world of mankind around us alienated from God and opposed to His rulership. The Devil or Satan includes also the fallen angels whom he controls.

The basis for our victory over this threefold enemy has already been laid for us in Chirst. With regard to the flesh we read in Romans 6: "Knowing this, that our old man is crucified with him, that the body of sin might be destroyed, that henceforth we should not serve sin. For he that is dead is freed from sin" (vv. 6,7).

With regard to the world we read in Galatians 6:14: "But God forbid that I should glory, save in the cross of our Lord Jesus Christ, by whom the world is crucified unto me, and I unto the world." This is why the Lord could tell us in John 16:33: "In the world ye shall have tribulation; but be of good cheer; I have overcome the world." Further light is thrown on this subject in I John 5:4,5: "For whatsoever is born of God overcometh the world: and this is the victory that overcometh the world, even our faith. Who is he that overcometh the world, but he that believeth that Jesus is the Son of God?"

Our victory over the flesh and the world is based on what Christ has done for us. This is true also with regard to our victory over Satan and his evil forces in the heavenlies. According to Ephesians 2:5,6 we have been seated together with Christ in heavenly places. We are seated with Christ who has been given a place and position that is above all the principalities and powers. Thus, though Satan is the prince of the power of the air, he is nevertheless subject to Christ. We hold a position of victory through being identified with Christ in His exalted position.

The defeat of Satan can also be traced to the cross of Christ. Our Lord said in John 12:31: "Now is the judgment of this world: now shall the prince of this world be cast out." That the cross was in our Saviour's mind when He said this is evident from the next two verses: "And I, if I be lifted up from the earth, will draw all men unto me. This he said, signifying what death he should die."

What Canaan Typifies

In the course of studies before us we will investigate a large number of incidents related to Joshua and Israel in the land of Canaan and will show how these relate to the Christian's daily warfare against the flesh, the world and the Devil. Canaan, the promised land for the Israelites, is not a type of heaven as some have thought and as some hymns portray it. Rather it is a type of the Christian's battle against sin and his victory over it as he seeks to live for the Lord. Canaan was a scene of conflict, not of complete peace and rest as heaven will be. The nations in Canaan become types of the principalities and powers we read about in Ephesians 6:12 where the Apostle tells us: "We wrestle not against flesh and blood, but against principalities, against powers, against the rulers of the darkness of this world, against spiritual wickedness in high places."

When Joshua led the people of Israel into Canaan, he and they not only had to overcome the human leaders and their armies in the Land of Promise, but also the evil spiritual forces under the direction of Satan who were the actual rulers of these heathen kings.

I have drawn more spiritual lessons for myself and the Back to the Bible Broadcast from Joshua's experiences and the Book of Joshua and its New Testament counterpart, Ephesians, than any other person or portions in the Bible. We as believers are warned to put on the whole armor of God, according to the Book of Ephesians, if we are going to enter victoriously into spiritual warfare against the powers of Satan. If we are to avoid a stalemate in our Christian lives, an experience similar to Israel's 40 years in the desert, we will have to choose to become spiritually aggressive.

Many of us tend to become defensive and hold an attitude of "Don't do this," and "Don't do that." There are things a Christian ought not to do but we would have fewer problems with the negative side of our Christian lives if we went on a spiritual offensive with Christ as our Armor and Victor.

Entering into offensive warfare is suggested under another figure of speech employed by our Saviour when He said: "Ye have not chosen me, but I have chosen you . . . that ye should go and bring forth fruit, and that your fruit should remain" (John 15:16).

We as believers need encouragement to move out in aggressive spiritual warfare, because we are inclined to look on the Christian life as a hard life to live. Many Christians, though delivered from their spiritual Egypt, still live in bondage to the old life. Theirs is a spiritual childhood in which they try to live the overcoming life by employing the methods of the world. When the Israelites were in Egypt they had no choice as to how they could live. They were under bondage to the Egyptians and had to submit. But there is no call for us as believers to be enslaved to the world.

There is another parallel in the experience of Israel and Christians. While the Israelites were in the desert, they were largely controlled by the flesh or the old self-life. Consequently they were always on the defensive. Murmuring and quarreling characterized their experience. A Christian who is marked by the same qualities or a church that is noted for its murmuring and quarreling is not on the offensive for the Lord. Theirs is a desert-life experience.

The third aspect of Israel's experience was when they entered the land. Then they faced the need of entering into offensive warfare. They came in as invaders with the objective of conquering. It was necessary that they destroy the enemy if they were to take possession of the land for themselves and their posterity.

We need to ask ourselves where we stand with regard to these three experiences. Are we still in the world enduring its bondage? Are we caught up in worldliness? Or are we in a desert experience in which we are on the defensive, making no headway? Or have we entered into spiritual warfare seeking to take possession of the things the Lord has for us?

Successful Second Fiddle

We have considered the first mention of Joshua and saw that it had to do with his leading the armies of Israel against the Amalekites. He is mentioned for the second time in Exodus 24:13 where he is described as a minister who waited on Moses. The words are, "And Moses rose up, and his minister Joshua: And Moses went up into the mount of God." In the language of our day Joshua played second fiddle to Moses. This is a most difficult position for anyone to master. He was near the top, yet not quite at the top. Yet Joshua held this position successfully for 40 years in the desert.

When he became Moses' successor, he again took the place of second in command. Only this time he was under a heavenly Master. Regardless of the sequence of command above him, Joshua served the Lord well. In fact, there was part of the time when he served two masters God and Moses, and he did this successfully and commendably.

Perhaps our first reaction is to say that such would be impossible. But this is not impossible when one is first submissive to the Lord and utterly devoted to His cause.

Few leaders ever pass a test of this nature with

distinction. Yet it is the only place where we can serve two masters successfully. Here is what the Scriptures say concerning Joshua in this regard: "As the Lord commanded Moses his servant, so did Moses command Joshua, and so did Joshua; he left nothing undone of all that the Lord commanded Moses" (Josh. 11:15). What a remarkable epitaph for a man to have. God commanded Moses, and Moses commanded Joshua and Joshua did exactly what Moses told him to do. It is clear from this that in obeying Moses, Joshua obeyed God. This was how he could successfully obey two masters.

Joshua and Aaron

Joshua's first responsibilities were in some respects not as great as those of Aaron who was made high priest to the nation of Israel. He was also right hand man to Moses and spokesman or prophet to him. Nevertheless Joshua was attached to the person of Moses in a special way and may even have looked after many of Moses' physical comforts.

As minister to Moses, Joshua went with him to the top of Mount Sinai where Moses received the Law and the blueprint for the tabernacle. This was unquestionably one of the greatest events in the life of Moses, for he was face to face with God for 40 days on this occasion. Aaron and his sons and several of the elders of Israel accompanied Moses and Joshua part of the way. Then Moses and Joshua went on together toward Sinai. As they approached the summit, a cloud covered it for six days and on the seventh day God called Moses to come up into His presence in the midst of the cloud. Joshua was not allowed to enter the cloud, but had to wait for 40 days for his leader to return.

Those must have been lonely days. During all that time he did not so much as catch a glimpse of Moses. The people of Israel down below in the valley saw the cloud and the fire and, no doubt, were frightened by it all. But Joshua was absolutely alone. Yet such periods of being alone can be very precious. They have been to me. I sometimes get away for a weekend if I can, and go to a motel or cabin somewhere just to be alone with God. I take my Bible and some books from my library for study and meditation.

Joshua was being prepared to eventually succeed Moses, so this time of meditation would be very beneficial. At this time, however, God spoke directly only to Moses and not to Joshua. This must have made his time of waiting a test of his faith, patience and fidelity.

Though at this time in his growth and development Joshua possibly held a lesser place than that of Aaron, it is very evident from the biblical record that Aaron did not have the spiritual caliber of the younger man. Moses, before he went on to the summit of Mount Sinai, left Aaron in charge of Israel but he failed God in this responsibility. When nothing was heard from Moses for several days, the people of Israel came to Aaron and said, "Up, make us gods, which shall go before us; as for this Moses, the man that brought us up out of the land of Egypt, we wot not what is become of him. And Aaron said unto them, Break off the golden earrings, which are in the ears of your wives, of your sons, and of your daughters, and bring them unto me" (Ex. 32:1,2). Then from these golden earrings Aaron made the people a golden calf.

The man who was to be high priest for Israel gave in to the demands of the people to make a golden calf for their worship. He should never have succumbed to such pressure regardless of how strong it was.

After 40 days Moses and Joshua came down from the mountain. When they came into the valley where the camp was located, they heard the noise of the revelry that marked the calf worship. After seeing what had happened, Moses asked Aaron: "What did this people unto thee, that thou hast brought so great a sin upon them?" (Ex. 32:21). Aaron pleaded with Moses not to get angry with him, then put the blame back on the people, thereby indicating a weakness in his own character. He did not show the backbone Joshua exhibited a little later when the same multitude wanted to stone him. He stood his ground and would not give in. Joshua was tested and found to be a vessel unto honor, sanctified and fit for the Master's use.

In righteous anger over the false worship Moses cleaned house. He took the golden calf and burned it and ground it to a fine powder. He then cast the powder into water and made the people drink it.

He also took the tabernacle or tent that marked the judicial center of the nation and set it up outside and far off from the camp. He called it the "tabernacle of the congregation." This was not the tent that later on became the center of Israel's worship under the law. This that Moses moved was a temporary one, but the significant fact is that he moved it to the outside of the camp. Up to that time it had been in the center and everyone had easy access to it. This was no longer true. The removal to the outside put everyone to the test who wanted to truly worship God.

Moses called on those men who were on the Lord's side to put to death the persons who were stubborn in their idolatry. The Levites rallied to his support and three thousand evil men died. Thus God through Moses put away sin from Israel. But when it came to the subject of worship, the removing of the tabernacle to the outside of the camp made it necessary for those who wanted to worship God to separate from the camp to do it.

Another incident connected with the removal of the tabernacle is that Moses entered it to worship God, and God gave His approval by having the cloudy pillar descend and stand at the tabernacle door. After a time of worship Moses returned to the people, but Joshua, "the son of Nun, a young man, departed not out of the tabernacle" (Ex. 33:11). He remained there in fellowship with the Lord and interceded for the people of God. This gives a clue to Joshua's inner life. He sought the things of God. This is what it is going to take from us if we are going to be faithful in the spiritual life. We have to take time to commune with God. There are some who say that they have no time for this; but the fact is we never have time for anything unless we take time for it. We have to make time, and we can make time for such communion if we want to.

A third time that Joshua's name is mentioned is in connection with his concern for the honor of Moses. The Lord instructed Moses to choose 70 elders from among the Israelites to help him administer the affairs of the nation. Moses obeyed and as the men were assembled, the Lord sent His Spirit upon them and they prophesied.

Two of the men, however, Eldad and Medad, remained in the camp; nevertheless the Spirit rested on them also and they prophesied (Num. 11:26). A young man ran and told Moses about this and Joshua, who apparently was standing by when the news was brought, urged Moses saying, "My lord Moses, forbid them" (Num. 11:28). Then Moses said to him, "Enviest thou for my sake? would God that all the Lord's people were prophets, and that the Lord would put his spirit upon them!" (v. 29). Though in this case Joshua was in the wrong he was, nevertheless, concerned for the welfare of his master. Joshua exhibited no jealousy. He did not have a self-seeking spirit. He was concerned only for the honor of the person he served. How Christ-like this is, for our Saviour came not to do His own will, but the will of His Father who sent Him. Such fidelity as Joshua expressed is rare but precious and to be treasured wherever found.

Chapter Two

JOSHUA'S INTRODUCTION TO FAITH

A Faithful Minority

Still another mention of Joshua outside the Book that bears his name is in Numbers 13:8. It tells us that he was chosen to represent the tribe of Ephraim as one of the 12 spies who were sent to investigate the land of Canaan. This experience stands out as proof of his love and devotion to his heavenly Master.

The name given him in Numbers 13:8 is Oshea, a name meaning salvation. Moses changed his name to Jehoshua (Num. 13:16) meaning "Jehovah is salvation," or "by whom Jehovah will save." In this change of name God was saying, "Here is a young man by whom I am going to save Israel." This change was made only two years after the people of Israel came out of Egypt. God honored Joshua's faithfulness, and by the change of his name signified what his future position would be. This is a principle we will find illustrated in the New Testament also. Jesus changed the name of Simon to Peter. Simon means "hearing" but Peter means "a piece of rock." Saul, who became the Apostle, had his name changed to Paul. Saul means "the great one," but when the Lord got hold of his life, he was given the name Paul meaning "the little one."

Joshua represented Ephraim among the 12 spies. The first report, the one from the ten spies, was discouraging due to their unbelief. They admitted the land was wonderful, that it flowed with milk and honey just as God said it did. But they also declared that the people of the country were strong, the cities walled and the children of Anak who were giants were in the land. The ten spies said they were like grasshoppers when compared to these large men.

The majority report had much to say about the difficulties and nothing about the power of God. The ten said the land could not possibly be conquered by Israel. No wonder it was called "an evil report."

Caleb and Joshua, on the other hand, showed their faith in God when they declared the land could be conquered. They had the courage and determination which, coupled with faith in God, would have carried them through to victory. They stated that, God being with them, the inhabitants of the land would be like bread to them. It would be just as easy to conquer those high-walled cities and those great giants as it was to eat bread.

The Israelites had sung the great song of triumph recorded in Exodus 15 after their deliverance from the Red Sea. All of the nation had sung it but apparently the ten spies had forgotten it. Joshua and Caleb had not. They remembered what God had done to deliver Israel from Egypt and from the Egyptian army and were confident that under His leadership Canaan would be theirs.

When they heard how the Israelites were delivered and protected by God, the people of Canaan became afraid. This was not known until many years later when Joshua sent two spies into the city of Jericho. Caleb and Joshua did not need to know this beforehand in order to be strong in faith. They believed God.

We must ever remember that Satan, our greatest spiritual foe, has been overcome by Jesus Christ our Saviour. We learn from Hebrews 2:14,15 that Christ in His death broke the power of Satan so that those that had been enslaved by him might go free from spiritual bondage. This is a foundational truth for us ever to keep in mind if we are going to enjoy fruits of that deliverance in our everyday experience.

The strong spiritual caliber of Joshua and Caleb stands out in the words of their report. Even though they were in the minority against a militant majority, they nevertheless said: "Only rebel not ye against the Lord, neither fear ye the people of the land; for they are bread for us: their defence is departed from them, and the Lord is with us: fear them not" (Num. 14:9). How graphically they express the ease of the victory over their foes. The Israelites will overcome the Canaanites as easily as a person eats bread.

How could this be? The reason is not hard to find. The battle would not be the Israelites' but God's. This is the secret of victory in our own Christian lives. The battle against the forces of evil is not necessarily a hard battle at all. We sometimes think so, even considering the Christian life itself to be a hard life. The problem with us is that we try to do in our own strength what God has promised to do for us. The Lord Jesus has already overcome the enemy so that our responsibility is simply to believe and trust.

The ten spies, like Joshua and Caleb, had seen God working for Israel before. They were in the group that came through the Red Sea. They were also among those who sang the following song: "The people shall hear, and be afraid: sorrow shall take hold on the inhabitants of Palestina. Then the dukes of Edom shall be amazed; the mighty men of Moab, trembling shall take hold upon them; all the inhabitants of Canaan shall melt away. Fear and dread shall fall upon them; by the greatness of thine arm shall they be as still as a stone; till thy people pass over, O Lord, till the people pass over, which thou hast purchased. Thou shalt bring them in, and plant them in the mountain of thine inheritance" (Ex. 15:14-17).

This is only a portion of the song of triumph that Moses and Israel sang after the victory at the Red Sea, but it is prophetic of what would happen to the enemies in the land of Canaan as a result of Israel's victory. The morale of the Canaanites would disappear. Their will to fight would be lost. Fear would grip them. And this is exactly what happened. Forty years later they were still afraid. However, it seems that the singing of the song of triumph had been largely forgotten by the ten spies. Two years after their deliverance from Pharaoh's army at the Red Sea the faith of these Israelites was largely gone. But with Joshua and Caleb this was not the case. They believed God and knew that the enemy would not be able to stand against them.

God has already taken care of the enemy of our souls, Satan himself. His power is broken. God expects us to believe this and trust Him for victory whenever we encounter Satanic opposition. We learn in Hebrews 2:14 of how our Saviour took on flesh and blood, that is, He became man that "through death he might destroy him that had the power of death, that is, the devil; and deliver them who through fear of death were all their lifetime subject to bondage." Christ not only died for our sins, but in dying He broke the power of the Evil One. This fact we will see illustrated in many ways in these studies.

Joshua and Caleb took their lives in their own hands when they admonished their fellow spies and the people to be courageous and believe God. This is often true of the person who believes God's Word. There are always those who will rebuke and despise us if we take our stand for God. The people turned on Joshua and Caleb and wanted to stone them. What a reward for the dangers they had encountered and the good advice they were giving! These two courageous servants of God were not abandoned. He intervened on their behalf. Whenever a man dares to stand on the Word of God, he will find that God takes his part. The promise of the Word is: "Commit thy way unto the Lord, trust also in him; and he shall bring it to pass."

Here is the account of this incident: "But all the congregation bade stone them with stones. And the glory of the Lord appeared in the tabernacle of the congregation before all the children of Israel. And the Lord said unto Moses, How long will this people provoke me? and how long will it be ere they believe me, for all the signs which I have shewed among them? I will smite them with the pestilence, and disinherit them, and will make of thee a greater nation and mightier than they" (Num. 14:10-12).

Because of Moses' intercession at this time Israel was not destroyed. At the same time, Joshua and Caleb were protected.

Consequences of Unbelief

The older generation that had come out of Egypt continued to murmur against Moses and Aaron. They stated they would rather have died in Egypt or in the wilderness than to have been brought to where they would fall by the sword and their children would be a prey to enemies in the desert.

Speaking to the same generation God said, "Your carcases shall fall in this wilderness; and all that were numbered of you, according to your whole number, from twenty years old and upward, which have murmured against me, Doubtless ye shall not come into the land, concerning which I sware to make you dwell therein, save Caleb the son of Jephunneh, and Joshua the son of Nun. But your little ones, which ye said should be a prey, them will I bring in, and they shall know the land which ye have despised" (Num. 14:29-31).

God said the whole nation would wander in the wilderness for 40 years, a year for each day in which the spies searched the land. During that time the older generation would die because they refused to believe Almighty God.

Concerning the ten spies the record is: "And the men, which Moses sent to search the land, who returned, and made all the congregation to murmur against him, by bringing up a slander upon the land, Even those men that did bring up the evil report upon the land, died by the plague before the Lord. But Joshua the son of Nun, and Caleb the son of Jephunneh, which were of the men that went to search the land, lived still" (vv. 36-38).

What we have here is an illustration of what the Lord is teaching us in Hebrews 6. This is a portion that has caused a great deal of discussion among God's people. "For it is impossible for those who were once enlightened, and have tasted of the heavenly gift, and were made partakers of the Holy Ghost, And have tasted the good word of God, and the powers of the world to come, if they shall fall away, to renew them again unto repentance; seeing they crucify to themselves the Son of God afresh, and put him to an open shame" (Heb. 6:4-6).

The subject in this portion is not salvation. The Lord is speaking about saved people who will not follow through and go on with Him in the Christian life. The Israelites who had seen God's glory and His miracles in Egypt and in the wilderness, tempted God and refused to listen to Him, were not allowed to enter Canaan. They had been enlightened. They had tasted of the good things. They had been made partakers. They came through the Red Sea and saw the power of the Holy Spirit, who led them by a cloud by day and the pillar of fire by night. When such deliberately refuse to go on with the Lord they cannot make progress in their Christian experience. Their only place is the desert till they die.

Joshua and Caleb were the only two adults who crossed the Red Sea who were allowed to enter the Promised Land. And the reason they were permitted to enter Canaan was that they believed God. They did not deny Him but were strong in faith. We, like them, need to learn how to trust God for everything and anything.

Joshua Appointed to Succeed Moses

So far, in following Joshua, we have investigated four references to him in the Pentateuch, the Five Books of Moses which precede the Book of Joshua in the Bible. There are several more references to him in these early Books, and the references provide us with clues to why he was a victorious man.

The next significant incident in Joshua's life had to do with his appointment as Moses' successor. The record of this event is found in Numbers 27, and we learn there that the appointment was made while Moses was still living. Moses knew that sooner or later another leader would be needed for Israel, and so he prayed to the Lord saying, "Let the Lord, the God of the spirits of all flesh, set a man over the congregation, which may go out before them, and which may

go in before them, and which may lead them out, and which
may bring them in; that the congregation of the Lord be not
as sheep which have no shepherd" (Num. 27:16,17).

The Lord's answer was immediate. He replied: "Take
thee Joshua the son of Nun, a man in whom is the spirit, and
lay thine hand upon him" (v. 18). God chose Joshua. He was
not elected by the people on the basis of a popular vote
which is the method followed in a democracy. Joshua's
responsibility would be to lead the people out of the desert
and into the land of Canaan.

God had a strong word of commendation for Joshua.
Surely all of us not only want to hear God say, "Well done,
thou good and faithful servant," but we would like to hear
also some of the things God said about Joshua. The Lord
declared that Joshua was a man in whom was the Holy Spirit,
meaning also that the Spirit of God controlled him. This is
something God wants to see in all of our lives.

In the thirty-second chapter of Numbers the Lord picked
out another factor in Joshua's life that greatly pleased Him.
The Lord contrasted the faith of Caleb and Joshua with that
of the ten spies in the following words: "And the Lord's
anger was kindled the same time, and he sware, saying, Surely
none of the men that came up out of Egypt, from twenty
years old and upward, shall see the land which I sware unto
Abraham, unto Isaac, and unto Jacob; because they have not
wholly followed me: save Caleb the son of Jephunneh the
Kenezite, and Joshua the son of Nun: for they have wholly
followed the Lord" (Num. 32:10-12). To live the life of faith
one must be filled with the Holy Spirit. This was the case in
Joshua's experience and is the reason for his wholly following
the Lord. Faith follows God.

It is wonderful that God could say such things about
Joshua, but He also wants to be able to say the same things
about us. This is the key to the victorious life. A person filled
or under the control of the Holy Spirit follows the Lord. This
speaks of definite obedience to the things of the Lord. Is God
able to say to us to do this and do that and we do it? God
will so speak to us if we will allow Him to.

The next mention of Joshua is in Numbers 34. There we learn that the Lord appointed Joshua as one of the men who was to divide the land, appointing the areas to be controlled by the various tribes. "And the Lord spake unto Moses, saying, These are the names of the men which shall divide the land unto you: Eleazar the priest, and Joshua the son of Nun" (v. 16,17). The Eleazar spoken of here was the son of Aaron.

Joshua's appointment to this position is also stated in Deuteronomy 1:38: "But Joshua the son of Nun, which standeth before thee, he shall go in thither: encourage him: for he shall cause Israel to inherit it."

This was all part of God's program of encouraging Joshua and preparing him for his future responsibilities. We read in Deuteronomy 3:21: "And I commanded Joshua at that time, saying, Thine eyes have seen all that the Lord your God hath done unto these two kings: so shall the Lord do unto all the kingdoms whither thou passest. Ye shall not fear them: for the Lord your God he shall fight for you."

Confrontation with the enemy began before Israel entered the land. They came from the east and found their pathway blocked by several nations of great strength, but with God's help these were wiped out completely. Moses was Israel's leader during this period, and it is to these events that he pointed Joshua so that he would be encouraged in the Lord, assuring him that no man would be able to stand against him as he led Israel into the land.

This could be classified as an "earnest" of Joshua's future victorious leadership. It was a demonstration of what God was going to do for him and through him.

God has provided us with a foretaste or "earnest" of our inheritance in Christ. We learn from Ephesians 1 that God has given to us the Holy Spirit. The Spirit's presence with us is called "an earnest." This might be likened to a down payment on a purchase. It is the pledge of the payment of the full amount. We read: "In whom ye also trusted, after that ye heard the word of truth, the gospel of your salvation: in whom also after that ye believed, ye were sealed with that holy Spirit of promise, which is the earnest of our inheritance until the redemption of the purchased possession, unto the praise of his glory" (Eph. 1:13,14).

The gift of the Holy Spirit and the sealing with the Spirit are the assurance of what God is going to still do for us. Part of that is His victory through us. It is for us to be of good courage and to follow the way God has mapped out for us. It is also the promise that our redemption will be completed.

The next time we find a reference to Joshua is when Moses gave him his final charge before taking over the responsibility of leadership. The account is in Deuteronomy 31 beginning with verse 7: "And Moses called unto Joshua, and said unto him in the sight of all Israel, Be strong and of a good courage: for thou must go with this people unto the land which the Lord hath sworn unto their fathers to give them; and thou shalt cause them to inherit it. And the Lord, he it is that doth go before thee; he will be with thee, he will not fail thee, neither forsake thee: fear not, neither be dismayed" (vv. 7,8).

What a remarkable promise this is. But do not limit it to Joshua only, though it was spoken first to him. If you carefully examine what God said, you will see that these same words are repeated in the New Testament for the benefit of those who dare follow Christ. Joshua was assured that the Lord would go before him. What did our Saviour promise us? That when He puts forth His own sheep He goes before them. He commanded us to go into all the world to preach the gospel and assured us He would be with us and even go before us and prepare the way.

Joshua was assured that God would not fail him. God never fails. He is the faithful One. Neither will He forsake any of us. He did not forsake Joshua and He will not forsake us though some of us sometimes think that He has. Read the promise in Hebrews 13 beginning with verse 5: "Let your conversation be without covetousness; and be content with such things as ye have [it is the failure to do this that causes us to sometimes think God has forsaken us]: for he hath said, I will never leave thee, nor forsake thee." Do we believe

Him, or will we charge God with lying? No, God will never leave us nor forsake us—"So that we may boldly say, The Lord is my helper, and I will not fear what man shall do unto me." When God calls us to a life of victory He endues us with all spiritual power necessary.

The last mention we find of Joshua in the Pentateuch is after he had been called to the leadership of Israel and installed in that position with the proper authority. We read in Deuteronomy 34:9: "And Joshua the son of Nun was full of the spirit of wisdom; for Moses had laid his hands upon him: and the children of Israel hearkened unto him, and did as the Lord commanded Moses." Whoever wrote these last four verses of Deuteronomy, possibly Joshua himself, told in them of Joshua's last meeting with Moses. God removed a workman, but He did not fail to carry on His work. His work does not cease. One servant may be removed, but another is raised up to take his place.

The new leader may not be called on to fill the place the other filled but to take his own place as leader. The work may need a new direction or new help. And those will be forthcoming when God chooses the new leader.

In Moses' case he was called to lead Israel out of bondage in Egypt and through the desert to the edge of the Promised Land. His was a difficult task but with God's help he performed it. Many were the heartaches and trials he endured with the people of Israel during those 40 years, but as God's man he was equipped to do God's work. That phase of Israel's journey and preparation was ended. Two great nations had already been conquered. A new step was ahead and new leadership was in the plan of God.

Joshua's training began early, part of which was the battle against Amalek. His training as leader of Israel's armed forces was now to come to fruition as Israel left the desert and entered Canaan.

God's preparations with this man were fully rounded out. Not only had God chosen him and ordained him publicly to his great office, but the hearts of the people had also been prepared to follow him. When God has a job to do, He works

it from both ends. There is nothing left undone. So where
God leads, we can safely follow.

Chapter Three

CANAAN-A TYPE OF
FAITH WARFARE

The Book of Joshua gives the history of Israel's entrance into and conquest of the land of Canaan under the leadership of Joshua. Canaan is not a type of heaven, but a type of spiritual Christian usefulness. A review of Israel's experiences covering their deliverance from Egypt to the conquering of Canaan and how these apply to the Christian life will be beneficial at this point. There are three stages in all.

First we saw the people of Israel in Egypt. They were slaves and had to be submissive to their slave masters, the Egyptians. They were not free, but under rules and regulations imposed by the Egyptian Pharaoh. Some Christians are still in that condition spiritually. They try to make themselves live a godly life by following certain rules and regulations instead of allowing Christ to indwell them and live through them.

The second stage involved Israel's emancipation from Egypt and their glorious deliverance at the Red Sea. Connected with this is the stay in the desert which lasted for 40 years. In this situation the people were a burden to God and to Moses instead of burden bearers. This can be true also of us who are Christians. We can burden others around us, perhaps our church leaders or church friends, instead of helping to carry the burden.

In their desert experience the Israelites were self-centered and largely useless to God. They constantly defended their own wrongdoing and considered little beyond their own self-interests.

It was not until they entered the land under Joshua's leadership, and this marks the third stage, that they became spiritual warriors and went on from victory to victory. They turned from being on the defensive to going on the offensive against the enemy.

There are two basic truths taught in the Book of Joshua, one is that Jehovah-God is a "man of war." The second is that "the just shall live by faith."

Many recoil from the first proposition that God is a God of war. Joshua and the Israelites are severely criticized by some, for in conquering and destroying the Canaanites they are thought to be out of harmony with the teaching of the Bible that God is a God of love. This is a frequent criticism of the Book of Joshua itself.

Let us look at it from the other side: How can God be a God of love and not be a God of wrath against sin? The fact is, if He were not a God of wrath upon sin, He could not be a God of love. Sin is at the bottom of all the world's problems. Righteousness is the opposite of sin and only as righteousness takes the place of sin will the world's great problems be solved. This in itself is a condemnation of sin.

We can thank God that a day is coming when Jesus Christ will finish the judgment of sin and establish righteousness in the earth. But we are not in that day as yet. God's program now is to show us how we can live victoriously in a world of turmoil with its many problems and troubles. We are to be a people of love, but there can be no true kingdom of love without sin being properly condemned and dealt with.

The reason we do not see this readily or at all is that man has such a low concept of sin. And this low concept of sin is the result of our lack of knowledge of God's holiness. In order to understand the awfulness of sin we need to know more of the holiness of God. If we would see how great sin is, we must not compare sin with sinners or sinner with sinner, but compare the sinner with God who is absolutely holy.

This will be revealed to us in the Scriptures. Let us take our Bibles and read them and see what they teach concerning God's holiness. As I have read the Book of Isaiah, for instance, for my devotional times, I have had to stop and rejoice in the holiness, righteousness and mercy of God. He is full of love and grace. There is no flaw in His character. My

God has become greater than ever to me, and that in itself makes sin the more sinful.

The exceeding sinfulness of sin is clearly shown in the fact that God gave His Son for our sins. He even forsook Him to the wrath of man and for judgment of our sin—your sin and my sin—the wickedness of sin can only be fully realized in the light of the price that was paid to provide salvation from sin. We begin to see something of the magnitude of the love of God as He reveals His wrath upon sin by sending His own Son to die for sinners.

As we study the Book of Joshua we find that he was commanded to completely exterminate the seven nations of Canaanites. Why should this be?

First of all, God gave the land of Palestine to Abraham. This is clearly stated in Genesis 15:18: "In the same day the Lord made a covenant with Abram, saying, Unto thy seed have I given this land, from the river of Egypt unto the great river, the river Euphrates." Why did God choose this land for His people? Was there no other land that He could have found for them? Why not the land that we know of as the United States of America? It is a wonderful land. But only one land suited the purposes of God with regard to Israel.

Israel did not go into Canaan to murder, to plunder and to steal the land of kindly, simple, loving peoples. The Israelites came as God's chosen people, as instruments to inflict proper judgment upon sin and sinners. God uses man to punish men, and such punishment was long overdue the Canaanites. They had forfeited their rights to the land and even to life.

This is what God said to Abraham with regard to God's program for him and the future nation of Israel: "And he said unto Abram, Know of a surety that thy seed shall be a stranger in a land that is not their's, and shall serve them; and they shall afflict them four hundred years; and also that nation, whom they shall serve, will I judge: and afterward shall they come out with great substance. And thou shalt go to thy fathers in peace; thou shalt be buried in a good old age. But in the fourth generation they shall come hither again: for the iniquity of the Amorites is not yet full" (Gen. 15:13-16).

It is evident from this that God in His longsuffering was going to give the residents of Canaan an opportunity to change their evil ways. In His grace He gave them more than 400 years, but they did not repent. Someone will object, possibly, and say that they knew nothing about God and His offer of life, but this objection will not stand. In Romans 2 beginning with verse 4 we read: "Or despisest thou the riches of his goodness and forbearance and longsuffering; not knowing that the goodness of God leadeth thee to repentance?" Here the Apostle is speaking of God's dealing with the heathen of Rome and points out that God was holding back judgment thus extending mercy, yet the heathen Romans were paying no attention. They despised God's grace. God was giving them time to repent but they were not considering God's offer.

Then the Apostle continues: "But after thy hardness and impenitent heart treasurest up unto thyself wrath against the day of wrath and revelation of the righteous judgment of God; who will render to every man according to his deeds." This is what God has to say concerning men in Rome in Paul's day or in any other place and time.

By the time Israel was delivered from Egypt, the cup of iniquity of the Amorites which included the other nations also in Canaan, was coming to the full. In Leviticus 18, verse 3 God said to the children of Israel: "After the doings of the land of Egypt, wherein ye dwelt, shall ye not do: and after the doings of the land of Canaan, whither I bring you, shall ye not do; neither shall ye walk in their ordinances." Then beginning with the 24th verse of this same chapter the Lord says, "Defile not ye yourselves in any of these things: for in all these the nations are defiled which I cast out before you." So the land was defiled because the people who had lived in it were defiled. God's indictment continues: "Therefore I do visit the iniquity . . . upon it, and the land itself vomiteth out her inhabitants. Ye shall therefore keep my statutes and my judgments, and shall not commit any of these abominations;

neither any of your own nation, nor any stranger that sojourneth among you: (For all these abominations have the men of the land done, which were before you, and the land is defiled;) That the land spue not you out also, when ye defile it, as it spued out the nations that were before you" (vv. 24-28).

Israel, then, did not come into the land under the impulse of lust of conquest. They came as the executioners of God's divine wrath against people so vile that the only course open to God was to judge them. We have seen the necessity of this before. God came and spoke in His wrath at the flood and destroyed a whole civilization for their sins. There were other times when He sent pestilences or earthquakes as judgments upon groups of people. God is no respecter of persons; He has pointed out in His Word the future judgments that will come upon the race, judgments not on mere localities, but on the entire earth. The cup of sin for this world is fast reaching the full mark.

Melchizedek lived in Jerusalem in those early days and was known as king of righteousness. He testified to the truth of God and was held in such esteem that he even received tithes from Abraham. Later on, in the New Testament, the writer to the Hebrews tells us that our Lord Jesus was made a high priest after the order of Melchizedek. We do not know where this man came from or how long he lived but we do know he was king of righteousness and witnessed to the truth of God. So in the midst of all the idolatry and evil practices that Canaan was notorious for and for which God destroyed Sodom and Gomorrah, there was an outstanding witness to the truth of God in Jerusalem in the person of Melchizedek.

Abraham also lived in the land and was a testimony to God. This man had no fixed abode, but wherever he went he gave his testimony. Isaac followed him and later Jacob. In spite of the weaknesses in all of these men, they each witnessed to the living God who demanded righteousness of men and judged them for their sins. We would like to think that some Canaanites believed God; but if so, their numbers

were few. The majority went on in their wilful, sinful ways.
They left God no choice but to bring judgment on them.

God is no respecter of persons. He was as severe against
Israel's sins as He was against those of other nations. It is true
that He chose Israel, a small nation, through whom He could
manifest His grace. This was God's prerogative. He is
sovereign and has the right to do as He pleases. God has
chosen to deal with nations and with individuals in mercy,
but His extending of mercy depends on their response to
Him. To those who claim His mercy He shows mercy. To
those who rebel He judges. God, being righteous, is against
sin and cannot tolerate it. Peter warned that judgment must
begin at the house of God so that even those on whom God
has showered His grace cannot expect Him to close His eyes
to anything evil that they do. The people of Israel found that
they reaped what they sowed. Never once did God condone
their sins even though He had called them to fulfill certain
tasks for Him.

Though Israel enjoyed the great victory at Jericho, she
suffered defeat before Ai because of Achan's sin. Until that
sin was properly taken care of—exposed, confessed and
repudiated—Israel could not be victorious.

In the Book of Judges we find that some 14 times
judgments were poured out on Israel for her sins during a
period of some 400 years. Time and again various parts of the
nation were put under captivity and then delivered as God
raised up judges to represent Him.

After the nation became divided the Syrians were made
God's scourge upon the northern ten tribes for their sinful
ways and defection from the faith. Eventually the northern
kingdom lost its independence and many of its people were
taken away as captives.

Later on the southern kingdom fell to the Babylonians.
Though after 70 years a small remnant returned, it was not
long until other conquerors ruled the land. When our Saviour
came, the Romans were the masters of Palestine. The revolt
of the Jews against the Romans in 70 A.D. proved to be a
terrible tragedy for that small nation. They were defeated

and dispersed. For nearly 2000 years they have been wanderers upon the face of the earth. Only in the last few years has the world witnessed a revival of the Jewish state.

God is not mocked. Whatever a man or a nation sows that man or nation will reap. Israel was warned and the Church is warned. God will not tolerate sin. He will not let any of us get away with it.

So we say then that the history recorded in the Book of Joshua shows us that God wars against sin. He shows how sin must be dealt with from His standpoint and ours. Then it goes on to declare how God gives victories to the person who will dare stand with and for God. This is the truth we want to emphasize again and again in these studies.

When the cup of sin of the Canaanites was full, God brought in Israel as His executioners of justice and judgment.

God is always at war with sin. This fact we must recognize. Consequently, Israel's entering into the land and overcoming its inhabitants was in line with this principle that God follows. At the same time, Israel as a conquering nation in Canaan provides a wonderful type of our spiritual warfare and conquest over sin in our daily lives and the entering in to possessing our spiritual possessions in Christ.

Steps for Spiritual Progress

In the first chapter of the Book of Joshua we are provided several steps concerning progress in spiritual things. In verse 2 there is this fact presented. The old method followed under Moses was no longer effective. It had to be abandoned. This was the method of the law. Actually, of course, in the history of Israel they were still under law, but their experience in leaving the desert and going into Canaan provides a remarkable illustration of the transition from law to grace. This is brought before us in Joshua 1:2: "Moses my servant is dead; now therefore arise, go over this Jordan, thou, and all this people, unto the land which I do give to them, even to the children of Israel."

We learn from II Corinthians 5:17 that if any man be in

Christ he is a new "creature [creation] : old things [methods, ways, means] are passed away; behold, all things are become new." The verse following tells us that all of this is from God who has reconciled us to Himself by Jesus Christ and has given to us the ministry of reconciliation. We are made the ambassadors of God; and, as Paul informs us, it is the love of Christ that constrains us to plead with men to turn to God. This was the principle to be used in conquering Canaan.

In the second place we must recognize that what we do for the Lord must be done on the principle of faith. We must take God at His word. Joshua 1:3 says, "Every place that the sole of your foot shall tread upon, that have I given unto you, as I said unto Moses." Faith takes what God has provided. God provided all of Canaan for Israel. It was up to the Israelites to believe Him and act upon that faith. Just so has God provided a complete life for the Christian. It is not only salvation from condemnation, but a life of victory over sin in the daily life as well as great changes for the future. But as Canaan had to be taken a step at a time, so must we progress with God a step at a time through faith. The principle is, "Every place that the sole of your foot shall tread upon, that have I given unto you." We cannot sit still, twiddle our thumbs, and expect God to do miracles. We must walk on with God one step at a time.

The third fact that is basic and essential to this whole Christian life is that nothing can stop or withstand faith when it is in action. In verse 5 of Joshua 1 we read: "There shall not any man be able to stand before thee all the days of thy life: as I was with Moses, so will I be with thee: I will not fail thee, nor forsake thee." According to this nothing can stop God's working when faith is operating in His people. The New Testament counterpart of this promise is Philippians 4:13: "I can do all things through Christ which strengtheneth me." Christ has already won the victories for us and now lives in us to produce this victorious living.

We learn in Joshua chapter 2 that Rahab was aware of the fact that the Canaanites were already defeated. They had no courage with which to face the foe. The people were

frightened and weakened by fear and had been from the time
Israel was delivered at the Red Sea. This is exactly how it is
in our spiritual life. The Devil is afraid. He knows what God
has done in Christ and trembles. This is why the Lord tells us,
"Resist the devil and he shall flee from you." It is through
reckoning on our death, burial and resurrection in Christ that
we have victory over the flesh. We are also assured through
the cross we have victory over the world. So Satan knows
that he cannot stand against a man or woman who dares to
act in God-given faith.

With God's promise of never failing or forsaking Joshua
went this admonition: "Be strong and of a good courage: for
unto this people shalt thou divide for an inheritance the land
. . . only be thou strong and very courageous, that thou
mayest observe to do according to all the law . . . turn not
from it to the right hand or to the left, that thou mayest
prosper whithersoever thou goest."

The child of God should be bold, for Christ indwells him.
We must not give way to seeming failures. Even where we fail
we must not give up. We should admit our failure,
recognizing the lack of faith that caused it, and then return
to God believing He will see us through because He never
fails. We must never go to the methods of the flesh in order
to try and make a success of the Christian life. It can't be
done.

In the fifth place we must know what is the secret of
continous victory. This is made clear for us in Joshua 1:8.
"This book of the law shall not depart out of thy mouth; but
thou shalt meditate therein day and night, that thou mayest
observe to do according to all that is written therein: for then
thou shalt make thy way prosperous, and then thou shalt
have good success." This is the only portion where we will
find the expression "good success." This has reference to
continuous victory and the secret is daily devotional meetings
with God. While Israel was in the desert they had manna
provided for them daily. Then when they came into the land
the manna ceased and they were to live on the "corn of the
land." Both the manna and the corn speak of spiritual food,

the one, the milk of the Word and the other the meat of the Word. This must be the daily diet of the person who would have victory in his daily life.

In accord with this is Psalm 1. There we learn that the godly man finds his delight "in the law of the Lord; and in his law doth he meditate day and night." As a result we learn that "he shall be like a tree planted by the rivers of water, that bringeth forth his fruit in his season; and his leaf also shall not wither; and whatsoever he doeth shall prosper" (vv. 2,3). The Psalmist is speaking of God's Word. It is this Word that makes us strong.

In the sixth place we must know that we need a will and a determination to go forth in the things of God. Satan will try to make us careless or indifferent in these matters. But we must respond as the people of Israel did when they were told what God's program was going to be. The officers went through the host telling the people: "Prepare you victuals; for within three days ye shall pass over this Jordan, to go in to possess the land, which the Lord your God hath given you to possess it" (Josh. 1:11). The people responded by saying, "All that thou commandest us we will do, and whithersoever thou sendest us, we will go" (Josh. 1:16).

Later on Joshua told the people to sanctify themselves for very soon God was going to do wonders among them (Josh. 3:5). This meant they were to set themselves apart to do the will of God. In verse 9 of chapter 3, Joshua called the children of Israel to come and hear the word of God for the purpose, of course, that they would do what God said. These were progressive steps with regard to preparing the people for what God had to say and what God was going to do. They remind us that the Christian life is a progressive life. God leads us step by step and from one victory to another.

Courage for Righteous Action

The Lord does not give us information so that we will merely have knowledge. His purpose is that we might act on what we know and thus do what He wants done. The Lord admonished Joshua to be of good courage, and the courage was to be followed by action. The same admonition was for Israel and the same action was to follow.

It could not have been an easy matter for the Israelites to accept the fact that Moses was dead. He had led the nation for some 40 years from the time of their deliverance from Egypt and their being brought to the very brink of the Promised Land. Two nations on the east side of Jordan had already been conquered, and all that was needed for Israel to enter Canaan was to cross the Jordan itself. The only leader Israel had known was Moses. Suddenly his ministry was ended. He was gone from their midst. Moses was dead, but God had not died.

All the old generation that had come out of Egypt had died in the desert. This was the result of their not having believed God. The only exceptions were Caleb and Joshua, and to Joshua was given the leadership of the new generation. So it was to this new generation under their new leader that God also gave the command to be strong and of a good courage, assuring them that He would be with them wherever they went.

Courage Based on Four Factors

Now courage of the kind that God was speaking of is not a natural virtue and does not come through a person determining to be bold. We cannot even pray it up in itself. There are certain basic factors that must be recognized and obeyed before this kind of courage is present. First of all, such courage does not exist apart from faith. Faith is its basis. I have to really believe something is true before I can be courageous enough to venture out on the basis of what I believe.

God's promise was, "Every place that the sole of your foot shall tread upon, that have I given unto you." That is the promise. Faith lays hold of the promise and is therefore the basis for courage. This laying hold of what God has promised can be called the law, or perhaps better yet, the principle of appropriation. The principle of appropriation means simply that not only must there be the promise of God for us, but we must go and claim for ourselves that which God has promised. Israel was told to go and take over the land and God would be with them. He had already given it to them, but they had to claim it by taking it. So courage is dependent upon faith, a faith that goes out and appropriates what God has given. God gives, but man must take.

We Christians have a remarkable promise in Romans 8:32: "He that spared not his own Son, but delivered him up for us all, how shall he not with him also freely give us all things?" Here is unlimited supply for whatever is necessary. The same is promised in Ephesians 1:3: "Blessed be the God and Father of our Lord Jesus Christ, who hath blessed us with all spiritual blessings in heavenly places in Christ." But in order for us to receive these things we must first believe what God has said and then accept it or take it. So then we see that while courage depends upon faith, faith has something that is basic to it also.

Faith has to depend upon the promise made. Someone makes a promise but how sure is that promise? Can it be depended upon? The answer lies in finding out who makes the promise. In our own country in an election year many promises are made to the people. Those of us who have watched the political scene know that many candidates make promises that cannot be kept. Some promises are kept but many are not. It is easy to make promises but we need to find out who it is that is making the promises.

It was God who promised that every place in Canaan which the Israelites claimed by treading thereupon He would give to them for their possession. The promise of God to Joshua was that as He was with Moses so would He be with His new leader. God promised not to fail him nor forsake him. He assured Joshua, "For the Lord thy God is with thee whithersoever thou goest."

God cannot lie, so when He says something, that should settle it for us. God speaks truth. "God is not a man, that He should lie; neither the son of man, that he should repent: hath he said, and shall he not do it? or hath he spoken, and shall he not make it good?" (Num. 23:19). This is the promise from our God, and He always keeps His side of the promises. There are times when He cannot do certain things for us simply because we are not obedient to Him. So it follows that we must be obedient by believing what God says and acting upon His promise. This is being obedient unto faith. It was to this line of conduct that God encouraged Joshua by saying, "Be thou strong and very courageous, that thou mayest observe to do according to all the law, which Moses my servant commanded thee: turn not from it to the right hand or to left, that thou mayest prosper whithersoever thou goest."

Let us review again these various observations. We are told to be courageous, but courage depends upon faith. Faith depends upon the promises. The fulfillment of the promise depends upon the faithfulness of the promiser. So, when we learn from the Scriptures that God has promised never to leave us nor forsake us, we can depend upon what He says

The fourth thing to notice is that faith in the promise is based upon daily meditation (v. 8). We do not know the promises and, therefore, they mean nothing to us until we go into the Word of God and learn what they are and begin to meditate upon them. Faith comes by hearing and hearing by the Word of God. The Book of the Law was not to depart out of Joshua's mouth, but he was to meditate in it day and night. Why? Because there he would find God's will for him and God's promises to him.

So it is for us. In the Bible we read God's promises and find His will for our lives. But we must meditate upon these things and apply them personally. It is not just a matter of reading what the Bible says, though we must read it in order to understand it. We can read the Bible through and this will give us a panoramic view of what it teaches, but our knowledge must go beyond mere head knowledge. We must stop and master it for the benefit of our own souls. And when we do, we have this promise: "Then thou shalt make thy way prosperous, and then thou shalt have good success."

So victory and growth in the Christian life are dependent upon our getting into the Word of God and giving our attention to it.

Result of Courageous Faith

The result of a courageous life by faith is practically unlimited in scope and achievement. Some of the promises in the first chapter of Joshua indicate this. For example, in verse 3 the Israelites were assured that every place they walked on in Canaan was to be theirs. This in itself was ground for courage and assurance to go forward. In verse 6 the land was described as an inheritance. It was something God had already provided for them and would not take back from them. In verse 7 they were promised that they would prosper wherever they went if they were faithful to what God had provided for them. In verse 8 prosperity and good success were assured them. And in verse 9 they were admonished to be fearless and undismayed because of God's presence with them. No matter what the enemy tried to do, no matter if things seemed to be adverse for awhile, Israel was not to give up but to press forward. Success was guaranteed.

The God who spoke these words of promise to Joshua is our God today. We will never grow in spiritual life until we recognize that the God of Moses and of Joshua, the unfailing God, is also our God. He has not changed. So the heart of the whole matter is for us to let God be God in our lives and rule and control us and be sovereign in His leading and direction.

When we take a panoramic view of the Book of Joshua, we will see how Joshua's courage was built up as he traveled the road of obedience. For example, with regard to the crossing of the Jordan the priests and the Levites bearing the ark were to move ahead and then the host of the Israelites were to follow. They were told, "Ye shall remove from your place, and go after it [the ark]." They could not just sit where they were encamped and expect things to happen. They had to "go after it." And courage was needed for this.

A little later, after Joshua had admonished the people,

and possibly in order to avoid pride on his part, he was met by the Captain of the Host of the Lord. Joshua came face to face with the real leader of God's people. How necessary this is with us. True, we have met the Lord Jesus Christ as Saviour, but have we met Him as Lord? Have we seen Him as our life? Have we recognized Him to be the indwelling One who wants to live out His life afresh in us? It will completely change our attitude toward Christian living when this takes place. Too many are satisfied merely to have a ticket to heaven; but God wants far more than that. He wants us to be individuals through whom the Lord Jesus Christ can live out His life before a lost world.

Chapter Four

THE GOALS AND CONDITIONS OF CHRISTIAN FAITH
(Joshua 1)

The first chapter of the Book of Joshua illustrates for us the goal and conditions of Christian living. A careful examination of its contents will rescue us from the one-sided approach to Christianity that so many persons have. We say "believe" and all of heaven is ours—with the emphasis on the "all." This is not a contradiction to what I have said so often: that everything we receive from the Lord is by faith. That is true. We believe for salvation, and salvation in all its parts is ours actually or potentially. However, there are aspects of salvation that we enter into only as we appropriate consciously and actively what God has provided for us.

We learn from I Corinthians 3 that there will be some Christians who will be saved yet so as by fire. This is what the apostle tells us: "Every man's work shall be made manifest: for the day shall declare it, because it shall be revealed by fire; and the fire shall try every man's work of what sort it is. If any man's work abide which he hath built thereupon, he shall receive a reward. If any man's work shall be burned, he shall suffer loss: but he himself shall be saved; yet so as by fire" (vv. 13-15). It is possible, then, for a believer to get to heaven and yet have no rewards. There will be no abundant entrance in a case such as this as Peter speaks of (II Pet. 1:11). This would be getting to heaven barely by the skin of our teeth. Would not this detract from some of heaven's joys?

There is a phrase current today concerning a poor man's city or a poor people's city. Will there have to be a poor people's heaven? If so, they will have made it so by their own lack of active faith in Christian living. God's people lose so much when they have no more truth than to believe Christ

48

for salvation from sin's penalty but know nothing about deliverance from sin's power and how to live the abundant life.

The Book of Joshua teaches us that there is a race to run and a crown to gain. It is true that everything we have is by faith, but faith that results in action. Salvation to so many is emancipation from the penalty of sin and hell and the assurance of going to heaven, but that seems to be the extent of their view of what salvation involves. In this way they are very much like the Israelites who were emancipated from Egypt and then lived the rest of their lives in the desert.

But who wants to live in a desert? God's plan for Israel was not only to bring them out of Egypt, but also to bring them into Canaan. It is the same with us. We have been brought out of sin through salvation in order that we might be brought in to the abundant life which is also part of salvation.

One night an elderly lady called me asking for spiritual help. She had been listening to the broadcast and was under conviction thinking that perhaps she wasn't saved because, as she said, she had not done a thing for Christ. She had been saved very late in life and could not go out and win souls and do work that she saw others do. For this very reason she doubted her salvation. At least she was concerned. Many of God's people are not. If the glories of heaven depended on what some Christians accomplish for the Lord while down here, the heaven they would go to would be a poor people's heaven!

Then there are many Christians who have been taught that they should expect nothing but frequent if not constant defeat in this warfare against the world, the flesh and the Devil. Such persons seem to believe that on this side of glory is defeat, and that victory will not come until we have entered into eternity.

This is far from the truth. The Book of Joshua teaches us that when we meet the required conditions, we can do all things through Christ who strengthens us. This is what Paul taught later and this is what Joshua believed and practiced.

The defeatist attitude toward the Christian life is seen at Kadesh-barnea where ten of the spies brought back the report that the land could not be conquered. They said they could not subdue the enemy and take possession of the country. If we interpret that into modern Christian living it would be the same as those Christians who say we have to struggle along the best way we know. Eventually we hope to get to heaven, but there is really no expectation of victory over evil forces today. They are too great and too many.

Such an attitude leads to disaster. We need to read Numbers 13 and 14 so as to be reminded of what happens to God's people when they reach a Kadesh-barnea—the decision point—and go back into the desert. The rest of their lives is lived in defeat. This happened to the generation of adults who left Egypt. God did not desert them even though they did not obey Him. He went with them, provided their food—manna and flesh—and waited 38 years until that whole generation was gone. There were only two exceptions to this, as we have already seen, Joshua and Caleb. They believed God was able to deliver all of Canaan into the hands of His people. Joshua was given leadership of the nation and led them into the Land of Promise.

The Book of Joshua sets forth by example and illustration the requirements necessary for a successful and overcoming life. In the New Testament the Books of Ephesians and Hebrews are the counterpart to Joshua.

Canaan in Hebrews

First of all, in the Book of Hebrews we find the land of Canaan is pictured as a place of spiritual rest and victory which every believer on earth may enjoy (Heb. 4:3). This rest of faith is in the Lord Jesus Christ Himself. This is why we read such statements as: "And Moses verily was faithful in all his house, as a servant, for a testimony of those things which were to be spoken after; But Christ as a son over his own house; whose house are we, if we hold fast the confidence and the rejoicing of the hope firm unto the end" (3:5,6).

Some may stumble over the expression "if we hold fast" thinking that we must hold on in order to be saved. The subject is not salvation in this passage. The writer is commenting on entering into the hope that God has set before each believer. In salvation, God holds fast to us. We are kept by the power of God. But the hope that we have of a victorious life, a life of rest and victory, a life of overcoming, a life of rejoicing is dependent upon our attitude toward God.

The passage goes on: "Wherefore (as the Holy Ghost saith, To day if ye will hear his voice, Harden not your hearts, as in the provocation, in the day of temptation in the wilderness . . .) But exhort one another daily, while it is called To day; lest any of you be hardened through the deceitfulness of sin. For we are made partakers of Christ, if we hold the beginning of our confidence stedfast unto the end" (Heb. 3·7-14). According to this we are to receive everything that God has for us in Christ.

Remember that God has highly exalted the Lord Jesus and given Him a name which is above every name. He holds a place of authority, a place of absolute victory over all His enemies. And one of the glorious things for us is that we are partakers with Christ in this. We have been raised with Christ and are to be partakers with Him and have victory over all our enemies. There is no need for any of us to remain frail, defeated, emaciated Christians. Any believer who fits that description is in that condition by choice. He either does not have what it takes to believe God and to follow after and to grow in grace and knowledge, or he does not want it, or he is ignorant of this great truth.

We are told we are made partakers "if we hold the beginning of our confidence stedfast unto the end." Again the subject here is not salvation from sin's penalty but the life of victory that should follow. If we continue on in faith, there is nothing that can stop us from enjoying all that God has for us. The danger is that, like the Israelites, we may harden our hearts. The warning is: "For some, when they had heard, did provoke: howbeit not all that came out of Egypt by Moses. But with whom was he grieved forty years? was it not with them that had sinned, whose carcases fell in the wilderness? And to whom sware he that they should not enter into his rest, but to them that believed not? So we see that they could not enter in because of unbelief" (Heb. 3:16-19). There is the same problem today. Some do not believe that God has a place of victory for us. We too ought to fear "lest, a promise being left us of entering into his rest," any of us should seem to come short of it. We too have had the gospel preached to us, not the gospel of salvation from condemnation only, but the gospel of overcoming also. Our hearing of it needs to be mixed with faith if it is going to profit us.

There is a rest remaining that is a rest of faith. Such rest does not mean that there will not be any problems or enemies or troubles. It does mean that we may have all of these things and yet our hearts will be at peace because we rest them in Christ.

In our morning devotions sometime back, we read about a servant of God who was passing through a region infested by robbers. He had perfect peace in his heart, believing that God would give him grace for whatever took place. He was accosted by a robber who took everything he had of material value. It was not much, but as the robber was turning away from him the servant of God said, "Wait a minute, I have something more for you." And he gave him a copy of one of the Gospels. Later on this minister of Christ found out that the robber was delivered from his evil ways through reading and obeying what he read in that portion of Scripture.

There is something left for us in Christ besides salvation from sin's penalty. There is victory and rest in Him when we completely turn our lives over to Him. Ephesians speaks of life in heavenly places. This is not heaven itself but our experience of oneness with Christ. We start from victory, we do not struggle toward it. He has accomplished everything for us, so it is for us now to enter into victory through Him. This is the kind of life the Book of Joshua illustrates for us.

Complete salvation is ours today both as a privilege and

as a birthright. Our inheritance is not all future. There is a possession and enjoyment of it that we may have now. Esau, you will recall, despised his birthright. It was a spiritual matter, but he was interested in physical and material things rather than spiritual things. In this he was like many Christians who today are despising their spiritual birthright.

God has great things, wonderful things for us. It was not until 1955 that I personally came into the knowledge of this greater truth of the Word of God. What this has meant to my own spiritual life is beyond expression.

Joshua a Type of Christ

The Book of Joshua begins with the statement that "the Lord spake unto Joshua the son of Nun." We need to reckon with this fact that what the Lord says and what the Lord does is all important with regard to salvation. It was God who undertook for the people of Israel and Joshua. It is God who undertakes for us. Salvation is not something we do for Christ but something He has done for us. The force of this will grow upon us, we trust, as we seek the spiritual messages to be found in the Book of Joshua.

The name "Joshua" means "Jehovah is Saviour." That is, God reveals Himself as the Saviour to save men from sin and its consequences. Joshua thus becomes a type of Christ, the Captain of our salvation.

Joshua came after Moses in the sequence of rulers over Israel. Christ came after Moses with respect to God's great principles of dealing with the human race. We learn in John 1:17: "For the law was given by Moses, but grace and truth came by Jesus Christ."

A further development of the type is seen in Romans 8:3,4: "For what the law could not do, in that it was weak through the flesh, God sending his own Son in the likeness of sinful flesh, and for sin, condemned sin in the flesh: that the righteousness of the law might be fulfilled in us, who walk not after the flesh, but after the Spirit." What Moses could not do under the law in bringing the people of Israel to the

Promised Land, Joshua was able to do. Joshua led the people into the land to a life of victory and conquest just as Christ provides us with victory over the world, the flesh and the Devil.

We read in Romans 10:4,5: "For Christ is the end of the law for righteousness to every one that believeth. For Moses describeth the righteousness which is of the law, That the man which doeth those things shall live by them." Here Joshua is again a type of Christ. Moses described the righteousness which is by the law, but Christ is the end of the law. We do not mean to say that the law came to an end when Moses died, but we have already seen a different approach to the work that had to be done after Moses. Joshua's victorious conquest was a matter of faith. He led his people on to victory. So it is with Christ. We learn, "In all these things we are more than conquerors through him that loved us" (Rom. 8:37). And in this same vein we read in II Corinthians 2:14: "Now thanks be unto God, which always causeth us to triumph in Christ." Joshua led the people of Israel to triumph and victory, and the Lord Jesus Christ leads us on to triumph and victory. This is the quality of spiritual life the Lord wants us to enter into today.

In the third place Joshua is a type of Christ in that when Israel suffered defeat he, Joshua, made intercession for the people before God. This was when they fled before the men of Ai, a defeat that was brought on by sin in the Israelite camp. We read, "And Joshua rent his clothes, and fell to the earth upon his face before the ark of the Lord until the eventide, he and the elders of Israel, and put dust upon their heads. And Joshua said, Alas, . . . God, wherefore hast thou at all brought this people over Jordan, to deliver us into the hand of the Amorites, to destroy us?" (Josh. 7:6,7). Christ Jesus is our Advocate who makes intercession for us. John wrote in his First Epistle: "My little children, these things write I unto you, that ye sin not. And if any man sin, we have an advocate with the Father, Jesus Christ the righteous [one]" (2:1).

So when we fail today, when there is sin in our lives,

Jesus Christ is the Advocate who takes our case before God. According to Hebrews 7:25, "He is able to save them to the uttermost that come unto God by him, seeing he ever liveth to make intercession for them."

We also find that Joshua was the leader who allotted and divided the land to the people of Israel. This is what our Lord does concerning our spiritual inheritance. Here is what Ephesians 1:11,14 says, "In whom also we have obtained an inheritance, being predestinated according to the purpose of him who worketh all things after the counsel of his own will . . . Which is the earnest of our inheritance until the redemption of the purchased possession, unto the praise of his glory." In this passage the Holy Spirit, we are told, is given as the earnest of our redemption.

Peter comments on this same truth. He says, "Which according to his abundant mercy hath begotten us again unto a lively hope by the resurrection of Jesus Christ from the dead, to an inheritance incorruptible, and undefiled, and that fadeth not away, reserved in heaven for you. [Part of this inheritance is ours now the earnest of it is given us now by the Holy Spirit.] Who are kept by the power of God through faith unto salvation ready to be revealed in the last time." (I Pet. 1:3-5).

Workmen Die, But God Lives

The first statement made in Joshua 1:2 is, "Moses my servant is dead." We have noted this previously but it needs to be emphasized. Moses was dead but not God. The work of God is in nowise hindered by the death of His servants no matter how eminent they may be. The workman may be removed, but the work goes forward as ordained by God. This is God's doing.

When we recognize that the spiritual life is God's doing, we will begin to grow. Until we do, we will not grow. God can change servants in order to show that He may use whatever instrument He pleases. He is not tied down by, or to, any certain individual. We have often heard the saying,

"Don't change horses in the middle of the stream," but God may do this when it pleases Him or suits His purpose. God is sovereign and can terminate the ministry of any of His servants when He pleases. He may change His principle of working any time He desires. A Moses can die, but God is eternal. He never dies.

I think of a remarkable organization that God has raised up in this century, starting it through one man. There came a day when God called that man home, and many people wondered if the organization would continue. I can say to the glory of God that it is not only going on, but it is larger than it ever was. I do not profess to understand God's ways and His reasons for doing things, but it is not necessary that I do. God is never dependent on any one man. No man is indispensable in God's work. When Moses died, God did not need another Moses but a man with other gifts and abilities. So it is God may vary His workmen but His work will continue, because it is God's work and not ours.

Had not God promised Moses: "I am the Lord, and I will bring you out from under the burdens of the Egyptians, and I will rid you out of their bondage, and I will redeem you with a stretched out arm and with great judgments: and I will take you to me for a people, and I will be to you a God: and ye shall know that I am the Lord your God . . . and I will bring you in unto the land . . . and I will give it you . . . I am the Lord" (Ex. 6:6-8)? It was the great "I AM" who said He would do these things, and He did. He never leaves Himself without a witness.

When our Saviour was about to leave the earth at the close of His ministry, He promised to send the Holy Spirit who would endue God's servants with power: "I will pray the Father, and he shall give you another Comforter, that he may abide with you for ever, Even the Spirit of truth; whom the world cannot receive, because it seeth him not, neither knoweth him: but ye know him; for he dwelleth with you, and shall be in you. I will not leave you comfortless: I will come to you" (John 14:16-18).

Again in John 16 our Lord said, "Nevertheless I tell you

the truth; It is expedient for you that I go away: for if I go not away, the Comforter will not come unto you; but if I depart, I will send him unto you. And when he is come, he will reprove the world of sin, and of righteousness, and of judgment" (vv. 7,8). Here we learn that we are but instruments in His hands. What is done by way of ministry and witness is His doing.

Paul wrote to the Corinthians: "Now then we are ambassadors for Christ, as though God did beseech you by us: we pray you in Christ's stead, be ye reconciled to God" (II Cor. 5:20). Again it is God working in us and through us to bring the message to hearts.

In I Corinthians the Apostle wrote: "Know ye not that your body is the temple of the Holy Ghost which is in you, which ye have of God, and ye are not your own? For ye are bought with a price" (6:19,20). So we belong to Him, and what good we do is to be credited to God.

This is seen again in Matthew 28:18-20: "All power is given unto me in heaven and in earth [all authority]. Go ye therefore, and teach all nations . . . I am with you alway, even unto the end of the world." One man cannot fill another man's shoes. Joshua could not fill the shoes of Moses. But it was the same God who led and endued Joshua with wisdom and power as filled Moses with power for his responsibilities. So though Moses was dead, God was not. God's work continues because God does not die.

God's Call to Conquer

Leading Israel into Canaan was God's doing. It was a divine undertaking impossible to man. This pictures the fact that the leading of each Christian into a life of victory, to be an overcomer, must be recognized as the work of God. Knowing this, however, we must also recognize that we are under responsibility to follow Him. This is suggested in the fact that after God made the announcement that Moses was dead, He did not put a period at that point. What He said was, "Moses my servant is dead, now therefore arise and go over this Jordan." This was the signal Joshua was waiting for.

God possibly waited 30 days while the nation mourned the death of Moses. Not once during this time did Joshua push himself forward to fill the breach in leadership though he had been duly appointed for this task earlier. He awaited God's orders. This is true in the Christian life also. We must wait on the Lord. Many times we are admonished in the Word to "wait on the Lord," but this waiting does not mean sitting by idly, twiddling our thumbs. It means we await His orders, ready to go into action. It is something like a waitress in a restaurant serving a table. She goes into action once she knows what the patrons want.

We must not only wait upon God, but we must also be careful not to go ahead of Him. This is where many of us Christians make a mistake. We decide that a certain direction is the direction we ought to go, then we get in a hurry and start out without God. God is never late. It may seem to us because we wait for a long time that time is running out. But the Lord assures us in John 10:4: "When he putteth forth his own sheep, he goeth before them." In the Orient a shepherd leads his sheep. He never drives them. We are not to go ahead of Him; we are to follow Him. And He has promised that when we follow Him, He "will make us fishers of men."

When the time came for Joshua to assume full command and lead the people across the Jordan River, he had God's reassurance back of him. God said, "There shall not any man be able to stand before thee all the days of thy life: as I was with Moses, so I will be with thee: I will not fail thee, nor forsake thee" (Josh. 1:5). What greater fortification could a person ask for than this? When God calls us to a task He stands back of us.

God has called all of us to be conquerors over sin. We need to know in this connection that God does not expect us to be conquerors in our own strength. He tells us clearly as He did Joshua that He, the Lord, will be with us. He was with Moses and with Joshua. He will also be with us.

Joshua's commissioning service was conducted by God. This is seen in verses 1-9. As we examine it in detail we must keep clearly in mind what we have already emphasized, namely that the Christian life when lived as it should be is God's doing in us. God leads and we follow. He promises to be with us. We find our strength is in the Lord and in the power of His might.

The Lord said to Joshua: "Arise, go over this Jordan, thou, and all this people, unto the land which I do give to them." Joshua was leader of the people and everything in Canaan was put into his hands as a trustee for the nation. It was Joshua's responsibility to divide the land, assigning to each tribe its particular portion.

In this Joshua is a type of Christ, for all of the spiritual blessings provided for us are in Christ and He holds them as a trust until we claim them for our own. In Ephesians, the New Testament counterpart of the Book of Joshua, we read: "Blessed be the God and Father of our Lord Jesus Christ, who hath blessed us with all spiritual blessings in heavenly places in Christ" (1:3). The heavenly things are in contrast to earthly things. The heavenlies is the sphere of the believer's spiritual experience, and Christ is the source of all our blessings in this sphere. Since we are identified with Christ, we have everything needful for this new life. This began at the new birth. Everything became ours in Christ the moment we were born again; but the things to which we are making reference are kept in trust by God until we come and claim them through Christ.

Peter teaches this same truth when he says, "According as his divine power hath given unto us all things that pertain unto life and godliness (II Pet. 1:3,4). In the following verse he tells us that "by these ye might be partakers of the divine nature." So in Christ we have all things needful.

We have life in Him according to Colossians 3:4: "When Christ, who is our life, shall appear, then shall ye also appear with him in glory." This passage does not speak of Christ who gives this life, but Christ who is our life. We can never grow in grace and become conquerors over sin until we recognize that we have all these things needful for spiritual life in Christ, and they are available to us because we are united to Him. John wrote: "He that hath the Son hath life; he that hath not the Son of God hath not life" (I John 5:12). Again speaking of our identification with Him, we read in Hebrews 2:11: "For both he that sanctifieth and they who are sanctified are all of one: for which cause he is not ashamed to call them brethren."

Even in service we are united to Him. In John 17:18, in His high priestly prayer, our Saviour said to the Father: "As thou hast sent me into the world, even so have I also sent them into the world." We serve because He sends us to serve, and He is with us while we serve.

We are also partakers with Him in His suffering. This we do not always like, it is not easy for us to take as human beings; nevertheless it is present as another ingredient of the Christian life. This is not necessarily physical suffering only. There are various kinds of suffering. We are appealed to "go without the gate and bear his reproach." This world opposes our Lord and reproaches us for following Him. In Philippians 1:29 we read: "For unto you it is given in the behalf of Christ, not only to believe on him, but also to suffer for His sake." Paul had a good deal to say about this and adds in Philippians 3:10: "That I may know him, and the power of his resurrection, and the fellowship of his sufferings."

We are also made partakers with Him of an inheritance. Paul wrote to the Romans: "The Spirit itself beareth witness with our spirit, that we are the children of God: and if children, then heirs; heirs of God, and joint-heirs with Christ; if so be that we suffer with him, that we may be also glorified together" (8:16,17). We share with Christ in an inheritance God has provided for us.

We are also partakers in future glory. In the same letter to the Romans Paul wrote: "For I reckon that the sufferings of this present time are not worthy to be compared with the glory that shall be revealed in us" (8:18). The words "shall be" indicate a future realization and this is confirmed in the verses following: "For the earnest expectation of the creature waiteth for the manifestation of the sons of God. For the creature was made subject to vanity, not willingly, but by reason of him who hath subjected the same in hope. Because the creature itself also shall be delivered from the bondage of corruption into the glorious liberty of the children of God" (vv. 19-21).

The Book of the Revelation takes up this refrain. We read in 1:6: "And hath made us kings and priests unto God and his Father, to him be glory." Then in Revelation 5:10 we are told: "And hast made us unto our God kings and priests: and we shall reign on the earth."

The believer is a heavenly man and is therefore a stranger and pilgrim on the earth. According to Hebrews 3:1 we are partakers of the heavenly calling. As strangers and pilgrims we are to "abstain from fleshly lusts, which war against the soul" (I Pet. 2:11). As pilgrims on the earth we are to live in the heavenly sphere, which can only be done as we receive these heavenly blessings through our union with Christ.

In Christ

We have heavenly possessions, which are ours for the taking, in Christ Jesus here and now. According to Ephesians 1 beginning with verse 17 it is possible for us to experience the exceeding greatness of his power to us-ward who believe. This is the key, this matter of faith or trust to entering into the blessing of the possessions we have in Christ. Christ holds these in trust for us, and we claim them not *from* Him but *in* Him. Christ is all these things to us we have been pointing out. We cannot have anything from God apart from having Christ Himself. God provides us nothing except as we find it in the Lord Jesus Christ. All His power, authority, spiritual blessings are in Christ.

There is a great deal of difference between getting something *from Christ* and having these things *in Christ*. He is the One who is become to us wisdom and strength and sanctification and redemption. Christ is made unto us everything we need. This means a great deal more than for Him to give us something out of His fulness. We are so limited in capacity that what we could receive would be very little. But knowing we are united to Him, all we need we find in Him. He is our strength. For this reason we are called on to be strong in the Lord and in the power of His might. God has nothing for any of us except as we find it in the Lord Jesus Christ.

All power is His whether it is power over sin or over the world or over Satan. Who among us in himself could withstand Satan? What one of us is complete conqueror over the flesh nature? What Christian can withstand in his own strength the temptations and allurements of the world? None of us can, but in Christ we can. He has all power over these enemies of ours, and that power is at our disposal because He is ours. All authority is in His hands; He has all power to do whatever He needs to do. Since we have Christ, we have everything we need. This is the promise of Romans 8:32: "He that spared not his own Son, but delivered him up for us all, how shall he not with him also freely give us all things?"

In Christ God has given us everything. When we have Christ we have everything. All is ours, for He has blessed us with all spiritual blessing in heavenly places in Christ. This is held in trust for us and is bestowed upon us as we by faith claim it.

As previously noted in Joshua 1:3 we have the law or principle of appropriation. God assured Joshua and the people of Israel that every place they walked on in Canaan God had given to them. The dimensions of the Promised Land are, "From the wilderness and this Lebanon even unto the great river, the river Euphrates, all the land of the Hittites, and unto the great sea toward the going down of the sun, shall be your coast." This was not a huge area. It was not as big as Europe or as big as the United States, but it was strategic both as to position and as to chemical wealth. It is a land bridge between the three great continents of Asia, Europe and Africa. The chemical wealth of the Dead Sea alone is exceedingly great. God's gifts are always generous, but Israel possessed the land only to the degree of her faith.

How like many Christians today. They have earthly goods because they have gone after them, but their spiritual poverty

is apparent. There has been no appropriation of what God
has provided. Spiritual poverty results when the things
Christians have in Christ lie unclaimed. A person may have a
substantial bank account put in his name, but unless he
writes checks against it and in that way claims it, it does him
no good. The Lord has given us a spiritual checkbook already
signed with His name. This checkbook covers all the riches
that are ours in Christ Jesus. He has invited all who thirst to
come to Him and drink. We are to receive of Him, claiming
and possessing by faith the divine riches provided for us.

Remember, everything Israel claimed was given to them
on a supernatural basis. If everything had been left without
counting God in, Israel would have had nothing. They were
delivered from Egypt because of supernatural power. They
passed through the Red Sea and witnessed the destruction of
the Egyptian army; yet they were helpless in themselves to
accomplish either thing. God gave them a supernatural
victory in both cases. When they met Amalek and overcame
that nation, it was again a case of God giving them the
victory. Moses prayed on the mountaintop and Joshua led
the army in the battle, but it was God who gave the victory.
Then when the people came to the east side of Jordan, they
destroyed two of the enemy nations and laid claim to the
conquered territory. But these victories were not the fruit of
their own strength or wisdom. It was God who fought on
their behalf. It was supernatural power that rolled back the
Jordan so the children of Israel could cross it; and it was
supernatural power that broke down the walls of Jericho.
The Israelites also found out that for 40 years the people of
Canaan had lived in terror of their coming. This was no
ordinary fear but a supernatural terror that God had instilled
in the Canaanites at the time of Israel's deliverance at the
Red Sea.

The point we are seeking to make is that all we have in
Christ Jesus is on the basis of the supernatural. There is
nothing natural about it. Eternal life with power and
authority over evil forces are all ours the moment we trust in
Christ. We possess them when by faith we claim them.

This spiritual provision is pictured for us in the land promised Israel. In Joshua 1:2 God says that the people would take the land which "I do give to them." According to verse 3 the promise of this land was made to Moses on behalf of the people, and again it is emphatically stated that it was given to them by God. In verse 6 we are told that it was an inheritance God assured the older generation under Moses that He would provide for the nation. In verse 15 it is emphasized again that the land of Canaan was a gift by God to His people. God's gifts are irrevocable. They are not taken back. God bound Himself with an oath basing it on Himself since there was no one higher, that He was giving that land to Israel.

God, however, did not present the land as a gift to an unwilling person or persons. It was necessary that Israel be energetic and possess the land. There was nothing there for those who were lazy or selfish. So it is in the spiritual realm. God's spiritual land is for those who through the energy of faith claim it.

The first generation that came out of Egypt came to Kadesh-barnea and, after hearing the report of the ten spies, decided they could not take the land. They refused to go in and claim it, consequently they did not get it. They went back out into the desert and died. According to Hebrews 4:2, "The word preached did not profit them (speaking of Israel), not being mixed with faith in them that heard it." They did not believe God, consequently they did not enjoy His gift.

The land became theirs legally the moment God uttered His promise. This promise was even made a long time before Israel came out of Egypt. It became theirs experimentally only as they entered the land to claim it and possess it. The principle back of this is given by our Saviour in Matthew 9:29 where He said, "According to your faith be it unto you." Only Joshua and Caleb of that first generation had faith to claim the land. They entered with the younger generation and possessed it many years later.

How few Christians claim all of God's provision for them today. We claim salvation. We have come out of Egypt and have a ticket to heaven. But there are vast spiritual possessions in Christ which we so often fail to claim. What a sorrow this is to the heart of God. In spite of Calvary, in spite of the resurrection of Christ, in spite of the giving of the Holy Spirit, so many Christians are saved yet so as by fire.

What a rebuke Abraham is to many of us in this respect. According to Hebrews 11:8: "By faith Abraham, when he was called to go out into a place which he should after receive for an inheritance, obeyed; and he went out, not knowing whither he went." He was obedient. Obedience is "faith in action." He went out not even knowing that God would give him the land. Faith and obedience are inseparable as the sun and the light it gives are inseparable. Abraham had faith and so he obeyed. God says to us, "Go claim these spiritual riches in Christ. They are yours. I have provided them for you."

Chapter Five

THE INWARD BASIS OF FAITH
(Joshua 1)

Incredible Promises—But True

God not only assigned the leadership of Israel to Joshua, but God encouraged His servant with what to many would seem incredible promises. It is for this same reason that we need to get into the Word of God on a constant basis for ourselves. Here we will find encouragement along the way by all kinds of promises made by God to us.

God first of all gave Joshua the assurance of divine authority back of him. He needed this, for it was no easy matter to follow one of the greatest men of history. This was enough to daunt any person, even the ablest of men. There was possibly no greater man on the earth than Moses, or has been since, by way of a human leader. Yet here was Joshua called on to immediately follow in his steps. How could he do it?

Joshua had God's "I will" to stand back of him. The divine assurance was, "There shall not any man be able to stand before thee all the days of thy life: as I was with Moses, so I will be with thee: I will not fail thee, nor forsake thee" (1:5). When God ordains our service, He morally obligates Himself to see us through to the end. This means that whatever He calls upon us to do by way of spiritual warfare, He obligates Himself to fulfill His purposes in us. Take for instance the promise in John 15:16: "Ye have not chosen me, but I have chosen you, and ordained you, that ye should go and bring forth fruit, and that your fruit should remain: that whatsoever ye shall ask of the Father in my name, he may give it you." Could any promise be clearer or more emphatic? When God makes a promise to us He obligates

66

Himself to fulfill it. Jesus says, "Just ask the Father for it in My Name" (John 14:13,14).

In this light look at Philippians 1:6: "Being confident of this very thing, that he which hath begun a good work in you will perform it until the day of Jesus Christ." The Lord's promise is not only that He will obligate Himself to do a work through us, but He will also do a work in us. What is more, He will not leave that work unfinished but complete it.

This is in accord with Hebrews 13:20,21. There the writer to the Hebrews prayed that the God of peace would "make you perfect [mature] in every good work to do his will, working in you that which is wellpleasing in his sight, through Jesus Christ; to whom be glory for ever and ever." It was by reason of such promises that Paul could say with assurance: "I can do all things through Christ which strengtheneth me."

Joshua needed just such an assurance as was given him as he led Israel in their conquering of Canaan. We need it also for the warfare that we are in. Joshua fought against men, but our warfare is against principalities and powers. Just as Joshua went on from victory to victory so can we as we let our "Joshua" the Lord Jesus Christ lead and direct us.

Israel suffered a temporary setback at Ai. This was a failure due to presumption and sin. This was not a contradiction of the promises God had made, but fitted into God's program of discipline and judgment when sin showed itself among His people.

In the second place, God gave Joshua the assurance of His divine faithfulness. We look again at verse 5 where we read: "As I was with Moses, so I will be with thee: I will not fail thee, nor forsake thee." This is reiterated in verse 9, emphasizing afresh the faithfulness of God.

Joshua had 40 years of experience and observations to fall back upon. He had been Moses' minister for that time and came to know some of the inside things with regard to God's special dealing with Israel's great leader. This is always a precious factor in life. It has been of great personal benefit to me to have had intimate fellowship with some of God's leaders, thus allowing me to see some of the aspects of their work not generally known among God's people. This was the way God dealt with Joshua allowing him to see many things that the average Israelite would know little or nothing about. However, if Joshua had not seen these 40 years of history under Moses, Joshua still had God's word and that is sufficient.

The promise given to Joshua is repeated for us in Hebrews 13:5. There again it is said, "I will never leave thee, nor forsake thee." There are times when we may feel forsaken and in the wisdom of God He may not remove this cloud from us at once; but we can be sure He sees us. He knows our problems and everything we are going through, and He is right beside us to help us. He may not make His presence known for a while in order to allow further testing of us, but such testing is in order to strengthen and encourage us. We must remember He is with us and He has promised never to leave us nor forsake us.

God changes not. The God of Joshua and the God of Moses is our God. Men come and go but God abides and He abides faithful. It is a wonderful truth to rest on that God who always was and always is and always will be is standing by us. His wisdom is infinite, He knows all things. There is no experience but what He knows about it and can cope with it.

Moreover, He has given us His Holy Spirit to be with us forever. For this reason there is nothing to give us fear. The Apostle John wrote: "Ye are of God, little children, and have overcome them: because greater is he that is in you, than he that is in the world. Satan is the one who is greater than any other created being, but he is only a creature and has no strength against the Spirit of God. The Holy Spirit is within us and will remain in us forever.

This assures us of victory over all satanic forces. This is why Paul could say in Romans 8:37, "In all these things we are more than conquerors through him that loved us." This is why Paul exhorts us in Ephesians 6 to be strong in the Lord and in the power of His might and to put on the whole armor of God. Our foes are not flesh and blood foes but principalities and powers in heavenly places. However, our armor, which is really Jesus Christ in us protecting us and delivering us, is sufficient for this fight. He has already conquered our foes and has been given a place of authority over them. "God," we are told, "also hath highly exalted him, and given him a name which is above every name: That at the name of Jesus every knee should bow, of things in heaven, and things in earth, and things under the earth; and that every tongue should confess that Jesus Christ is Lord, to the glory of God the Father" (Phil. 2:9-11). Our Lord has overcome the enemy, so what we need to do is to know Him and the power of His resurrection and the fellowship of His suffering even as Paul desired for himself.

In John 14:12 Jesus said to His disciples and also to us: "Verily, verily, I say unto you, He that believeth on me, the works that I do shall he do also; and greater works than these shall he do; because I go unto my Father." By this He meant that He would send the Spirit of God so that we would do even greater works because of the Spirit's work in and through us.

We also read in Mark 11:22,23 where Jesus admonished the disciples to have faith in God. People often just say, "Have faith." But that is inadequate. We must have faith in God. He is the only One for us to have faith in. When faith is in God we have this promise: "For verily I say unto you, That whosoever shall say unto this mountain, Be thou removed, and be thou cast into the sea; and shall not doubt in his heart, but shall believe that those things which he saith shall come to pass; he shall have whatsoever he saith." So we must learn to know our God. This is the important thing.

God's call to Joshua was given clearly. Israel's new leader was urged to be strong and of a good courage. This was repeated several times. God had revealed Himself as the giver of every good and perfect gift. Furthermore He had set forth the basic principle of faith as the means of appropriating what He had provided. Every place the Israelites walked in Canaan was land God had given them. God had also promised His abiding presence and vowed His absolute faithfulness to

His servants. This was not only a message for Joshua, but for us also. When the Lord Jesus stated that all authority had been given to Him and commanded us to go to the end of the earth with the message of the gospel, He assured us that authority was to follow us. Christ promised to be with us, even to the end of the age. We can believe that and act upon it.

God called upon Joshua to involve himself with respect to God's work. God is calling on us because we have exactly the same promises. We are to go forth and reveal Him to a lost world as the Giver of every good and perfect gift. He has shown us His promises, assured us of His presence and called on us to step out in faith. We are to get involved. We are to be responsive to His call. We are to evidence action. Three times Joshua is admonished by the Lord to be strong and of good courage. Then when Joshua challenged his brethren to follow him, they agreed providing he would be strong and full of courage.

Such are the qualities essential for a soldier engaging himself in aggressive spiritual warfare. The enemies Joshua faced were human, yet back of them were the evil spirits of the unseen spirit world. Therefore the weapons he had to use had to be more than weapons of man's warfare. They had to be of a superhuman quality, for Joshua could not depend upon himself and the Israelites. He needed God's strength. The counterpart is, of course, our own battle against evil beings which we can wage only in the strength of Christ.

Birthright in Christ

The believer has a birthright in Christ. This has to do with our position in Him as born-again members of His family. This is not a position belonging to us because we are members of the human race, but because through trusting Christ we have become children of God.

Part of our trouble in our use of the Word of God is that we don't meditate upon it. We read it but don't take time to let its teaching soak in. We even memorize it, but our efforts do not go beyond what is needed to memorize. For this reason our knowledge of it lacks depth.

Consider the first chapter of Ephesians. There we are told that we have been blessed "with all spiritual blessings in heavenly places in Christ." What are some of these blessings? The passage lists them for us. One of these is the fact that we were chosen in Christ before the foundation of the world, that we should be holy and without blame before Him in love (v.4). God has chosen us to show us His favor, and through us His power, so that a dying world may know what the power of an Almighty God can do in a life.

In verse 5 we learn we have been predestinated to the adoption of children by Jesus Christ. Predestination has to do with a goal that is ahead, so we have the promise here that God will undertake for us so that we reach the place of mature sons. Mere relationship is not the main thought in this portion as is the matter of position. God will see to it that we are placed as mature sons at the right time.

Verse 7 tells us that we have redemption through Christ's blood, the forgiveness of sins according to riches of His grace. Notice that the source of all these blessings is Christ. The forgiveness of our sins and our acceptance before God are due to the Lord Jesus Christ.

Beginning with verse 19 we have the climax of the Apostle's prayer for God's people. Paul prayed that we would know "what is the exceeding greatness of his power to us-ward who believe, according to the working of his mighty power, Which he wrought in Christ, when he raised him from the dead, and set him at his own right hand in the heavenly places, far above all principality, and power, and might, and dominion, and every name that is named, not only in this world, but also in that which is to come: and hath put all things under his feet, and gave him to be the head over all things to the church, which is his body, the fulness of him that filleth all in all."

This passage tells us that the power given to us who believe is the power that raised Jesus Christ from the dead. Humanly speaking resurrection is an impossibility. Men have developed remarkable knowledge in science and medicine these days, but they have not been able to produce life. The ability to produce life would be necessary for the raising of the dead. What man cannot do, however, God can and does do. And that same power that raised up Christ is operative to bring new spiritual life to us who are His children.

It is because of the presence of such divine power in the believer that we can follow in our experience the admonition of Ephesians 6:10. There we are told to "be strong in the Lord, and in the power of his might." The tendency among Christians when they face opposition to living the Christian life, or find themselves opposed in spiritual warfare, is to draw back thinking the cost is too high. It is not the money cost in such things that trouble us as much as some other factors. Perhaps we find we are in the minority, something that has been true down through the years, so is no new factor at all. However, when things are not popular we tend to shrink from them. Let us not forget, though, what happened to Israel at Kadesh-barnea when under Moses' leadership they refused to go in. This was 38 years before the incident we are studying in this series took place. The Israelites under Moses backed off because they believed the task was too much for them. It was, had they been left to their own resources, but their trust should have been in God who would have given them the victory.

So we believers who are now admonished to be strong in the Lord and encouraged in the power of His might should learn from Israel's experience and go forward with the Lord. Thank God for those Christians who are willing to take up this challenge today!

Young people, Christians and non-Christians alike are seeking for what they call "reality." Many of them are frustrated when they look at us who are supposed to be mature in Christian things, and they find that we are not. We talk about Christian standards, but too often we live selfishly following our own standards. Where then is the challenge for young people today who want to follow Christ? Where is the reality for them in the adults who should be showing the way?

It was the older generation of Israelites who revolted against God at Kadesh-barnea according to Numbers 14. It was those who were over the age of 20 and had the responsibilities of homes and families. They were supposed to set the example for the younger people; but instead they defected, not having the spiritual qualities of faith and trust in God that were needed for such a decision. It is no wonder God said that generation had to go back into the desert and would not be permitted to enter the Promised Land.

God then added that those little children of theirs whom the parents had thought would be "cannon fodder" for Israel's enemies would eventually enter Canaan. When the older generation had died and the younger generation had come to maturity, God would again give His people the opportunity to enter the land.

That younger generation was not guilty of delinquency, a word so often attributed to youth in our day. The delinquents were the older generation. The young people failed to see reality in their parents. Undoubtedly this is part of the reason today why our youth are troubled and often act irresponsibly.

We as believers must be strong and of good courage. We have everything to gain and nothing to lose in following the Lord fully. Our strength is in Him, not in ourselves. We are admonished to be strong in the Lord and in the power of His might.

Not many are called to lead a great nation as was Joshua. Yet all of us Christians who have reached adulthood have certain responsibilities of spiritual leadership whether in the church or in the family. Joshua felt weak but God assured him: "You be strong, for I will be your strength." This is God's promise to us also.

Joshua felt very inadequate. God reassured him, admonishing him to be of good courage and not to worry about his inadequacy. The Lord promised to take care of any situation that he would face. It would only be natural for

Joshua to have some fear as he considered the great task before him, but God quieted his fears, giving him boldness.

There may have been times when Joshua felt like quitting. He had played second fiddle for 40 years. He had not been called on to carry the full responsibility of leadership. There was always someone else to fall back on. Now there was no Moses to make decisions or to hear God's word and pass them on to Joshua and the people. Joshua was the one who stood between Israel and God. The Lord encouraged him not to be dismayed, assuring His servant that He, the Eternal God would be with him and never leave him. God said to him that as He was with Moses so He would be with him. Again and again God told him to "be strong and of a good courage."

May God be able to bring us to such a low estimate of ourselves that He can get us to the place where we will let Him be our strength. Frankly, many of us fail because we are too big for God. God cannot do what He wants to do because we want to do it ourselves. This is sin on our part. That which is not of faith is sin.

Many exclaim, "I've tried and I have tried but with no success." This is our trouble. We have tried, but we have tried in our own strength and abilities. It is no wonder we have failed. Let us admit our failures so that God can be strong on our behalf. The world speaks of the "survival of the fittest" but God does not. He gives power to the faint and strength to those who have no strength within themselves.

Paul learned this lesson well and wrote about it in II Corinthians 12. God said to him, "My grace is sufficient for thee: for my strength is made perfect in weakness." In answer to this Paul stated: "Most gladly therefore will I rather glory in my infirmities, that the power of Christ may rest upon me. Therefore I take pleasure in infirmities, and reproaches, in necessities, in persecutions, in distresses for Christ's sake: for when I am weak, then am I strong" (vv. 9,10).

Paul came to the place where he saw that any spiritual power he possessed had its source in our Lord Jesus Christ. In stating this same general truth from another standpoint, Paul said, "For ye see your calling, brethren, how that not many wise men after the flesh, not many mighty, not many noble, are called: But God hath chosen the foolish things of the world to confound the wise; and God hath chosen the weak things of the world to confound the things which are mighty; And base things of the world, and things which are despised, hath God chosen, yea, and things which are not, to bring to nought things that are" (I Cor. 1:26-28). What the world calls weak God makes strong so that His work may continue and prosper.

We need to translate this truth into the realm of our spiritual warfare. Our ability to overcome, victorious living on our part, is God's responsibility, for it is part of our birthright. We can be strong in Him and of a good courage for the result is sure. He supplies the strength. It is our responsibility to act in faith.

This was the message the Lord made very clear to Joshua when He commanded him to lead the people into the land. It was a weighty task, but God was going to be with Joshua just as He had been with Moses. And just as Israel's Joshua led them into their inheritance, our Joshua, the Lord Jesus Christ, leads us into our inheritance.

Joshua had not forgotten the first stop the Israelites had made at Kadesh-barnea and how they turned against him and Caleb and others who dared to believe God. There is always opposition for those who want to go on with God, and this can be very discouraging.

There are those who will tell us that we must stay under the law if we are going to make progress in the Christian life. But the Lord tells us we are not under law but under grace. Our strength lies in what comes from God, from the God of grace. Eternal life finds its source in Christ, for He said concerning His own, "I give unto them eternal life; and they shall never perish, neither shall any man pluck them out of my hand." Until we see this truth we will never have the power of God in our lives. As long as we try to keep ourselves we ignore the power of God and what He wants to give us. Defeat is all we can expect under such circumstances.

Sad to say there are others who, when they come to understand that they can be overcomers and enter into spiritual possessions here and now in Christ, back off when they realize that spiritual warfare with Satan and his hosts is involved. They are content to remain in the wilderness rather than to make progress in divine things. They are satisfied with having their sins forgiven and an assurance of heaven, but they do not want to develop and mature in spiritual things. Existence in the spiritual wilderness satisfies them.

Chapter Six

THE INWARD BASIS OF FAITH
(Joshua 1) (Continued)

Babes in Christ

Some may be inclined to say that the person we have been discussing who wants to remain in the wilderness cannot be a Christian at all. Such overlook the truth that a person can be a babe in spiritual things. In fact, all of us who have been born again began as babes in Christ, but there is no need for us to remain babes. For a person to be a Christian at all he must be born again. But not all Christians reach the same degree of maturity.

Concerning babes in Christ Peter wrote: "As newborn babes, desire the sincere milk of the word, that ye may grow thereby" (I Pet. 2:2). It is normal that a babe in Christ should desire the milk of the Word. But, on the other hand, the baby stage in Christian things is not the spiritually mature stage. This Paul made clear in his Letter to the Corinthians: "And I, brethren, could not speak unto you as unto spiritual, but as unto carnal, even as unto babes in Christ. I have fed you with milk, and not with meat: for hitherto ye were not able to bear it, neither yet now are ye able. For ye are yet carnal: for whereas there is among you envying, and strife, and divisions, are ye not carnal, and walk as men?" (I Cor. 3:1-3). What Paul has listed here are signs of spiritual carnality, signs of spiritual babyhood. How many spiritual babes we have today!

The same charge is made against certain believers in the Book of Hebrews. The writer stated: "Of whom we have many things to say, and hard to be uttered, seeing ye are dull of hearing. For when for the time ye ought to be teachers, ye have need that one teach you again which be the first principles of the oracles of God; and are become such as have need of milk, and not of strong meat. For every one that useth milk is unskilful in the word of righteousness: for he is a babe" (Heb. 5:11-13). This is God's evaluation of the spiritual babe, not mine. If we still think only in terms of the milk of the Word and of the matter of the beginning of our salvation, we endanger our own spiritual growth. The passage continues: "But strong meat belongeth to them that are of full age, even those who by reason of use have their senses exercised to discern both good and evil" (v. 14). It is no wonder that the next chapter in Hebrews begins with the admonition for Christians to progress from the foundational things and go on to maturity.

Self-Discipline Through the Word

Considering again what God said to Joshua we find this expression: "Only be thou strong and very courageous" (Josh. 1:7). The goal God had set for him was that he might "observe to do according to all the law, which Moses my servant commanded thee: turn not from it to the right hand or to the left, that thou mayest prosper whithersoever thou goest." The word "very" is emphatic and strong. Joshua was going to need to be very courageous, for he had to deal first with himself before he could deal with others. It is easier for us to see the faults in others and admonish them or exhort them to go on with God than it is to practice self-discipline.

God calls upon each one of us for absolute obedience. He did this with Joshua and this is ever His standard. Some persons may want us to follow directions other than those God gives; but if one is to have complete victory and be an overcomer he must follow God's plan explicitly.

This was why Joshua, as we have said, needed to be very courageous. He had to practice self-discipline before he could expect others to be helped through him. This self-discipline comes through the Word of God. The tendency of man, and much of the teaching and preaching of today shows it, is to "Do this," and, "Do not do this." Christians are often scolded for not doing certain things and scolded for some things they do. There is a need for a critical examination of our lives, but one has to be sure he is admonishing the right persons. There is no point in telling babes in Christ they have to go out to work because as babes they are not ready to work. They have to be trained and to be made strong and be able to partake of strong meat before they can work for the Lord as they should.

There are some people who are too lazy to work. The majority of persons, however, when they find they have growing muscles want to do something with them. Spiritually speaking it is the same way. But in this area we can talk our heads off to babes in Christ, telling them what they should do and should not do without first feeding them the kind of spiritual food that will cause them to grow. We cannot discipline ourselves in the Bible sense of the term until we learn that Christ indwells us to live His life in us, and that self-discipline comes from Him.

We are living in a day of rapid and often great change. We are frequently told that we must keep up with the times, and there are philosophies and methods that must be changed if we are to have any impact for God in this day and age. There may well be some truth in this, but we must also remember that there are some things that do not change. God's basic principle of operation in the heart of the Christian has never changed and never will change. We must stick to the good, old truth of the Word of God just as God has given it to us.

It was to this very Word that God sent Joshua for his strength and courage. It is one thing to say to a man that he should be very courageous, but there must be something to base this on. There must be some source to which he can go to find this courage. This is why God said in Joshua 1:8: "This book of the law shall not depart out of thy mouth; but thou shalt meditate therein day and night, that thou mayest observe to do according to all that is written therein: for then thou shalt make thy way prosperous, and then thou shalt have good success."

Obedience to the Word of God is the source of our strength and courage. There is no short cut. Satan is not concerned about how much work a Christian does or how much activity he enters into as long as he does not take time in the Word of God. When he does, then Satan becomes alarmed for he knows that it is then that spiritual fruit will result from the Christian's activities and ministry. Satan knows better than we do that we do not get far, even though we run around and do all kinds of things, as long as we do not take time in the Word of God to gain strength. We are just so many little people trying to do a job too big for us. Satan knows, and we should know, that a baby Christian cannot do the job of a mature Christian. But as soon as we begin to get into the Word of God, then trouble with our enemy begins. The reason is that faith cometh by hearing and hearing by the Word of God (Rom. 10:17).

When we begin to believe God, things begin to happen. As long as we do not trust God, and refuse His strength and life, nothing of any consequence takes place. It is the Word of God that is powerful as we read in Hebrews 4:12: "For the word of God is quick [life giving], and powerful, and sharper than any twoedged sword, piercing even to the dividing asunder of soul and spirit, and of the joints and marrow, and is a discerner of the thoughts and intents of the heart."

When we start reading and meditating upon the Word of God, the Holy Spirit begins to pierce our hearts with it. He points out to us what is wrong in our lives. He exposes our sin and shows us His righteousness. These are things Satan does not want to see happen and is the reason why he wants to keep us from the study of the Bible.

I learned this lesson early in my ministry. I attended seminary where I learned all about the Word of God. I learned to do research in it and learned many things about it, but I did not learn the Word itself. It was after I got into the ministry and learned from the Word itself that faith comes by hearing and hearing by the Word of God that I began to study the Word and meditate upon it. It was then that I began to meditate on it and then sowed it in my preaching, trusting God to give the increase.

The Lord Jesus said in John 6:63: "It is the spirit that quickeneth; the flesh profiteth nothing: the words that I speak unto you, they are spirit, and they are life." Spiritual life comes to us through the Word. The Saviour assures us of this Himself.

The Psalmist wrote concerning the godly man: "But his delight is in the law of the Lord; and in his law [Word] doth he meditate day and night. And he shall be like a tree planted by the rivers of water, that bringeth forth his fruit in his season; his leaf also shall not wither; and whatsoever he doeth shall prosper" (Ps. 1:2,3). It is by giving ourselves to the Word of God in this way that the promises in these verses are realized. But someone may ask how it is possible to meditate on the Word of God day and night? That is not hard to answer. During the day we can read it and memorize it. During the night hours when we lie awake we can quote it and think upon it. If we should have a tendency to wake at night and start worrying about things, we will find release from our anxieties by thinking on some promise from the Word. Recall some Bible verse that has been memorized and meditate upon it. It will do wonders.

We read further in II Timothy 3:16,17: "All scripture is given by inspiration of God, and is profitable for doctrine, for reproof, for correction, for instruction in righteousness: That the man of God may be perfect, throughly furnished unto all good works." Without the Word the results spoken of in this passage could not be realized. No wonder Jeremiah recorded the fact that the Lord likens His Word to a fire and to a hammer that breaks the rocks in pieces (Jer. 23:29).

Then there is the 119th Psalm that from beginning to end deals with the Word of God. It shows how essential the Word is in every phase of our lives. So we must get into the Word. There is no short cut. We have to pay the price of time and effort, but it pays eternal dividends.

Our Manual of Instruction

Just how it is that God can take the written Word and make it a living Word with us has never been explained. It is beyond human explanation. But we do know that the Holy Spirit takes the written Word of God and conveys to us through it the Living Christ. The Spirit takes what God said and makes it a living Word within us. This marvelous work of the Holy Spirit is such that without it we could never expect success. "It is the spirit that quickeneth; the flesh profiteth nothing: the words that I speak unto you, they are spirit, and they are life" (John 6:63). "For the word of God is living and active and sharper than any two-edged sword, and piercing as far as the division of soul and spirit, of both joints and marrow, and able to judge the thoughts and intentions of the heart" (Heb. 4:12, N.A.S.). Our responsibility is to get into the Word for ourselves and, as we have pointed out already, meditate on it day and night.

The Word of God is our manual of instruction for spiritual warfare. This will unfold more and more as we get into these future chapters in Joshua. If we are to be the kind of Christians God wants us to be we must take time to get into the Word. This must be a deep settled purpose with us for there is no short cut. As we have already emphasized we must pay the price of time even if it means a little less sleep or giving less attention to some things that we may count precious otherwise. It takes more than just a casual reading of the Word. Meditation and delighting in it are prerequisites to victory through it.

To meditate on the Word means to digest it. It also means that we set our hearts upon it with a determination to obey it. When this is done we will find that God's promises are fulfilled in us. This is what will make our way prosperous and give us good success.

The Lord admonished Joshua: "Neither be thou dismayed: for the Lord thy God is with thee whithersoever thou goest" (1:9). God stayed with the people of Israel in the desert even though they had little accomplishment to show for the 40 years they spent in the desert. Yet God was faithful to them providing manna and water, and shade by day and light by night. The lives of many of them while in the desert were characterized by quarreling and murmuring, yet God was true to them though He must have been very disappointed in them. Their lives must have been a heartbreak to Him. Finally the nation (i.e., a new generation) began to obey God and followed Him, showing it by their obedience to Joshua. It was then they began to conquer and possess the land. Eventually they had rest from their enemies. Joshua took to heart this admonition of the Lord and was blessed in his obedient faith.

One of the first things Joshua did following this encouragement from the Lord was to command "the officers of the people, saying, Pass through the host, and command the people, saying, Prepare you victuals; for within three days ye shall pass over this Jordan, to go in to possess the land, which the Lord your God giveth you to possess it" (vv. 10,11). Those three days were days of preparation of a special kind. And after they were completed Joshua gave orders for the people to march.

Questionable Separation

A rather sad note enters in with regard to some of the tribes. They did not all have the same degree of separation from the evil around them nor the same degree of surrender to God. Beginning with verse 12 of Joshua 1 we read: "And to the Reubenites, and to the Gadites, and to half the tribe of Manasseh, spake Joshua, saying, Remember the word which Moses the servant of the Lord commanded you, saying, The Lord your God hath given you rest, and hath given you this land. Your wives, your little ones, and your cattle, shall remain in the land which Moses gave you on this side Jordan; but ye shall pass before your brethren armed, all the mighty men of valour, and help them; Until the Lord have given your brethren rest, as he hath given you, and they also have possessed the land which the Lord your God giveth them: then ye shall return unto the land of your possession, and enjoy it, which Moses the Lord's servant gave you on this side Jordan toward the sunrising" (vv. 12-15).

The background for this lies in the fact that while Moses

was still leader, the Israelites conquered some of the kings on the east side of Jordan and took possession of their lands. It was good land with strong, walled cities and a countryside ideal for the raising of cattle. Two and a half of the tribes, Reuben, Gad and half of the tribe of Manasseh asked to stay on that side of Jordan. Someone has entitled their decision as "the choice of world borderers." These tribes wanted Canaan, but not that part of Canaan across Jordan. A reading of chapter 32 of Numbers gives the historical background for the whole transaction. We read in the New Testament in Mark 5:1-17 what the descendants of those tribes were like when our Saviour came to live among men.

Like Lot these two and a half tribes chose what appealed to the eye. They were more concerned with physical and material things than spiritual. They illustrate a type of carnal Christians. Every believer is given the right to choose what level of Christianity he wants, but he must remember the consequences when God's best is rejected.

A definite statement concerning this matter is given to us in Psalm 106:15. There we learn that God gave certain ones their request but sent leanness to their souls. Lot and his wife also made an unfortunate choice in their day and lost everything.

It must be said on behalf of these two and a half tribes that their warriors were willing to help the other tribes take the land across the river and possess it. But the Reubenites and Gadites wanted to return to the other side of Jordan where things were more appealing to the eye and where there was ease, comfort, plenty and riches as the world would look at it. They tasted of the blessings of the promised land and helped the others to secure it, but they themselves hankered after the world, its pleasures and indulgences and were eventually trapped and ensnared by it. This is always the danger of those who would live on the border and not get into the land.

God has His best for the few who will dare to stand the test and endure the hard places they come to. Yet these hard places are made easy in Christ Jesus. His yoke is easy and His burden is light the Scriptures tell us.

The choice made by the Reubenites was in keeping with their family head, Reuben the first-born of Jacob. His conduct was such that he lost his birthright. He was never the leader the first-born was intended to be. We read in I Chronicles 5:1: "Now the sons of Reuben the firstborn of Israel, (for he was the firstborn; but, forasmuch as he defiled his father's bed, his birthright was given unto the sons of Joseph the son of Israel: and the genealogy is not to be reckoned after the birthright."

The two and a half tribes started out nobly, but they were the first to defect and go into heathen worship. They were also the first tribes of the northern kingdom to be taken into captivity. This took place quite some time before the northern kingdom lost its identity.

The lesson for us here is not so much how a man begins his Christian life but how he ends it. This is what counts.

When the descendants of these tribes are brought to our attention in the New Testament we find them keepers of swine in disobedience to the command of God under the law. The Lord Jesus cast demons out of the man of Gadara and these demons entered into a great herd of swine and "the herd ran violently down a steep place into the sea" (Mark 5:13). There were nearly 2,000 animals involved, and the Gadarenes were so deep in their backsliding that they implored the Lord Jesus to leave their country. They wanted no further exposure of their evil ways.

The Unity of the People

Though we have considered the subject of so-called "border Christians" fixing our thoughts on the experiences of the two and a half tribes that decided to stay on the east side of Jordan, their spiritual defection did not show up until a later date. At the time covered by these Scriptures in the Book of Joshua there was a wonderful unity between the tribes. The danger was largely a hidden one and did not become an open danger until later. The experience of Lot, Abraham's nephew, shows what happens under similar conditions. Lot separated from Abraham and went down into the rich valley of the Jordan River. At first everything seemed to go well, but little by little the interests of Lot and his family became centered in Sodom and God was largely forgotten. The pull of the material became stronger than the spiritual. It did not take long.

As we have stated, however, at the time Israel was ready to enter Canaan there was real unity among the tribes.

Such unity is seen in the response of the leaders of Israel to Joshua's instructions. They said, "According as we hearkened unto Moses in all things, so will we hearken unto thee: only the Lord thy God be with thee, as he was with Moses. Whosoever he be that doth rebel against thy commandment, and will not hearken unto thy words in all that thou commandest him, he shall be put to death: only be strong and of a good courage" (Josh. 1:17,18). These men showed they were one in spirit and purpose with Joshua in fulfilling the commands of the Lord. Such encouragement was needed and when given was appreciated. It showed real harmony in Israel at that time.

There have been marked divisions in Christendom over the last centuries. Dissensions and disunity have often been present where there should have been harmony and fellowship. Now there is a movement on foot that is attempting to bring all branches of Christendom into one big union. But there is a marked difference between unity which the Spirit of God produces and a union which men form. The present ecumenical movement is man's attempt to overcome divisions among Christian organizations by bringing them into one big organization. This does not mean unity, however, for the very basic doctrines of Christianity, as well as Christ Himself, have been pushed aside in order to effect this union. We dare not be misled by such a man-made organization, but we must at the same time seek to be strong in the unity that the Spirit of God produces.

True spiritual unity is not possible apart from the work of the Spirit of God. That He has provided such a unity among God's people is taught in the Scriptures. We read in I Corinthians 12:13: "For by one Spirit are we all baptized into one body, whether we be Jews or Gentiles, whether we be bond or free; and have been all made to drink into one Spirit." This is true unity.

Another statement on this subject is Ephesians 4:3: "Endeavouring to keep the unity of the Spirit in the bond of peace." We endeavor to keep this unity through being filled or being under the control of the Holy Spirit. We must put ourselves at His disposal and allow Him to bring us together as believers in Christ.

Joshua had the assurance as he began his march into Canaan that he had the full allegiance of the Israelites. As God's man he could count on them to stand back of him. Insubordination was not going to be tolerated for one moment.

I shall never forget an action on the part of some of my friends that expressed their confidence in me and faithfulness to me as a servant of God. This took place in my early ministry. I had been pastor of a small church in which I had the joy of leading the majority of the people to a saving knowledge of the Lord Jesus Christ. There was a spirit of allegiance and harmony in the group that came only from the Lord. It was difficult for me to leave them even though I knew the Lord was leading me to do so. I remember one little fellow, some eight or ten years of age, coming up to me, hugging me and crying his heart out as he said, "Brother Epp, you just can't leave." That was a time the Lord was calling us to this Broadcast ministry, and we had to obey the Lord.

Sometime later I was back in that same neighborhood conducting some meetings and some of these friends helped me. A slander was started against me in a neighboring church which I did not know about at the time. A few of the leaders of my former pastorate found out about it, traced it down, found the person who had started the evil story and made him retract his lie. He admitted he had lied; and at the insistence of these church officials he went back to the people to whom he had talked about me and confessed he had lied. The brethren from my former pastorate straightened this matter out and stopped the lie from being spread any farther. Then, after it was all over, they came and told me about it. Such an experience binds Christians together and also to the Lord. This was a genuine attempt to preserve the unity of the Spirit, and it succeeded.

The leaders of Israel under Joshua gave him implicit obedience so that the work of God could be done. This was the key to the success of that great venture in conquering and possessing the land. This is also the key to spiritual success on our part—obedience to Christ.

The Lord said about David, "I have found David, the son of Jesse, a man after mine own heart, which shall fulfill all my will" (Acts 13:22). The purpose of our hearts must be like that of David's. We must determine to obey God. The Holy Spirit indwells us for this very purpose. We have Christ in us the hope of glory. He has come to live in us that He might live out His personal life of obedience through us. He was obedient to the heavenly Father, coming not to do His own will but His Father's will. We want to do the same, but we cannot do it except as Christ does it in us. There must be a heart response on our part. This must result not only in mere words, but in actions.

This obedience, then, would be in line with James 1:22-25 which says, "Be ye doers of the word, and not hearers only, deceiving your own selves. For if any be a hearer of the word, and not a doer, he is like unto a man beholding his natural face in a glass: For he beholdeth himself, and goeth his way, and straightway forgetteth what manner of man he was. But whoso looketh into the perfect law of liberty, and continueth therein, he being not a forgetful hearer, but a doer of the work, this man shall be blessed in his deed."

In this connection the Lord Jesus has a very strong warning for us in Matthew 7:21: "Not every one that saith unto me, Lord, Lord, shall enter into the kingdom of heaven; but he that doeth the will of my Father which is in heaven."

In order to realize unity among ourselves as God's people, we must place ourselves at God's disposal so that we might be one in Christ. This is the only way there can be oneness in Him among us down here. Christ, who is the Head of the Body, must be given complete control of every member of the Body.

Chapter Seven

THE OUTWARD BASIS OF FAITH
(Joshua 2)

The Defeated Foe

In the second chapter of the Book of Joshua we learn about the defeated foe. In the first chapter we found how God has called us to a life of overcoming, a life of victory. We are instructed how we are to do it. It is by faith. He gives us wonderful promises and assures us He will be present with us at all times. We have a number of illustrations furnished us as to what God expects to be done.

In Joshua 2 a concrete illustration is given of something that is necessary to help us understand what God is undertaking in our lives. If we master this chapter, especially certain verses in it, we will begin to see how God in Christ has already won every victory for us. But it is up to you and me as individuals to by faith cash in on this particular victory.

Joshua sent two spies into the land to find out what they could concerning the city of Jericho. This city was the first great fortress to be overcome, and its king was not asleep. He had an intelligence department that apparently brought him word of the movements of Joshua's armies; and the coming of the two spies was not lost to the king. His officers reported that two of the Israelites had entered Jericho.

The kings of Canaan are types of the principalities and powers mentioned in Ephesians 6:12. It is possible that the King of Jericho was the most important of all of these kings and becomes a type of Satan himself. The Devil is not asleep. He is quite aware of the activities of Christians in their work for the Lord. It becomes the purpose of the Evil One to hinder the believer in his ministry. We do not point this out so as to dismay any one, but to emphasize that eventually

90

there will be victory for the believer who walks in the strength of the Lord.

There was a distinct difference in the purpose of the spies sent by Joshua and those that had formerly been sent by Moses. The spies in Moses' time were not sent because Moses questioned God's promises, but because the people doubted and wanted information to substantiate their doubts. It was the people who wanted to send in the spies to find out whether the land was worth going after. Theirs was a negative approach because they did not believe God. They were looking for evidence to support their unbelief. In the case of Joshua, he believed God and he sent the spies after evidence to substantiate faith and not doubt. The Israelites were committed to entering Canaan, and Joshua wanted to discover the wealth of the land and the strength of the foe.

We need to learn more about the inheritance we have in Christ Jesus. We need to know the spiritual wealth that is ours in Him. We also need to get information on the strength of Satan just as Paul warns in II Corinthians 2:11: "Lest Satan should get an advantage of us: for we are not ignorant of his devices." We need the information Peter furnishes when he says, "Be sober, be vigilant; because your adversary the devil, as a roaring lion, walketh about, seeking whom he may devour" (I Pet. 5:8). We need to know the reality of the foe, and the strength of the foe; yet at the same time we must recognize that he is a defeated foe and is afraid of God and of any of God's people who dare to believe God for absolute victory.

That is what happened in the heart of the King of Jericho. He was filled with fear. This is true of the demons under Satan. We are victorious when we go against them in the strength of Christ.

Rahab and the Spies

Joshua's two spies entered Jericho, finding refuge in the house of Rahab. She was a woman of low morals, but apparently she had a spiritual awakening of some kind though she was not a saved person at the time the spies first met her. She hid them under stalks of flax on the roof of her house, and when the King of Jericho sent soldiers to arrest the Israelites, she lied about them saying they had already made their escape.

It is easy to understand why the King of Jericho would be apprehensive about such visitors. He knew they had come to investigate his fortifications in preparation for Israel's invasion. The king had good reason to be uneasy.

We have already pointed out that the King of Jericho is a type of Satan. Before we develop our analogy relating to this particular incident, however, let us remind ourselves that we should know something of Satan's devices so that he will not catch us unawares. Peter warns us to be sober and vigilant because the Evil One is seeking our destruction. We are to resist him steadfast in the faith. When we do there is no need to anticipate failure. According to Ephesians 1:18-23 the power at our disposal is unlimited.

The King of Jericho wanted Rahab to produce the spies who had sought refuge in her home. He was alarmed at their presence in his city. Satan is no less alarmed when Christians begin to move forward in the things of the Lord. The evil powers watch us and try to thwart our efforts when we become involved in spiritual warfare. But there is nothing that need cause fear in us because we have the promise that greater is He that is in us than he that is in the world.

The persons who have real cause for fear are the Devil and his demons. That they show fear when the circumstances are right is clear from the following incident: "And there was in their synagogue a man with an unclean spirit; and he cried out, Saying, Let us alone; what have we to do with thee, thou Jesus of Nazareth? art thou come to destroy us? I know thee who thou art, the Holy One of God" (Mark 1:23-25). The demons well know that there is a judgment day for them. Those involved in this incident were fearful that that day had arrived.

Some will say the demons would naturally be afraid of Christ, but they would not be afraid of us. They are afraid of us if we are walking with the Lord Jesus Christ. Satan is a defeated person according to Hebrews 2:14,15 and can have no power over us when we assert this fact with regard to our position in Christ. The power of Satan was annulled through Christ's death on the cross, so there is no reason why we should give in to him or give him any place of control in our lives.

We also learn from Philippians 2:9-11 that after Jesus Christ finished His ministry on the cross and was raised again from the dead, God highly exalted Him and gave Him a name that is above every name. This means that He was given authority above all principalities and powers, and that all beings in heaven or on earth or under the earth will confess that He is Lord to the glory of God the Father. This has not yet been realized for all the universe but the demons and Satan acknowledge His authority over them. Satan knows what his limitations are, just how far he can go as well as what he cannot do.

Satan cannot stand against us when we dare to believe God and claim the power God has for us, the same power God showed when He raised Christ from the dead and gave Him a place above all principalities and powers.

The Devil does not fear us as such. He does fear Christ who is in us, however. John assured us in his First Epistle: "Ye are of God, little children, and have overcome them: because greater is he that is in you, than he that is in the world" (I John 4:4). The Devil is no match for the One who indwells us. Our strength, our power, our victory, our ability to overcome Satan is in Christ and we are in Christ.

When the King of Jericho commanded Rahab to give up the two men she hid in her house she lied to him. She said they went out at dark and she did not know which direction they took. Rahab's lie cannot be condoned. Such deceit cannot be justified as far as Christians are concerned. We must remember, however, that she was a pagan woman whose heart and mind were just being opened to spiritual things.

In spite of the fact that she lied, God used her to help preserve His servants. God used an enemy of His people to shelter two of them. This is in line with Proverbs 16:7 which says, "When a man's ways please the Lord, he maketh even his enemies to be at peace with him."

The same truth is brought out in the experience of Jeremiah. He was put in prison because he had dared to tell his countrymen and king that God had given Jerusalem over to Nebuchadnezzar, the Babylonian ruler. His own king and leaders were angry with him and threw him in a dungeon, but when Nebuchadnezzar came and did as God said he would do to the city and its people, he freed Jeremiah and gave him the choice of going to Babylon or to go back to his own home outside Jerusalem. God in His grace made Nebuchadnezzar to be at peace with Jeremiah and to protect him and help him when his own countrymen would have taken his life.

Something of what was going on in Rahab's mind is disclosed in her conversation with the two men after she brought them out from their hiding place. Her words were, "I know that the Lord hath given you the land, and that your terror is fallen upon us, and that all the inhabitants of the land faint because of you. For we have heard how the Lord dried up the water of the Red Sea for you, when ye came out of Egypt; and what ye did unto the two kings of the Amorites, that were on the other side Jordan, Sihon and Og, whom ye utterly destroyed. And as soon as we had heard these things, our hearts did melt, neither did there remain any more courage in any man, because of you: for the Lord your God, he is God in heaven above, and in earth beneath" (Josh. 2:9-11).

What a testimony this was coming from the person who was not a saved person in the way we use that terminology! For 40 years the Canaanites had been in fear of the Israelites. This must have been a revelation to these men of the terror that had laid hold of the whole population of Canaan, leaders and people alike. They knew that they could not stand against Israel's God.

Just so is the Devil aware of his own defeat, and he would like to keep us from finding it out. Rahab had begun to see something about God, recognizing Him as God of heaven and

earth before whom no earthly power could stand. Even
before she was saved God gave her credit for believing that
He existed and for acting upon that knowledge. She is added
to the gallery of the great heroes of faith in the 11th chapter
of Hebrews. We read: "By faith the harlot Rahab perished
not with them that believed not, when she had received the
spies with peace." In her case faith produced godly fear. The
fear of the Lord is the beginning of wisdom. Cannot we also
believe God concerning victory over Satan? Why cannot we
go in faith and claim the victory which is in Christ Jesus? We
can with Paul thank God who gives us the victory through
our Lord Jesus Christ. God always makes us to triumph in
Christ. When we advance in this area of spiritual warfare, we
will find that the fear of God's judgment is already upon the
enemy. The demons believe there is a God and they tremble.
Let us appropriate the victory that is in Christ, advancing
from faith to faith.

Rahab's Faith

It needs to be repeated again and again that in our
spiritual warfare as believers we fight against a defeated foe.
This does not mean there will not be a battle, but it does
mean we do not need to be worried about the outcome.
Satan is not afraid of us but he is afraid of Christ, and as long
as we walk with Christ, victory is assured. As we press
forward in aggressive warfare on the spiritual battlefield, we
will find as did the two spies in Jericho that terror has
already laid hold of the enemy; and they anticipate nothing
but defeat. The powers of darkness tremble when we come in
the strength of the Lord.

Rahab knew what had happened to the morale of the
Canaanites. She herself shared their belief and conviction that
the nations of Canaan were doomed. But she saw more than
this. If the God of Israel is God in heaven above and in earth
beneath and can judge as He pleases, He can also save. So she
made a very definite plea for herself and her father's house.
She said, "Now therefore, I pray you, swear unto me by the

Lord, since I have shewed you kindness, that ye will also shew kindness unto my father's house, and give me a true token: And that ye will save alive my father, and my mother, and my brethren, and my sisters, and all that they have, and deliver our lives from death" (Josh. 2:12,13). Her primary concern seemed to be for her family and included herself only when she said, "and deliver *our* lives from death."

The two spies gave her reassurance putting their own lives on the line. They said, "Our life for yours, if ye utter not this our business. And it shall be, when the Lord hath given us the land, that we will deal kindly and truly with thee" (v. 14).

As they were leaving her they gave her last minute instructions: "We will be blameless of this thine oath which thou hast made us swear. Behold, when we come into the land, thou shalt bind this line of scarlet thread in the window which thou didst let us down by: and thou shalt bring thy father, and thy mother, and thy brethren, and all thy father's household, home unto thee. And it shall be, that whosoever shall go out of the doors of thy house into the street, his blood shall be upon his head, and we will be guiltless: and whosoever shall be with thee in the house, his blood shall be on our head, if any hand be upon him" (vv. 17-19). Rahab had a home located on the city wall which made it possible for her to effect the escape of the two spies, and would make it easily identifiable during an attack.

This preservation of the family of Rahab brings before us the subject of household salvation. A Christian can believe for the salvation of his household, but he must also be faithful and show them the way to God through Christ Jesus. An individual can be saved only through personal faith, but a saved member of the household can do much in bringing others of the family to that decision.

The only safe place in Jericho was Rahab's house. There was no safety in the king's palace. There was no safety for other homes in Jericho whether on the walls or in the city. We are told that the walls were 90 feet high and 30 feet wide, but they were not going to be able to stand against the invading forces of Israel. In fact, the very method God used to break down the defences of the city made the wall the most dangerous place of any. At the moment designated by God the walls collapsed with the exception of that part where Rahab's house was located. This was God's undertaking and He honored the faith of Rahab and the promise of the spies.

It is also significant that it was a scarlet cord or rope that Rahab was to display in her window. This was symbolic of the blood of Christ which according to I John 1:7 cleanses us from all sin. In Hebrews 9:22 we are told that "almost all things are by the law purged with blood; and without shedding of blood is no remission." The protection that came to Rahab's household reminds us also of the incident of the Passover in Egypt. God instructed His people to sprinkle blood on the doorposts of their houses. He assured them that when the death angel came to slay the firstborn in Egypt, the houses protected by the blood would not be entered. They would be spared. The scarlet cord in Rahab's window protected her household just as the blood on the doorposts protected the Israelites in Egypt.

The New Testament makes special mention of Rahab with regard to this. James wrote: "Likewise also was not Rahab the harlot justified by works, when she had received the messengers, and had sent them out another way?" (2:25). Rahab had a faith that worked. She aided the spies in their escape from Jericho and hung a scarlet cord from her window. This was faith in action.

Rahab's faith brought her triumph. When Joshua and his soldiers entered Jericho the record says, "And Joshua saved Rahab the harlot alive, and her father's household, and all that she had; and she dwelleth in Israel even unto this day; because she hid the messengers, which Joshua sent to spy out Jericho" (Josh. 6:25). Grace overshadowed all her sin. Wherever she is spoken of in the Bible, she is called Rahab the harlot which emphasizes the kind of sinner she was; but God in marvelous grace saved her because she dared to believe Him.

Rahab's salvation from death is a type of our salvation

from sin if we will dare to believe God. The salvation He provides saves us from more than the guilt of sin, for it saves us also from sin's power and makes it possible for us to live useful lives for the Lord. The Bible tells us that Rahab became the wife of an Israelite and the great grandmother of David, the family line from which Christ came.

This is a marvelous picture and evidence of the grace of God. It is important that we come to understand something of the contrast between the severity of God and His holiness and perfection on the one hand, and His grace and love as shown in Jesus Christ on the other. God abhors sin to such a degree that none of it will enter heaven. Neither can we hope to walk forward in victory with Him if we allow known sin in our lives. But over against that God is so full of love and grace that He can cause the most wicked of sinners to become the greatest of men.

How can the love and grace of God do this for sinful men? In Romans 3:26 Paul clarifies this for us: "To declare, I say, at this time his righteousness: that he might be just, and the justifier of him who believeth in Jesus." God was just in that He punished sin—our sin—when His Son died for us. In the second place He became the Justifier of them who believe in His Son. So on the one hand He is severe because of His holiness and perfection. On the other hand He is full of love and grace toward sinners because His own Son bore the penalty of their sins on the cross. This grace of God leads us on to victory and triumph in Christ. It was so in Israel's experience as they went into Canaan. It will be ours as we commit our lives and wills to the Lord. We, too, can conquer in the power of the indwelling Christ.

Rahab triumphed because she recognized conditions for what they truly were. She told the spies that there was no further strength left in the Canaanites. What they had learned of God's deliverance of Israel from Egypt and the Red Sea and of the destruction of the kings who had tried to halt Israel's progress had brought fear upon the Canaanites. This was an encouraging fact for the spies who said to Joshua: "Truly the Lord hath delivered into our hands all the land;

for even all the inhabitants of the country do faint because of us." This, as we have seen, applies in our spiritual lives to the effect that all the principalities and powers under Satan are under fear and trembling at the victory of the Lord. Any child of God who will dare to believe Him, will get on his knees and pray, and then will go forward with Christ, brings fear to the powers of darkness. They already are defeated.

It was for this reason that Peter wrote: "Humble yourselves therefore under the mighty hand of God, that he may exalt you in due time: Casting all your care upon him, for he careth for you. Be sober, be vigilant; because your adversary the devil, as a roaring lion, walketh about, seeking whom he may devour: whom resist stedfast in the faith" (I Pet. 5:6-9).

Satan's lion-like qualities and roaring need not frighten us. We are assured of complete victory over him for the same passage in I Peter goes on to say: "But the God of all grace, who hath called us unto his eternal glory by Christ Jesus, after that ye have suffered a while, make you perfect, stablish, strengthen, settle you" (v. 10). When we go forth in the Name of Christ we have One with us indwelling us Whose power is vastly superior to that of Satan's.

James also, as we recall, emphasizes the fact that we have victory over Satan because of the power of God. His words are, "But he giveth more grace: Wherefore he saith, God resisteth the proud, but giveth grace unto the humble. Submit yourselves therefore to God. Resist the devil, and he will flee from you" (Jas. 4:6,7).

Sometime ago I received a letter that illustrates how Satan can be successfully resisted. The letter was from a woman whose husband was unfaithful to her and had left her. As she was praying over this very serious situation, the truth suddenly came to her that if she would humble herself before God as the Word told her to and resist Satan and claim the victory through the blood of Christ, Satan would be defeated in this whole experience. She did this; and in her letter to me she stated that her husband, after three years' absence, had returned to the home and wanted to reestablish it on proper grounds. She wrote that the only reason he gave for returning was that he felt God "was calling him to come back—and He was." The Lord would do this kind of thing in more lives if His people would trust Him and obey Him in this matter of resisting Satan.

Divisions of the Book of Joshua

The Book of Joshua can readily be divided into three parts. The first has to do with Israel's entrance into the land. This is covered in the first five chapters. The second section has to do with Israel's conquering the land and is covered in chapters 6 through 12. The third section deals with possessing the land and includes chapters 13 through 24.

The record in Joshua is historical and is a true record since it is part of the Word of God. It was given, however, to provide more than just a mere history of Israel's experiences. According to what we have already seen in I Corinthians 10, these experiences were recorded for our benefit as believers in this age so that we can more readily learn spiritual truths that will lead us into spiritual growth and lives of victory over sin and Satan. So as we consider these various divisions of the Book of Joshua, there are a number of preliminary matters that must be clearly understood in order for us to get the most out of the spiritual lessons involved.

Chapter Eight

CROSSING OVER BY FAITH
(Joshua 3)

We know there was a definite moment in history when Israel entered Canaan. It was a definite experience that took place at a certain time. As we have seen, entering into Canaan does not represent the first part of the Christian life, that is the new birth. Entering Canaan represents the decision to become involved in spiritual warfare. So far as Israel is concerned, 40 years elapsed between these two experiences, that of leaving Egypt and entering Canaan. In many Christians' lives there is a time element between the new birth and the decision to yield to Christ for a life of triumphant warfare. Yet, according to the Scriptures, these two decisions could be and should be simultaneous. Unfortunately, in most cases, time elapses between these two decisions and in some cases a great deal of time.

The Book of Joshua does not deal with the new birth either in type or symbol. Israel's experiences in Canaan represent the life of a regenerated person, a born-again person in his spiritual warfare. It covers the more abundant life. It is not a picture of heaven as some have thought. But it is necessary we understand clearly that before there could be an entrance under Joshua into Canaan, there had to be an exodus from Egypt under Moses.

Some Contrasts

Some contrasts between the two, the exodus under Moses and the entrance under Joshua, will prove helpful here. An exodus, of course, speaks of a going out. An entrance speaks of that which leads in. The exodus for Israel was a going out from bondage and slavery. The entrance was in order to

101

conquer and to possess. In the Christian life the exodus speaks of release from the world and from sin and from Satan. The entrance into Canaan speaks of the overcoming life in which the believer learns to possess his possessions in Christ.

These two truths are also included in the transaction of the cross. Christ dying for our sins speaks of the exodus, taking us out of sin. But He also died to sin and we were identified with Him in this aspect of the cross also, and this has to do with entrance to Canaan which was made through the Jordan River.

Some have wrought confusion because they have referred to these two aspects of the work of Christ as two separate works of grace. Those who hold this view believe that the exodus, that is the coming out through the Red Sea or our salvation experience, provides us with only a portion of that which is ours in Christ. These persons also believe that there is a second work of grace in which, by a certain experience, we receive everything that God has for us and we enter in and take possession of it all. This may sound good but it is not scriptural. The whole of the Christian life is a process of continuing grace beginning with the new birth. It is a matter of growth. If there is a time element between these two things of which we are speaking in our experience, it is due to lack of faith on our part and not the lack of provision on God's part.

When the children of Israel were in Egypt, they were in bondage. Even after God had sent Moses to deliver them there was a long period of time necessary to prepare them to even want to come out. The plagues, the added work load placed on the Israelites by the Egyptians, and the other testings all were designed not only to break down Pharaoh's opposition, but to bring the Israelites to the place where they wanted to leave Egypt. The same thing can be seen today with regard to people who are not concerned about salvation or coming out from their sins. In many cases God allows trials and testings of various kinds to bring them to the place where they are ready to come out from their spiritual Egypt.

When the people of Israel were ready to come out of Egypt, God sent one more judgment, that of the slaying of the firstborn. This pictures for us what judgment on sin involves. Sin brings death. God, however, provided the way of escape, a way by the blood on the doorposts. The applying of the blood in this manner speaks of the remission of sin, and the escape of the Israelites from that judgment illustrates salvation from the judgment of sin.

The second part of this same salvation, separated in time in Israel's experience, but so far as the saint or Christian is concerned they are simultaneous, is the exodus by power. This took place at the Red Sea where God, by His show of power, completed the work of delivering Israel from bondage. It in effect represents the new birth.

Now, a birth is not the work of the child being born. The birth process is the work of the mother who labors to bring forth her child. So also the new birth is altogether the work of Almighty God, the work of the Holy Spirit in bringing us out of death into life.

It was God who divided the Red Sea and then destroyed the enemy. Pharaoh and his army perished, so there was no chance of Israel being recaptured by them. This was altogether the work of Almighty God. This speaks to us of Jesus Christ the Way who broke Satan's power and made it possible for us to be delivered from it. These are truths that apply to us as we accept them by faith.

The Israelites had a barren desert before them, but this was not the end; it was merely the beginning. It was a place to learn to depend on God for everything. They had passed through the "from" stage; when they finally came to the Jordan River, they entered the second stage or the "into" stage. This is the second aspect of the cross work of Christ. It is that particular part of it which by the grace of God makes it possible for us to participate in death to sin, to the world, to self, to Satan and to enter into the active resurrection life which is the victorious life. It is the entrance to the abundant life. Jordan speaks of the gateway to the life of conquering. It is the road that leads to the possessing of our spiritual possessions in Christ Jesus. These are abundant as we have already seen from Ephesians 1:3. We have been blessed with all spiritual blessings in heavenly places in Christ.

So Christ has not only brought us out, but He has made an abundant entrance for us. It need not take us 40 years like it did the people of Israel to enjoy this. It need not even take us two years which was the length of time it took Israel to go from the Red Sea to Kadesh-barnea the first time. Sad to say, they did not enter at that time. So far as the physical journey from the Red Sea to Kadesh-barnea was concerned, it involved only a few days at the most. From the spiritual standpoint there need be no such interim.

Exodus and Entrance Complementary

The Red Sea exodus and the Jordan entrance are complementary in their spiritual significance. They are closely related in their meaning. This is suggested in Psalm 114 where no note is made of the 40-year period of desert wandering. "When Israel went out of Egypt, the house of Jacob from a people of strange language; Judah was his sanctuary, and Israel his dominion. The sea saw it, and fled: Jordan was driven back. The mountains skipped like rams, and the little hills like lambs. What ailed thee, O thou sea, that thou fleddest? thou Jordan, that thou wast driven back? Ye mountains, that ye skipped like rams; and ye little hills, like lambs? Tremble, thou earth, at the presence of the Lord, at the presence of the God of Jacob" (vv. 1-7).

The Red Sea and Jordan are listed as separate events but they are recorded here as though they followed each other without any interval. And in each case it was the presence of the God of Jacob who wrought the miracles.

Though complementary, there are significant differences in the two events. The crossing of the Jordan was more than a mere repetition of the crossing of the Red Sea.

Some writers in commenting on these two crossings have suggested that since the generation that stood on the banks of the Jordan to enter Canaan had not experienced the Red

Sea crossing, they needed a similar experience which crossing the Jordan provided.

There is undoubtedly some truth in this, but we must not overlook the fact that some things can be known through faith without our having to pass through the actual experiences. We would emphasize again that the crossing of the Red Sea and the crossing of the Jordan were not identical events.

The opening up of the Red Sea provided a way out of Egypt. On the other hand, the heaping up of the waters of Jordan opened the way into Canaan.

Spiritually speaking, these two miracle experiences present two distinct aspects of the Christian's experience. The one speaks of a going out, the other of a going in. The older generation made an exit from the house of bondage, whereas the new generation was about to enter the Land of Promise. The older generation did not have to fight and conquer the army of Egypt, for the Lord destroyed Pharaoh and his host in the sea. But in order to possess the land of Canaan the younger generation had to conquer their enemies before they could take possession. It was with one master stroke that the Red Sea swallowed up Israel's enemies and God brought His people out of bondage. The conquest of Canaan was not accomplished in a moment. The time was long and the going was hard. The new generation under Joshua had to fight before they could possess the land.

In type the crossing of the Red Sea pictures to us what Jesus Christ did on the cross when He brought us out from under the bondage of sin and broke the power of Satan. This initial phase of our salvation we had no part in. It was all the work of Jesus Christ. We do bear special responsibility to obey and closely follow our Leader as we enter into warfare against the powers of evil, seeking as we ought to possess our spiritual Promised Land. The victory lies in Christ, but we must fill the capacity of spiritual warriors totally surrendered to our Captain.

The older generation faced a barren wilderness after their

escape from Egypt. The new generation under Joshua had for their goal a land flowing with milk and honey.

When we first come out of our spiritual Egypt, out of sin and bondage and condemnation into eternal life, we are faced with a sort of spiritual desert. There is a place where we first learn to know God and His ability to provide for us and properly train us. Following that we enter into the Jordan experience and pass over into the land of promise.

The method used to open up the Red Sea was quite different from that of opening up the Jordan River. At the Sea Moses stretched out his hand and the Lord caused the waters to go back. He brought a strong wind which parted the waters and provided a safe path for His people.

At the Jordan neither a wind nor a staff were used. God used the Ark of the Covenant to open the way for the Israelites. In both places, however, divine power was necessary. It was used differently in each case, yet it was indispensible. At the Red Sea God freed His people from slavery. At Jordan He gave them entrance into a land where their possessions lay.

So far as our Lord's work in redemption is concerned, the entrance into Jordan can be likened to what He did when He ascended on high after He had completed His work of emancipation from sin for us here on earth. Not a great deal is taught in the Scriptures concerning the ascension of our Lord and its meaning for us. We usually sum it up for ourselves as knowing that He went to the right hand of the Father after having ascended from earth. We must remember, however, that He first came from above, from heaven to the earth and became man so that He might die for our sins. After His death, burial and resurrection He ascended on high to sit at the right hand of the Father and was placed above all principalities and powers. His present work is to make intercession for us, to provide a life of victory while we are here upon this earth.

In the Old Testament we have an illustration of Christ's ascension in the battle with Amalek where Moses ascended the mountain to pray while Joshua descended into the valley to fight. The spiritual lesson is that while we fight in the valley today our Lord prays for us in glory.

A further truth with regard to Christ's ascension is that in order to reach the right hand of the Father, our Lord had to pass through the domain of the prince of the power of the air. In this He overcame Satan and all his hosts. The Lord Jesus Christ broke Satan's power at the cross and demonstrated that victory in ascending to the right hand of God. Ephesians 1:19 takes on new meaning as we look at it from this angle: "And what is the exceeding greatness of his power to us-ward who believe, according to the working of his mighty power, Which he wrought in Christ, when he raised him from the dead, and set him at his own right hand in the heavenly places, Far above all principality, and power, and might, and dominion." It is to this that Colossians 2:15 also makes reference, where we read: "And having spoiled principalities and powers, he made a shew of them openly, triumphing over them. . . ." He openly triumphed over Satan when He passed through his domain.

In our identification with Jesus Christ we have been made to sit with Him in the heavenlies. This is a very important truth for us to grasp. We are down here on this earth so far as our physical body is concerned. Yet in our spiritual position before God we are in heavenly places in Christ Jesus and in Him overpowering all of the satanic evil forces.

We wonder if something of this is not noted in Psalm 114 where the statement is simply made that at the Red Sea the waters fled as though there was no opposition. But with reference to the Jordan the language is: "the waters were driven back." The difference may simply be what we have pointed out here with regard to Satan. There were powerful enemies opposing the crossing of the Jordan but these could not withstand the power and the purpose of God. They were driven back. So it is in our crossing over to our seat in the heavenlies, the principalities and powers ranged against us were driven back.

The Ark of the Covenant

At the Red Sea the Israelites were commanded to stand still and see the salvation of the Lord. In contrast, at Jordan they were instructed to fix their eyes on the Ark of the Covenant, follow behind it a certain distance and cross the river when the waters were rolled back.

The Ark of the Covenant of the Lord played a tremendous part in Israel's history in the desert and also later on in the land. Like everything else in the tabernacle the Ark had spiritual significance. It was the most outstanding piece of furniture in the tabernacle and represented the presence of God. It was more than that, however, for it also typified the Person of the Lord Jesus Christ.

First of all the Ark contained the two tables of stone on which the law was written by the finger of God. These spoke of the holiness of Almighty God. The Lord Jesus Christ was altogether holy and perfectly obedient to the Father.

In the second place on top of the Ark was a cover made of gold called the mercy seat. This again represents Him who was sent forth by God to be our propitiation—mercy seat—through the presence of the sprinkled blood. We read in Romans 3:24: "Being justified freely by his grace through the redemption that is in Christ Jesus: whom God has set forth to be a propitiation through faith in his blood, to declare his righteousness for the remission of sins that are past, through the forbearance of God." This is rather heavy and technical language, but it means that God sent forth His Son Jesus Christ to be the One through whose shed blood God was able to reveal His mercy and grace to us. So in verse 26 we learn, "To declare, I say, at this time his righteousness: that he might be just, and the justifier of him which believeth in Jesus." God is just because God is holy. He cannot overlook sin. So in atoning for sin He gave His Son Jesus Christ to become sin for us. It was in this way that He could show forth His wonderful grace and have us declared righteous and at the same time remain just.

The Ark, as we have already indicated, speaks of the

presence of God. The Ark, located in the Holy of Holies, represented God's continual dwelling with men.

In summing this up we see that Christ is the archetype of the Ark. He is the Obedient One who kept God's law perfectly. He is the Merciful One who makes it possible for a Holy God to show mercy to sinful men. In the third place, Christ manifested the presence of God among us when He dwelt here upon earth. Now He indwells each believer, for we are His temples.

Just as the Israelites were to keep their attention focused upon the Ark as the great entrance was to be made into Canaan, so we are to keep our spiritual eyes fixed on Jesus Christ. This is what we read in Hebrews 12:2: "Looking unto Jesus the author and finisher of our faith." This is basic for our whole Christian life. We must keep our eyes on Him not only to see Him, but also to follow Him. This is exactly what the Israelites were instructed to do with regard to the Ark at the crossing of Jordan.

The people of Israel, when they came out of Egypt, were told to stand still just before they crossed the Red Sea. They were to wait and see the salvation of the Lord. Then, after God had saved them they were to start walking on the basis of that salvation. Theirs was a physical salvation at the Red Sea, but the lesson for us is a spiritual one. After we see the salvation of the Lord then we are to walk accordingly.

At the Jordan the people were to pause for three days. Then the Ark was to move and they were to follow it. At the Red Sea the angel of the Lord, together with the cloud, stood behind them to protect them from the enemy. The Egyptian army followed after them but was not able to come up with them. The Israelites were not to fight the Egyptians nor to protect themselves in any way. Their deliverance was entirely from the Lord.

The situation concerning the Ark was different. It went before them into the danger spot and stood in the midst of the river. There was no threat from enemies behind. All the threat was from before them. Their fighting lay ahead. So it is important with us that we keep our eyes on Christ who goes before us. He said of His own work with us: "And when he putteth forth his own sheep, he goeth before them, and the sheep follow him: for they know his voice" (John 10:4). So it is as we enter into spiritual warfare having first been born again we follow our Shepherd. Our Saviour spoke of this in John 10:27 where He said, "My sheep hear my voice, and I know them, and they follow me." Then He added, "And I give unto them eternal life; and they shall never perish, neither shall any man pluck them out of my hand." They shall not perish, or in the language of Joshua and the Old Testament, they shall not go back into Egypt. That way is barred to them. Then He adds, "No man shall pluck them out of my hand." God promises to take us through the spiritual warfare that lies ahead. No matter what the storm or stress, we are safe with Him. No one can pluck us out of His hand. This is a wonderful assurance which is ours because we are in Christ Jesus.

The older generation that left Egypt did not have to fight the Egyptian army. That was taken care of for them by the Lord. The new generation entering into Canaan, however, had to take the offensive against the enemy. But they did this not on their own, but as they followed their Captain. He promises that we shall have tribulation in this world, but we are to be of good cheer for He has overcome the world (John 16:31). He has chosen us, not we Him, that we should bear fruit and that our fruit should remain (John 15:16). As we follow Him He makes us fishers of men (Matt. 4:19). As He puts us forth, He goes before us.

All the power necessary for the conquest of Canaan was already provided for the Israelites when they crossed the Red Sea. This great potential, however, was not experienced by them until they accepted it by faith. In the first blush of victory as they sang about the triumph of their deliverance at the Red Sea, they not only rejoiced at their redemption from Egypt and their preservation from the army of Egypt, but they also looked forward to the effect this great deliverance would have on the people of Canaan. The Israelites sang, "The people shall hear, and be afraid: sorrow shall take hold on the inhabitants of Palestina, Then the dukes of Edom shall be amazed; the mighty men of Moab, trembling shall take hold upon them; all the inhabitants of Canaan shall melt away. Fear and dread shall fall upon them; by the greatness of thine arm they shall be as still as a stone; till thy people pass over, O Lord, till the people pass over, which thou hast purchased. Thou shalt bring them in, and plant them in the mountain of thine inheritance" (Ex. 15:14-17).

It was a tragedy that the older generation forgot the fact that God's deliverance of Israel at the Red Sea had struck terror to the hearts of the Canaanites. But as we learned in Joshua 2:9-11 that fear stayed with the Canaanites all the time the Israelites were in the desert. So the new generation under Joshua crossed the Jordan by an act of faith. They entered the land to conquer it and to possess it.

Again we need to be reminded that this points to the fact that every blessing of God is ours actually or potentially the very moment we are born again. We have been blessed with all spiritual blessings in heavenly places in Christ. These blessings become ours in reality as we appropriate them by faith. The inheritance which is the sum total of blessing in Christ is ours as a gift from God. Yet there is much that becomes ours simply as we by faith lay hold upon it.

How sad it was that after the Israelites had been conquering the land for five years Joshua had to say, "There remaineth yet much land to be possessed." Why were the Israelites so slow in possessing what God had provided for them? We might well ask ourselves why we are so slow in possessing our spiritual heritage in Christ. Why don't we go in and take what is ours by faith?

Someone has said, "What is enfolded in regeneration should be unfolded in sanctification. What is ours should become ours. What is possible should become actual. What is potential should become potent."

So in the Book of Joshua we see the process of becoming what we ought to be. We also see why much that ought to have been was never fully realized. There is a wonderful inheritance that we have right here, that is kept in trust for us in Christ, and it is ours as we learn to possess it and take it.

Our actual possession of these things will depend upon our attitude toward them. Paul said concerning his own mind on these matters: "All these things I count but dung for the sake of the knowledge of the Lord Jesus Christ." He saw there was much in store for him and he had not yet attained to all of it, but he determined to follow after Christ so that he might receive what was provided for him. This was why he pressed toward the mark for the prize of the high calling of God in Christ Jesus (Phil. 3:7-15). This should also be our goal. We are seeing these things reflected in historical events in Joshua. We should let them impel us toward their realization in our day-by-day experience.

Conquest and Rest

What was historical for the people of Israel pictures experiences in the spiritual life of the child of God. The Israelites were to cross over into the land of Canaan which was, after conquest, to be a land of rest for them. The child of God is to enter a place of rest for we are told, "There remaineth therefore a rest to the people of God" (Heb. 4:9). To the Israelite the place of rest was a land. To the Christian it is a Person. It is in Christ "in heavenly places." We have been blessed with all spiritual blessings in heavenly places in Christ. Christ is our inheritance as Canaan was theirs. In Christ we have everything, and without Him we have nothing. We have claimed Him as Saviour, now let us look to Him as Lord and make Him Master of our lives.

The sphere of the Israelites was an earthly one, but the sphere of the believer is a heavenly one, a spiritual one. Their sphere of living and working had its boundaries. It was a country. Our sphere has no boundaries. Their enrichment as a nation was temporary but ours is eternal. What is set forth historically in the Book of Joshua is set forth spiritually in the Epistles. What was the portion of this one nation is now the privilege and portion of every Bible-believing truly born-again Christian. It may seem contradictory that we have to fight in order to rest, but both the Book of Ephesians and the Book of Hebrews emphatically associate rest with conflict.

In Ephesians 1:3 we learn that we have been blessed with all spiritual blessings in heavenly places in Christ. In the second chapter (v. 6) the Apostle tells us we have been made to sit down in heavenly places in Christ Jesus. It is right there in those heavenly places that we are to wrestle against principalities and powers—the very subject of chapter 6 of Ephesians.

The expression "the heavenlies" is used in Ephesians five times. It is defined as the sphere of the believer's experience in our identification with Christ. So then in speaking of "the heavenlies" we do not mean a place in heaven somewhere far beyond the clouds or the stars. What is meant is the believer's spiritual experience with its conflicts, testings and victories. It is the New Testament equivalent, as we have pointed out, to the land of Canaan spoken of in Joshua.

To grasp this line of truth firmly we must understand at least two things. First of all, every Christian is and has in Christ from the moment of his conversion all the potential of salvation. Everything that Christ has for us was at our disposal, either actually or potentially, the moment we were born again. It is kept in trust for us so that we might by believing attain to it.

The second thing is that each Christian should by faith claim these riches in Christ. It is one thing to have them reserved for us, it is quite another thing to enter into the blessings and privileges now.

When we speak of what we have the moment we believe in Christ, we are dealing with our spiritual standing in Him. This is not altered by what we do or what our experiences may be. Our position before God is fixed and unalterable the moment we trust in Christ.

When we speak of claiming by faith these riches in Christ, we are speaking of our state or walk here on earth among men. It is here that by faith we claim that which is ours in Christ.

Entering the Land

Israel's entrance into Canaan was a very crucial step in their progress as a nation. The method of entering in is the subject of the first five chapters of Joshua. There were three distinct steps in this project, all of which have a typical significance for us today.

It was by an act of faith that Israel entered Canaan. The people lined up behind the Ark as they were told, and as soon as the priests entered the Jordan the waters rolled back. The spiritual blessing which this history typifies must also be entered into by an act of faith. We do not sit and idly twiddle our thumbs and all at once find ourselves spiritual. There is a decision to be made as we enter this spiritual land of conquest.

In the second place, the land which was entered had to be fought for. Israel had the assurance that the enemies would be defeated, but Israel nevertheless had to fight. This is also true in the spiritual warfare that we are engaged in. Faith must be backed up by effort. Faith that does not produce action is not faith. That is why we are told in Ephesians that after we put on the whole armor of God and are ready for the battle we are to pray "always with all prayer and supplication in the Spirit, and watching thereunto with all perseverance and supplication for all saints" (Eph. 6:18). This is our method of overcoming the enemy once we have entered the land.

In the third place, the land which Israel entered and conquered had also to be possessed. But in a country such as Canaan which was already occupied there was no way of possessing it without first dispossessing the enemy living in the land. In many cases we will find as we study the Book of Joshua that though the Israelites conquered many portions they did not entirely drive out the inhabitants. They merely conquered the people, subdued them and made them pay tribute. Thus the Israelites could not possess the land as long as their enemies were in it.

The application to the spiritual life is obvious. There are obstacles in our way to spiritual victory which must be put aside if we are to take complete possession of every faculty of our being and place ourselves in subjection to Christ. We learn in II Corinthians 10:3 5: "Though we walk in the flesh, we do not war after the flesh: (For the weapons of our warfare are not carnal, but mighty through God to the pulling down of strong holds;) Casting down imaginations, and every high thing that exalteth itself against the knowledge of God, and bringing into captivity every thought to the obedience of Christ." We are in a spiritual conflict and the weapons at our disposal are the Word of God and prayer. Through these we cast down "imaginations," which are the reasonings of the natural man's mind, and we bring into subjection every thought to the Lord Jesus.

Some Christians will say that they cannot help what they think. But we can. We have the weapons in Christ Jesus to bring this thought life of ours under His complete control. Only then will He be able to think His thoughts through us.

A Progressive Order

With regard to our entering the land in a spiritual sense we see that the order is progressive. First there must be entrance before there can be conquering. Then there must be conquering before there can be possession.

Now let us consider three steps or movements with the Jordan River as the central feature. As Israel is about to enter the land three distinct steps were to be taken and the Jordan River was at the heart of it all.

We have already seen in Joshua chapters 1 and 2 that the Israelites had come to the River Jordan. This ground we have covered quite well. In the second place it was necessary that they go through the river. This is described for us in Joshua chapters 3 and 4.

In the third place they proceeded from the river. This we are told in chapter 5 and the chapters following. So there was preparation to cross the river; then a passage through the river; and finally the purification after they had crossed the river.

It was an inward preparation that was necessary in the preparation to cross the river. After repeating the promises of God, Joshua told the people to get themselves ready, to get into the Word, to believe it, and to be strong and of a good courage. This was all inward preparation.

In the second chapter the preparation was outward. There we learn of the two spies who were sent to Jericho in order to see exactly what God had already done by way of preparation in the country and in the hearts of the Canaanites. They would be readily conquered because they were fearful and demoralized.

The inward preparation reveals faith as a principle. The Israelites had to learn what it meant to believe. Then faith had to be exhibited or practiced in order to bring out the action believed in. Another way of saying it is that the inward and divine blessings are promised in chapter one, but in chapter two the human conditions are exposed for all to see.

With this before us we can now consider chapters 3 and 4 of Joshua where we can examine closely the passage through the river.

The people had prepared themselves. Everything was ready. All that was needed was for them to act on faith and cross the river. Here they were ready to enter into the life of blessing. At the Red Sea they had been separated from the life of bondage, but at Jordan they were separated unto a life of blessing. In other words, the act is from one thing to something else. This is sanctification in its essence—separation from something unto something.

Events which lay behind them could not be changed. They had been delivered from Egypt. This corresponds to our spiritual birth. We cannot be unborn once we are spiritually born.

In the second case, something lay before the Israelites toward which they now had to press. This is seen in the spiritual realm when we consider what Paul said about "forgetting those things which are behind, and reaching forth unto those things which are before."

To the Israelites the Red Sea was their way of exit and the River Jordan was their way of entrance. There must be a Red Sea experience before we can have a Jordan experience. There must be salvation before there can be an entering into the progressive Christian life. Time is no factor. In the case of Israel 40 years elapsed between the two events. They can be, however, simultaneous. Too often, however, they are separated by a period of time.

Crossing the Jordan does not typify passing into eternity. Some of the old hymns and gospel songs reflect this viewpoint, such as the one beginning with the words, "On Jordan's stormy bank I stand." This song makes it appear that the Jordan River represents physical death and the other side of it is heaven.

This popular view has been a source of much confusion. It has also resulted in a loss of a great deal of spiritual truth when a book such as Joshua is read. The crossing of the Jordan illustrates the passing of a Christian from one level of Christian experience into another level of Christian experience with the Lord. It marks the end of the self-life and the beginning of the Christ-life. The self-life is the life lived on the principle of mere human effort, whereas the Christ-life is lived on the basis of faith and obedience to the indwelling Christ.

Israel left the desert which represents the self-life and came into a land flowing with milk and honey, a place of conquest, of triumph and of rest. Between those two aspects of life was the Jordan River, a river speaking of human impossibilities. How does a believer come out of a life of selfishness into a life centered in Christ, a life of conquering and living victoriously and restfully in Him?

Are you looking for a life on a higher plane? Or have you thought that this was not for you? Your problems may be ever so great and you may face mountains of impossibility, but the Lord has good news for you. Here is what the Lord Jesus told His disciples at one time: "Have faith in God. For verily I say unto you, That whosoever shall say unto this mountain, Be thou removed, and be thou cast into the sea; and shall not doubt in his heart, but shall believe that those things which he saith shall come to pass; he shall have whatsoever he saith" (Mark 11:22,23).

Israel, too, faced impossible situations. First of all, there was the Jordan before them which was then at flood stage. Beyond the river were seven great nations, all of them larger than Israel. Back of those seven nations, encouraging them and energizing them, were the forces of Satan, the spirit world of evil that he controls, and which is mightier than any man. This whole historical setting is a perfect analogy of the warfare faced by every child of God.

We must ever remember that our wrestling is not against flesh and blood beings. We are ranged against principalities and powers in heavenly places. Ours is a warfare that lasts as long as life lasts. It rages between the forces of heaven and the forces of hell. On the one hand is Satan seeking to possess us and control us for evil. On the other hand is God who through Christ Jesus is seeking to possess our life for righteousness. The battle rages even in our very hearts, for Galatians 5:17 says, "The flesh lusteth against the Spirit, and the Spirit against the flesh: and these are contrary the one to the other: so that ye cannot do the things that ye would."

God has a master plan for victory and this plan is centered in Jesus Christ our Lord. This is not something that we do ourselves, but it is in Christ who, by becoming man and dying on our behalf, being buried and raised again, has overcome Satan. We are identified with Him in His death and burial and resurrection. Thus there is nothing that can stand in the way of God's plan for absolute and complete victory for us if we will lay hold of what is ours by faith.

Just as the overflowing Jordan River could not stop Israel when God told them to move forward, neither can the gates of hell prevail against the Church of Jesus Christ. You and I are members of that Church.

We have already seen something of the significance of the Ark in the life of the Israelites. It plays a prominent part in this third chapter of Joshua. The ten references to it are the key to the victory Israel had over the Jordan River.

As we have seen, the Ark represented the presence of God with the Israelites. It was a visible evidence of that presence which God had promised to Joshua. As God had been with Moses so He would be with Israel's new leader. A similar promise lies for us in the assurances and instructions our Saviour gave the disciples. He promised to lead them out and to be with them wherever they went. In His final instructions to them to go into all the world and preach the gospel, He also added that He would be with them and empower them. These are promises for us also. He has promised never to leave us nor forsake us.

We cannot escape the responsibility laid upon us with regard to these things. Do we want to advance in the Christian life and become mature and victorious believers? Or do we want to stay as some of the Israelites did in the desert and be useless? Do we want the Christian life based on self and when it is over enter into glory just by the skin of our teeth, or in the language of I Corinthians 3:15 to be saved just so as by fire? Do we want to spend our days down here as spiritual paupers and send nothing on ahead for rewards?

The crossing of the Jordan centered in the Ark. It was carried by the priests into the river and it was the last object to be moved after the Israelites had passed through.

The Ark represents Christ who is the center of our spiritual life. He is the Alpha and the Omega of our salvation. He is the Author and Finisher of our faith. He is the One who began our spiritual life and He is the One who is going to bring it to completion. Our eyes must be upon Him just as the Israelites were instructed to watch the Ark. The effectiveness and growth of our spiritual lives will depend upon the attention we give to Christ.

The instructions given Israel for crossing the Jordan were from God and these form the background for the spiritual lessons we will draw for our own benefit and learning.

The Process for Crossing Jordan

We read in Joshua 3:1: "And Joshua rose early in the morning; and they removed from Shittim, and came to Jordan, he and all the children of Israel, and lodged there before they passed over." From Shittim to the Jordan River was a distance of some six or eight miles. Then they were brought hard up against the overflowing waters of the Jordan which formed an impassable barrier, marking Jordan as a place of impossible passage for the Israelites. The people had been in camp but now they were made to move. Just as a bicycle cannot be steared unless it is moving, even so we must be moving before God can direct the path we are to take. If we merely sit and wait we need not expect God to do something.

An outstanding example of this principle is found in the case of Abraham's servant who was sent to bring back a bride for Isaac. The Lord's leading was evident in his life; and when he had found the proper bride, Eliezer said, "I being in the way, the Lord led me." It was when he was in the way that the Lord was able to lead him. It was when he was moving, not when he was standing still. It was not when he was contemplating or planning the journey and thinking through the problems he would have to face, but when he was actually on the move that God was able to direct him.

Abraham's own life illustrates this same principle. According to Genesis 12 the Lord said to His servant, "Get thee out of thy country, and from thy kindred, and from thy father's house, unto a land that I will shew thee." He did not tell Abraham where it was nor that his posterity would eventually possess it. The Lord merely instructed Abraham to get out of Ur of the Chaldees and to go to a country God had chosen for him. Abraham, however, had to be "on the go" in order to be led. Abraham departed and took Lot with him. They finally came to the land of Canaan; but it was not until they arrived there that God appeared to Abraham and said that He would give that land to Abraham's seed.

We have seen how the first two chapters of Joshua are

chapters of preparation both of Joshua and the people for this step forward. The third chapter is one of action as God prepares His people to move. There was a brief delay of three days, but when this was over the officers of the nation went among the people and instructed them as to what they were to do. In more than one place in Scripture we are told to wait on the Lord. And not all waiting is of the same nature. Israel had already started the journey to Canaan so this halt was only temporary. There was a great deal of activity of different kinds involved in preparation for that stupendous crossing.

Have we gone forward to follow the Lord? We must make a decision. We are called to go forth with Him. If you who read this have not made that decision to this point make it now. Say in the language of these studies, "Lord, I am going to enter into this land. I do not know all that is ahead, but I am waiting for Your orders."

Chapter Nine

CROSSING OVER BY FAITH
(Joshua 3) (Continued)

There is a time for action and there is also a time for waiting. There are times when we get in too big a hurry and are too impatient to wait on the Lord's time. On the other hand, there are some who lag behind and are not ready to move forward when they should. We need to remember that God is never too late. If we really want to do His will, He will always do His part on time.

So there was a three-day delay when the people reached the Jordan River. This gave them the opportunity to become quiet before God and made it possible for Him to give them final instructions. It was when they were ready to hear that the orders were given.

The same is true in our spiritual experiences. We must make a decision and then act upon that decision. After we have acted on our decision, it may be that God will have us wait for a while. This may sound like a paradox but it is not. We need to learn to be calm before the Lord and await His time and timing for the events in our lives. The reason for Israel's delay at the Jordan, and often the reason for a delay after God has made plain to us that we are to move ahead, is in order to see if we are in earnest. When this is evident, then further instructions are given us.

The officers moved among the people and commanded them saying, "When ye see the ark of the covenant of the Lord your God, and the priests the Levites bearing it, then ye shall remove from your place, and go after it" (Josh. 3:3). They needed to watch the Ark, for its movement was to determine theirs. When it went forward, they were to move forward.

As we have pointed out repeatedly the Ark represents the

presence of the Lord. Without His being with them Israel could not have existed as a nation during the years in the desert nor entered into Canaan to conquer and possess it. The fact of the Lord's presence with them was settled by strong assurances from Him. These are recorded in Exodus 33. This was just after the people of Israel had sinned in worshipping the golden calf and God had urged them through Moses to go forward. God said that He would send an angel before them to drive out the Canaanites and the other inhabitants of the land. But God refused to go up Himself in the midst of the people of Israel for they were a stiffnecked people (Ex. 33:3).

This decision could not satisfy the heart of Moses so he pleaded with the Lord: "Now therefore, I pray thee, if I have found grace in thy sight, shew me now thy way, that I may know thee, that I may find grace in thy sight: and consider that this nation is thy people. And he said, My presence shall go with thee, and I will give thee rest" (Ex. 33:13,14).

Keeping the Ark in View

Thus it was important that the Ark of the Covenant which represented the presence of the Lord would be in sight of the people as they made the historic crossing of the Jordan. Joshua said, "Behold, the ark of the covenant of the Lord of all the earth passeth over before you into Jordan." This was a visible token to Israel that God would go into the river first and part its waters and remain as the protection of His people while they safely crossed over to the other side. Then God commanded Joshua to tell the priests to come up out of the Jordan; when they did, the waters returned to their former level.

So it is, as we have already indicated, that Christ is the Author and Finisher of our faith. He perfects our salvation. In life's experiences He goes before us; we are to follow Him. His presence with us preserves us. What He begins He will consummate.

There is no getting through from the self-life to the

Christ-life unless one has a clear view of the Lord Jesus Christ. An illustration will help clarify this. There is the account in the Gospels of how Peter started to walk on the water, the result of Christ's permission and enabling. Peter had no difficulty as long as he kept his eyes on the Saviour; but the moment he began to look at the waves and noted the violence of the elements he began to sink. Then he cried out to the Lord Jesus for help. He turned his eyes on Him once again and the Lord took care of the situation.

This is what we need to learn to do with regard to Christ. We must look away unto Jesus. If we keep our eyes on the problems, the circumstances and the frustrations of life they will overcome us. But if we look constantly to Christ for help, we will grow and develop in spite of our circumstances. A gospel chorus puts the matter quite well:

> Turn your eyes upon Jesus
> Look full in His wonderful face,
> Then the things of earth will
> grow strangely dim
> In the light of His glory and grace.

Let us learn to keep our eyes on Jesus at all times whether the problems are financial, or health or whatever they may be, for we will find that our safety lies in Him.

Another part of the instruction given the Israelites concerning the Ark was that they were to leave a space between them and it. The words are, "Yet there shall be a space between you and it, about two thousand cubits by measure: come not near unto it, that ye may know the way by which ye must go: for ye have not passed this way heretofore" (Josh. 3:4). The people were to keep an open space of some 3,000 feet between them and the Ark until it was in the bed of the river. Some 3 million persons were involved in this crossing and had they crowded up close to the Ark, only a handful of them would have seen it. It was kept far enough in the distance so that the people could see it. This was undoubtedly one reason for the instructions—near enough to see it, yet not too far so that it was out of sight.

There is always a danger of following too far off. This was true of Peter at one time. It resulted in him denying His Lord, and Peter was not convicted of his sin until he caught a glimpse of the Lord Jesus. Then Peter went away weeping in his repentance.

There is still another reason for keeping that certain distance between the Israelites and the Ark. That was the need for reverence.

This is a much needed lesson for many believers today. We sometimes speak of Him familiarly as our "older Brother." There is truth in this but it is not an expression to be used in the sense we would of an older brother after the flesh. There is a tendency among us to what we might call a "first-name-calling approach" to our Lord. This is characteristic of our time, but it is not a practice to be followed with regard to Him. We must reverence Him, for He is the Lord of Glory. We must keep a certain distance, close enough to see Him, but not too far away as to lose sight of Him.

The Ark was going to point the way for the people to go. For this reason they needed a clear vision. They had never traveled that way before, so they needed an unobstructed view of the Ark.

How true this is of many of us believers as we face the decision to fully enter the new life in Christ. We have never crossed the Jordan before which spells death and then resurrection, that is death unto self and new life in Christ. We need a clear vision of Him. It seems as impossible to us to shake off the desire for self things as it was for the Israelites to cross the Jordan River. Victory comes from following the instructions God has given.

How many times believers have failed to be overcomers in their spiritual lives. This failure has been so marked in some of us that we have wondered if a life of victory is possible at all. Some might advise us to "Let go and let God." But this formula does not fit in to this particular transaction. This is a case where we are to follow our Lord as He has commanded us. The people were to go into the river after the Ark. Just so we are to follow Christ.

We read of Him in I Corinthians 1:30 as our Wisdom, Righteousness, Sanctification and Redemption. This is why He is able to take us through the place of death into life. There are no bridges over this Jordan River. The way is not over, it is through. He is our Righteousness when we sin and fail. But we are restored to fellowship when we confess our sins. Christ is always our Righteousness. He is always our Wisdom. He leads us on. He is everything we need—the Alpha, that is the beginning; the Omega, the end; and everything in between.

We read in Ephesians 1:22 that God "put all things under his feet, and gave him to be the head over all things to the church. Which is his body, the fulness of him that filleth all in all." Jesus Christ is filled with all the fullness of God and we are united with Him. We are complete in Him, so it is no wonder that we can do all things through Him who strengthens us. We find everything we need in Christ.

The river to the Israelites was an impassable barrier, seemingly making the command of God impossible for them to attain. But with God nothing is impossible.

My wife and I saw the Jordan River in flood stage; it looked very formidable to us. It looked impossible to the Israelites in Joshua's day but nothing is impossible with God.

Just so many of God's people have tried through the years to overcome the self-life and have failed. They have wanted the fruit of the Spirit to be manifest in their daily conduct but this has somehow eluded them. But none of us need be discouraged. The Spirit-controlled life, the victorious life, is God's goal for us, and with Him nothing is impossible.

One day a rich young ruler came to Christ and showed interest in spiritual things. When he learned, however, that he would need to give riches a lesser place in his life and give first place to God, he refused. After he left, the Lord Jesus commented on his conduct and attitude and assured the disciples that nothing was impossible with God.

God announced to Abraham and Sarah when they were

both very old that Sarah would have a son. Humanly speaking this was impossible, but Isaac was born according to promise.

When Jeremiah prophesied concerning Israel, it did not look as though that nation would ever again be in a position to be used of God. Yet he told how they would be finally delivered from all their troubles and trials and would be brought back and permanently settled in their land. We are beginning to see some of the first steps in the fulfillment of those prophecies today. As Jeremiah considered these things he exclaimed: "Ah Lord God! behold, thou hast made the heaven and the earth by thy great power and stretched out arm, and there is nothing too hard for thee" (Jer. 32:17).

When things seem to be too hard for us let us fix our eyes on Jesus. Ponder for a moment as did Jeremiah that our Lord has made the heaven and the earth. There is nothing impossible to Him.

After Job's heartrending experiences when it seemed he had lost everything in life, he came to a new concept of God and one of the things he confessed was: "I know that thou canst do every thing, and that no thought can be withholden from thee" (Job 42:2).

In saying that nothing is impossible with God we mean that no good thing is impossible with Him. God cannot sin, therefore God cannot lie. How thankful we should be that God is altogether righteous. When He makes a promise He keeps it. When He says He will do such and such a thing, He does it.

So far as our responsibility to God is concerned we must exercise faith, or in other words, believe Him. We are told in Hebrews that without faith it is impossible to please God. When He makes us a promise, and we trust Him to fulfill it, then God works on our behalf.

Faith, in order to be the right kind of faith, must be in the Lord Jesus Christ. Our trust must be in Him. Self may seem unconquerable but not when we reckon on God. The greatest obstacle to the overcoming life to us as believers is the self-life. This we have seen in Israel's wandering in the desert for 40 years. Their wandering was due to their selfish, self-centered desires instead of trusting God. But when the new generation of Israelites came to the Jordan, they were ready to do as God said and cross over to the other side.

Self Nature Not Renovated

The Red Sea typifies God's judgment on sin, but the passage of the Jordan typifies God's judgment on self. The old self-life of the Christian is not renovated as a result of salvation. God does not make it over as some men would rebuild an engine. The old self must be put in the place of death. It must be crucified. This is exactly what happened. In Galatians 2:20 Paul said, "I am crucified with Christ." Romans 6:6 says, "Knowing this, that our old man is crucified with him, that the body of sin might be destroyed."

Perhaps the hardest truth to accept and the last truth that many of us accept is that the old self nature was crucified in Christ. It was put to death with Christ on the cross. So far as our position before God is concerned the self nature is crucified. In our experience here on earth we must reckon this so by definitely putting off the old self and putting on the new self. We are to reckon ourselves dead indeed unto sin but alive unto God. Paul says, "I am crucified with Christ, nevertheless I live, yet not I but Christ liveth in me." This new self in us is Christ. The Lord regards the believer as united to Christ. When it comes to making this a reality in our daily experience we come to a place of decision. We may call it a time of crisis, a time when we pass through the "Jordan River." This is not a second work of grace. This is the working of God's grace from beginning to end of the Christian life. We experience His blessings moment by moment as we believe and trust in God.

When the believer comes to view himself in this way as having died and not yet having arrived at the completion of his Christian experience, something begins to happen. The Bible tells us that we are dead and our life is hid with Christ in God. This is Jordan. This is the new passage to a new kind of life. This is the experience that is pictured for us in the 4th chapter of Joshua. It is something that takes place at a very definite time in all of our experiences. It is not that we try to die, but we learn to reckon on a death that is already past.

Some may say that we are not dead to sin because we find sin creeping up on us every day. This is the way we look at it, but this is not the way God looks at it.

By way of illustration, consider a man on death row. He is condemned and awaiting execution. The time may be just a day away or several weeks away. Every avenue of escape from the penalty has been sought but none has been found, so he is to be executed. Legally he is as good as dead though physically he is not dead. He has lost all his liberties and his rights and privileges to any future existence in society.

Christ has condemned the sinful self to death. It no longer has any rights with regard to us. All of its privileges and liberties have been taken away. The moment we accepted Christ as Saviour this became a fact to us. We do not always act on the basis of this fact, but it is something we should claim constantly. This we must reckon on and trust the Holy Spirit to do His part, making this truth effective in our daily experience. We know that we have died to the old self. A burial has taken place and we have been raised to a new life; we trust the Holy Spirit to make this effective.

This is not a reckoning that is once and for all. This is, as we have indicated, a continuous thing. Paul said in one place that he died daily. What did he mean? There was a sense in which he died once for all, but in another sense he died every day. One had to do with his position before God, the other had to do with his daily experience or practice before men. The Lord Jesus said in Luke 9:23: "If any man will come after me, let him deny himself, and take up his cross daily, and follow me." For a man to take up his cross in this sense means to recognize daily that he has died to sin. We constantly reaffirm that we have died and that we are alive in Christ.

So in our early morning prayers and devotions we must reckon on this fact. Reckon on the fact that we have died to sin and that we are alive to God. This must be made a constant attitude throughout the day. We must put ourselves at God's disposal for anything He wants.

This crossing of the Jordan experience is a crisis which was really included as part of the Red Sea maneuver.

We must remember that the sin nature is not dead but we are dead to sin. The sin nature uses these mortal bodies through which it expresses itself, but what was once at the disposal of sin should now be at the disposal of the Lord so that we bring forth fruit unto righteousness. The sin nature has no longer the right to this vehicle of the body through which to act. Our bodies belong to God.

A third command was given with regard to Israel as they prepared to cross the Jordan River. The Ark was upon the shoulders of the priests who stood close to the edge of the water. The Israelites were some 3000 feet behind waiting for their orders. They came in these words: "And Joshua said unto the people, Sanctify yourselves: for to morrow the Lord will do wonders among you" (Josh. 3:5). The word sanctify means to set apart. The Israelites were to set themselves apart for God. The reference here then is to a prepared heart. God was going to do something special for them and they needed to be prepared morally and spiritually for it. We read in Ezra 7:10: "For Ezra had prepared his heart to seek the law of the Lord, and to do it, and to teach in Israel statutes and judgments." Here was a definite purpose of heart that Ezra had of seeking the Lord through His Word, first for his own spiritual benefit, and then so that he could teach it to others.

A heart that is prepared in the sense that Joshua commanded the children of Israel is a heart from which self has been put away. If God's leadership was to be followed, then man's leadership had to be left behind. God could not lead Israel until Israel was prepared to follow.

Isaiah said, "Behold, the Lord's hand is not shortened, that it cannot save; neither his ear heavy, that it cannot hear: but your iniquities have separated between you and your God, and your sins have hid his face from you, that he will not hear" (59:1,2). God will not direct us and perform

wonders for us unless we set ourselves apart for Him. This is
the import of Colossians 3:1: "If ye then be risen with
Christ, seek those things which are above, where Christ
sitteth on the right hand of God."

This is an act of faith on our part as Romans 6:13 tells
us, it is an act of yielding. God is holy and we must be holy
also "in all manner of conversation" as Peter says (I Pet.
1:15,16). Then and only then can we clearly see the way that
we should go.

Place of the Bible in Victory

We cannot enter into spiritual warfare until we make a
definite decision to do so. We decide to appropriate by faith
the fact that we have died with Christ to sin and to self and
to the world and have been raised again with Him to live in
the place of victory. This is the most important decision for
us to make once we are saved. Search the Scriptures and you
will see this for yourselves. We must not trust to feelings.
This is the way some Christians conduct their lives, feeling
that God will do this or that God will do that, but this is not
a safe procedure. Others again look for dreams and visions.
Some open their Bibles and put their finger on a verse and
take that as God's mind for them. We must be very careful in
this area and check every impression by the Scriptures. It is
through His Word that we learn the direction we are to go.

I am not speaking here of such information as a
missionary needs with regard to the place of service. There is
no passage in the Bible that says to any of us we are to go to
Africa or South America. But in the Word there are
instructions for us to follow, principles to guide us that will
lead us unerringly. The Word of God does not contradict
itself. It will not lead us astray. So it is through God's Word
and not merely through experiences that we know the way to
go.

In verse 6 of Joshua 3 we read: "And Joshua spake unto
the priests, saying, Take up the ark of the covenant, and pass
over before the people. And they took up the ark of the

covenant, and went before the people." This is only the first part of the order. The priests were to take the Ark of the Covenant and go ahead of the people, not to pass over Jordan, but to get to the head of the line. As we have noted several times before there was to be a distance of 3,000 feet between the priests carrying the Ark and the first of the people. This distance was to be maintained until the priests with the Ark entered the water.

The Ark as a symbol of the Lord Jesus Christ went ahead of the nation just as Christ is to go before His people. But just as the Ark must precede, the people had to follow. "Behold, the ark of the covenant of the Lord of all the earth passeth over before you." The Ark was first just as Christ leads each one of us. We must follow. This is our responsibility.

Just as the Lord promised the Israelites that they would see great wonders when they obeyed the Lord, we too will see wonders happening in our lives when we are obedient. If we have never tried the Lord in this way before, it is time we began; not for the sake of wonders that we may see, but because He deserves such allegiance from us. And the things He does for us are a proof that we belong to Him. They are a proof of His presence with us.

We know that the Lord is with us, for this information is given repeatedly in the Gospel of John, chapters 14, 15 and 16. There we learn that the Holy Spirit has been given to us and will be with us and in us forever. He is to lead us into all truth, teaching us the things that the Lord wants us to know. We were not left orphans when the Lord Jesus ascended from this world because He gave us the Holy Spirit to indwell and empower us.

The overcoming life in us becomes a proof of the indwelling of the Lord in our hearts. If we are not living an overcoming life we have no proof, at least of a visible nature, of our redemption or salvation. In I John 4:4 we are told: "Ye are of God, little children, and have overcome them: because greater is he that is in you, than he that is in the world." Or again in the same Book in 5:4,5 we read: "For

whatsoever is born of God overcometh the world: and this is
the victory that overcometh the world, even our faith. Who is
he that overcometh the world, but he that believeth that
Jesus is the Son of God?" In other words, if I say that I
believe Jesus is the Son of God and that I have accepted Him
as my Saviour, He indwells me. If He indwells me, then I
should be able to give proof that I am following Him and that
He is doing wonders for me.

He will change our lives completely. This is His guarantee.
Once we recognize that we have died with Him and are
buried with Him and have been raised with Him and keep
looking away unto Him, our lives will be different. This will
make us overcomers in the best sense. The habits of our lives
will change. The evil things will begin to fall off and works of
righteousness will be in evidence—the fruit of the Spirit in
other words. People will begin to understand that something
has really taken place within us.

They may have already seen a change as is apparent in
gross sinners who, having expressed the world's vile ways, are
saved and start attending church and reading their Bibles.
This gives proof that a change in disposition has taken place.
But there is something more needed, and this step of which
we speak takes us beyond even the changes just suggested. It
is then that people see something in us and want what we
have for themselves. This is proof to them that Christ is in us.
This is exactly what Joshua meant when he said, "Hereby ye
shall know that the living God is among you, and that he will
without fail drive out from before you the Canaanites" (Josh.
3:10). The proof that God controls us is in evidence when we
follow Him completely.

Any one who lacks victory lacks proof of his salvation.
We are not speaking here of sinless perfection or that a
person who is saved never sins any more. But to those who
may be watching our lives our lack of triumph is proof to
them that we do not have what we claim. There are people
around us who are watching to see if the real thing is in us.

Remember the Lord Jesus Christ asked according to Luke
6:46: "Why call ye me, Lord, Lord, and do not the things

which I say?" The word "Lord" is used here to mean one who is in complete control of another. It goes beyond addressing Christ as Saviour. The word "Jesus" means Saviour. The word "Christ" means the Anointed One. It speaks of the Holy One indwelling us and coming again. But the word "Lord" means He is Master. He is the One in absolute control of our lives. So let us repeat again our Saviour's question: "Why do you call me Lord . . . and do not those things which I say?"

Paul said in I Corinthians 12:3, "No man can say that Jesus is the Lord, but by the Holy Ghost." We cannot honestly say that Jesus Christ is Lord of our lives until the Holy Spirit has control of our lives. This comes as we yield ourselves wholly to Him. This is the subject illustrated by the crossing of the Jordan.

The priests were to precede the people into the Jordan River. To me this illustration has meant more for my life so far as the Christian walk is concerned than possibly any other portion in the Word of God. Beginning with verse 13 we read: "And it shall come to pass, as soon as the soles of the feet of the priests that bear the ark of the Lord, the Lord of all the earth, shall rest in the waters of Jordan, that the waters of Jordan shall be cut off from the waters that come down from above; and they shall stand upon an heap. And it came to pass, when the people removed from their tents, to pass over Jordan, and the priests bearing the ark of the covenant before the people; And as they that bare the ark were come unto Jordan, and the feet of the priests that bare the ark were dipped in the brim of the water, (for Jordan overfloweth all his banks all the time of harvest,) That the waters which came down from above stood and rose up upon an heap very far from the city Adam . . . " (Josh. 3:13-16).

There is the whole thing before us. We must get our feet wet so to speak. Faith is venturing forth. Do not stand at the edge of the water until it parts, for it never will. At the Red Sea the people had to wait until Moses stretched out his staff and the waters parted. But that had to do with another phase of our redemption. Here the subject is the Christian walk and in this we are instructed to step in, move forward, believe God, and then step out on the other side. We know from the Scriptures that we have died to self and the old self nature and are now alive unto the Lord Jesus Christ. This is true in our position before God, and we must make it a reality in our experience by believing the Word and acting upon it. We cannot be neutral in this matter.

Four progressive steps are brought before us here. The first one is that faith reckons on God's ability to do anything. There is nothing impossible with God. Faith also desires and therefore it asks. This is the second step. In the third place faith expects something to happen. The fourth step is that faith accepts the answer and therefore acts upon the Word of God. Faith marches forward. However, this is never done by us alone. All we are and have is in Christ.

A Step of Faith

It is a never-to-be-forgotten experience when we hear a promise of God and step out on it in faith and then see God doing things on our behalf. The priests who carried the Ark of the Covenant into the Jordan River saw God work. It would not have been enough for them to have stood close to the edge of the water and to have believed on the great ability of God to stop the flow several miles upstream and pile up the waters as though there was a great dam there. If we were asked, "Is God able to do such a thing?" We undoubtedly would answer yes. But if each of us had to answer the question, "Will God do this for me?" what would our answer be?

Every Christian is as precious in God's sight as the people of Israel were precious in His sight. What He promised them He did for them, and what He has promised you and me He will do for us. If we step out in faith, God will work on our behalf. With the danger of making this sound repetitious, I would say again that if we believe that we have died with Jesus and have been buried with Him and raised again and reckon on this fact, then step out in faith to walk in spiritual warfare and victory with Him, we will see remarkable things happen in our lives. They will be as remarkable to us as those that took place when the people of Israel followed Joshua.

The Israelites did not make the mistake at the edge of Jordan of merely reckoning on God's ability to do what He promised. They did not stand to see what God would do. When they received their marching orders to go into the river and the priests led with the Ark, then the waters parted.

These priests got their feet wet. That is the only way faith operates. We have tried this method over and over again at Back to the Bible Broadcast, and we know it works. This radio ministry would not be in existence today if it had not been for this passage of Scripture and God speaking to our hearts through it. We stepped out in faith back in 1939 and drove 400 miles, leaving everything of our former ministry and life behind us and planted our feet in Nebraska, believing that God had a work for us to do here. It was not an easy decision, and the course of our lives has not always been easy since then. We have had our Jerichos—our places of triumph. We have also had our Ais—our places of defeat. We have seen remarkable things happen. We thank God for the glorious victories He has given along the way.

We stepped out in faith believing God for new stations. We signed contracts when there was no money in sight to meet the obligations. But God had said, "Go," and we had to obey.

This is what happened when the priests stepped into the waters carrying the Ark. Humanly, the passage of the Jordan at that time and place seemed impossible. Yet it ended in victory because God gave the victory. It was a victory that had been won 40 years before at the Red Sea. Israel was now claiming, even though belatedly, some of the power that had been potentially hers for those long years. As we have pointed out before, our victory was won for us by the Lord Jesus Christ when He died, was buried, and rose again and then ascended to the right hand of God. Through the Holy Spirit He makes real to us the things He won for us so long ago. We need to exercise faith in order to enjoy the victory already provided.

Israel's walk in Canaan was to be a walk of faith. They had the promise that every bit of ground they walked on God had given them. We, too, in this day, as believers in Christ, are blessed with all spiritual blessings in heavenly places in Him. But these things must be claimed as we, too, walk a step at a time by faith.

To unbelievers this type of life seems hazardous. The decisions we make and the direction we go make them think, looking at things as they do, that we lack common sense. Businessmen in the field of radio have asked me what my background is and who has underwritten the work I represent? All that I can tell them is that it is God through His people. They shake their heads and say they do not understand.

Back in 1939 I stood in a radio station discussing with its managers the matter of financing a gospel radio program. They asked me how I was going to meet my obligations and I said, "My Partner pays the bills."

"Well, who is your partner?"

I said, "God." They were startled to say the least. They had never heard of such a thing. They finally answered that it I had God for a partner, they could risk taking on the Back to the Bible Broadcast. They used the word "gamble" and undoubtedly that is what it seemed to them. But they let me sign the contract.

Several years went by with God blessing step after step. Station upon station was added. One day one of these men who had allowed me to sign the original contract met me at a meeting and said, "Well, it looks as though your God has taken care of you." He had begun to see that this work was God's undertaking.

Let us learn to trust God. In our everyday walk let us exercise faith. We take risks in any kind of life we live, so why not risk everything on God? The farmer takes risks. He plows the land, sows the seed, putting money and time into his work. Certainly a farmer who is a child of God trusts Him for the harvest.

Other people take risks in their investments in other ways. In this they often trust men, but they take risks in order to gain more. So why not trust God? Why not believe Him? Barnabas and Paul did. They were described as "men that have hazarded their lives for the name of our Lord Jesus Christ" (Acts 15:26).

Here is a wonderful promise God gave through Isaiah: "When thou passest through the waters, I will be with thee; and through the rivers, they shall not overflow thee: when thou walkest through the fire, thou shalt not be burned; neither shall the flame kindle upon thee" (43:2). This is God's promise. Will we believe Him? When we live according to the will of God, He fulfills what He promises. When we dare to believe God, we need never fear the outcome.

In Joshua 3:13 God said that when the priests stepped into the waters the waters would part. In verse 16 we have the record of them stepping into the Jordan River and the waters piling up, making a safe passage for the people. But this took place only after those involved had acted upon their faith. This was the crisis act of decision followed by action.

With regard to our own decision to enter into spiritual warfare with Christ, we know that we were identified with Christ in His death, burial, resurrection and ascension. God says it is true and we believe it. So on this basis we say "No" to the flesh and "Yes" to the Lord Jesus Christ. We step out by faith and things begin to happen. This is the crucial decision we must make.

When the priests stepped into the waters of Jordan they stepped into the place of danger. The Israelites were to keep the Ark in view as they crossed over the Jordan for their safety rested with it.

It is not hard to visualize this historic event. The priests moved into the river carrying the Ark and the water stopped flowing. It began to pile up at a place out of sight of the Israelites some 16 miles up the river. It was not necessary for the Israelites to see this great volume of water piling up higher and higher. All they needed to do was to believe God and keep their eyes on the Ark which represented the presence of God.

There is a practical lesson for us in this. When we are in the midst of this spiritual warfare we do not always see where the danger lurks. We may not see how the Devil is working behind the scenes, but we do not need such information. What we are to do is to keep our eyes on Jesus, and the distracting influences of the world, the flesh and the Devil will not ensnare us.

The people of Israel were not to center their attention on the Land of Promise but on the Ark. Neither are we to be looking for signs of victory, but to look to the Victor. When we keep our eyes on Jesus, the victory will follow. There is a gospel song many of us enjoy singing, one line of which says, "Once it was the blessing, now it is the Lord." At one time we wanted things, but in this new approach to the spiritual life our eye is upon Him and our desire is centered in Him. As we keep our eyes on the Lord, the enemy will flee. Satan will harass us, but our victory lies in looking at Christ, not at the Devil.

Remember, we have the promise in James 4:6,7: "But he giveth more grace. Wherefore he saith, God resisteth the proud, but giveth grace to the humble. Submit yourselves therefore to God." This is the important thing. We must look to Him and submit to His control. We are to commit our way to the Lord, trust in Him and He will bring it to pass. This is the attitude of heart necessary for conquest. We must get our eyes on Christ. Then James continues: "Resist the devil, and he will flee from you."

That victory that lies in Christ is also the truth taught through the Apostle Paul: "But thanks be to God, which giveth us the victory through our Lord Jesus Christ" (I Cor. 15:57). It is because of this that the Apostle then appeals to us to be "stedfast, unmoveable, always abounding in the work of the Lord, forasmuch as ye know that your labour is not in vain in the Lord" (I Cor. 15:58).

When the Israelites crossed over the river they then stood

on the victory side. This pictures, as we have pointed out before, what it means to be crucified with Christ, buried with Him in death and then resurrected in spiritual life. It was this phase of experience that Paul spoke of when he said, "That I might know him and the power of his resurrection, and the fellowship of his sufferings, being made conformable unto his death; if by any means I might attain unto the resurrection of the dead." Paul said in effect, "I have trusted Him, I have died with Him, now I am living together with Him." Thus the entering into the land by the Israelites after the passage over the Jordan serves as a picture of the resurrected life, the ascended life, the life of spiritual warfare which results in victory and rest.

This crossing of the Jordan also serves as one of the best pictures of the principle of faith in action. It shows that when we appropriate what God has promised He will do for us according to His Word. So whether it is a matter of beginning this life of victory or of any other decision we have to make along the way, let us find out what God says and that will settle it. We will believe Him and step out on the basis of what He has said.

Psalm 37:5 is the verse the Lord gave us back in 1939 as we claimed His promises to begin the Back to the Bible Broadcast: "Commit thy way unto the Lord; trust also in him; and he shall bring it to pass." God did it and we thank Him for it.

When Israel crossed the Jordan they established a beachhead at Gilgal. The Ark remained firm in the place of danger while the people traveled in safety through the dry riverbed. The last persons to come up out of the river were the priests carrying the Ark. This is a picture to us of Christ who was victorious in and through death. It also carries the promise that we together with Him will be victorious, for He stands and has stood in the place of danger protecting us while we acted on the promises of God.

When John the beloved disciple was on the Isle of Patmos and saw the Lord, he was reassured and comforted. John testified, "And when I saw him, I fell at his feet as dead. And he laid his right hand upon me, saying unto me, Fear not; I am the first and the last: I am he that liveth, and was dead; and, behold, I am alive for evermore, Amen; and have the keys of hell and of death" (Rev. 1:17,18). Christ the victorious One dispels fear by His presence with us.

A Message to the World

The latter part of Joshua 4:18 tells us that when the priests who carried the Ark of the Covenant stepped out of the Jordan River, the waters of the Jordan began to flow again. The typical significance of this is that our death and burial with Christ and resurrection is a matter of the past. If we can say that we have appropriated this by faith then we are ready to enter into the spiritual battles that are before us. Preparation for these is much needed. We do not want to report defeat or failure when our Lord returns, an event that does not seem to be too far in the future.

The effect of the crossing of the Jordan was not limited to the Israelites and the people of Canaan. It was reported wherever there were men. Here is part of the record: "For the Lord your God dried up the waters of Jordan from before you, until ye were passed over, as the Lord your God did to the Red sea, which he dried up from before us, until we were gone over: *That all the people of the earth might know the hand of the Lord*, that it is mighty: that ye might fear the Lord you God for ever" (Josh. 4:23,24).

The application to us is that God has accomplished a work through the Lord Jesus Christ that not only takes away the guilt of sin and condemnation, but has provided victory for our lives. It is when we live this life of victory that the world knows that God has done something for us and through us. Our world today is seeking for reality. It looks for something real in the Christian and in the Church, the Body of Christ. Are they seeing it? If not, why not? If they do not find it in us, it is because we have failed to enter by faith and appropriate that sphere of Christian experience which has to do with conquest and rest.

The immediate enemies of Israel in Canaan were terrified by the miracle at the Jordan River: "And it came to pass, when all the kings of the Amorites, which were on the side of Jordan westward, and all the kings of the Canaanites, which were by the sea, heard that the Lord had dried up the waters of Jordan from before the children of Israel, until we were passed over, that their heart melted, neither was there spirit in them any more, because of the children of Israel" (Josh. 5:1).

It was not the numerical strength of Israel that made their enemies afraid. Neither was it the military equipment the Jewish soldiers carried with them. It was the drying up of the Jordan River. It was what the Lord had done, not what Israel was or had accomplished.

The world today needs to see what God can do. He has already demonstrated His power in Christ, but if we do not appropriate it for ourselves the world will not see it. The church in the main has lost its message and its character. There is too much dabbling in power politics and in efforts to change the social structure of peoples and nations instead of preaching the gospel of the Lord Jesus Christ that changes lives.

The Canaanite nations got the message from the passage of Jordan that God was almighty. They knew then that judgment for their wicked ways was near at hand.

The world today needs to know that God is almighty. The problems of this present age seem to be insurmountable. Men have no solution for many of them. And where the church has entered into these things the problems have not abated. What the world needs to see from us is that only God is adequate to deal with the mountainous troubles besetting the world. The true Church is but a mere handful as compared to the vast unbelieving multitudes of mankind, yet the world should be impressed through us with the nearness of God's judgment on the nations.

There is power even in the weakest saint, when he claims it, to cause even Satan to tremble. James 4:7 tells us that if we submit ourselves to the Lord and resist the Devil, the

Devil will flee from us. The weakest Christian on his knees can cause Satan to run in fear. The reason is that Christ has overcome him and has broken his power. For ourselves, however, we have to claim this so that we can resist Satan in the faith.

The Prophet Daniel saw this side of Christian victory and wrote: "The people that do know their God shall be strong, and do exploits" (Dan. 11:32). The Prophet knew both by faith and by experience how great and powerful God is and how He works through trusting saints to do His will.

Chapter Ten

THE MEMORIALS OF FAITH
(Joshua 4)

According to Joshua 4:19 the passage of the Jordan was effected on the tenth day of the first month and the Israelites "encamped in Gilgal, in the east border of Jericho." Their objective was to take Jericho, city and fortress, so they established their beachhead at Gilgal which was between the river and their objective.

The word "Gilgal" means "the reproach has been rolled away." For the Israelites this meant that the reproach of the wilderness wanderings had been rolled away. Their self-centered, carnal life had been left behind. The place of spiritual defeat and of failure had been removed. Even the reproach of Egypt itself was gone. This does not mean that Israel experienced no further failure or defeat. Sin did creep in occasionally but its power had been broken.

This is true also in our experience as believers. According to II Corinthians 5:17: "If any man be in [in union with] Christ . . . old things are passed away; behold, all things are become new." This does not mean that we may not sin again or become carnal, but it does mean the old life dominated by sin is gone as far as our position in Christ is concerned. When we take the position that we have died to the old self, the old flesh, and are now alive unto God, then the reality will be manifested.

Gilgal, a Base of Operations

Gilgal became the base of Israel's operations for the next several years. When they went out against their enemies, the Israelites eventually returned to Gilgal. Sometimes they returned every night after a battle if they were close enough

144

to their headquarters. It was here they returned after the victories and after their failures also. This was the place for readjustment, for replenishment, for refreshment both spiritually and physically. This was their rest camp and also their place of spiritual encouragement. When they failed at Ai they went back to Gilgal and God showed them where they had sinned and how to judge it.

We, too, need to establish a place that we call "Gilgal." We need to establish a regular devotional life. If we do not have one, we are only cheating ourselves.

In Joshua 1:8 God made it very clear to His servant that the Word of God should never be neglected. It should be meditated upon daily. In Ephesians 5 we have this admonition: "And be not drunk with wine, wherein is excess; but be filled with the Spirit; Speaking to yourselves in psalms and hymns and spiritual songs, singing and making melody in your heart to the Lord; Giving thanks always for all things unto God" (vv. 18-20).

Again in Ephesians we learn of the need of spiritual replenishing. Paul prayed for the believers in these words: "That he [God] would grant you, according to the riches of his glory, to be strengthened with might by his Spirit in the inner man" (3:16). This is the place of our Gilgal. And the reason for this is that Christ may dwell in your hearts by faith, not only to be our Saviour but to dwell as our spiritual life within us. We are to be rooted and grounded in Him in love so that we may be able to comprehend with all saints what is the breadth and length and depth and height of this love. It will lead us on also to know the love of Christ which passes knowledge. Paul also prayed that we might be filled with the fulness of God. He can do this for us because He is able to do exceeding abundantly above all that we ask or even think.

Gilgal, a Place of Remembrance

Gilgal was not only established as a home base for Israel during the conquest of the land; it also became a place of remembrance. Joshua was instructed to establish a memorial at Gilgal. The record is, "And it came to pass, when all the people were clean passed over Jordan, that the Lord spake unto Joshua, saying, Take you twelve men out of the people, out of every tribe a man, And command ye them, saying, Take you hence out of the midst of Jordan, out of the place where the priests' feet stood firm, twelve stones, and ye shall carry them over with you, and leave them in the lodging place, where ye shall lodge this night" (Josh. 4:1-3).

Later on in the chapter we read of the setting up of another memorial, this time in the river itself. "And the children of Israel did so as Joshua commanded, and took up twelve stones out of the midst of Jordan, as the Lord spake unto Joshua, according to the number of the tribes of the children of Israel, and carried them over with them unto the place where they lodged, and laid them down there. And Joshua set up twelve stones in the midst of Jordan, in the place where the feet of the priests which bare the ark of the covenant stood: and they are there unto this day" (vv. 8,9).

These two memorials made of stones were to be reminders to Israel of their safe passage through the Jordan River. From the standpoint of the types involved these two memorials remind us of the two aspects of our identification with Christ. First of all, the stones in the Jordan speak of the Israelites having died to the past. Whenever an Israelite came into that area he would see the stones and would be reminded that it was there Israel passed through the place of death as it were. The second set of stones was set up at Gilgal, the place of Israel's first night's lodging. They speak of new life out of death. These stones were taken out of the river as the Israelites marched through, then brought with them to the camping site. They therefore speak of Israel's new life on the other side of Jordan—a resurrection life.

With regard to our own experience, we have the first set of stones that were set up in the riverbed itself as a reminder that we died and were buried with Christ. This marked death to the old self and to sin. The doctrinal aspect of this truth is given in Romans, chapter 6. In our position before God we are dead to sin, and in our daily experience we are to reckon this fact as true.

The second set of stones which were set up at Gilgal are typical of the fact that we rose with Christ into new life. Colossians, chapter 3 tells us that if we are risen with Christ we should seek those things which are above where Christ sits at the right hand of God. We are to set our affections on things above and not on things on the earth because we have died and our life is hid with Christ in God.

These two monuments then typify to us the fact of our having died with Christ and our having been raised with Him and being alive in Him today. We are called to reckon this so in our daily experience. This calls for faith in action. We are to present or yield our bodies unto Him so that He can live in them through us and use us for His own.

It is interesting to note that Joshua set up the memorial in the riverbed right at the spot where the priests holding the Ark stood while the Israelites passed safely over. It was Joshua himself who placed these stones at that particular spot. He did this at the command of God. He did not delegate it to someone else. It was his responsibility to raise this memorial.

In this action Joshua is a type of Christ. Remember, that the name "Jesus" and the name "Joshua" both mean "Saviour." Only Joshua was allowed to raise this memorial of Israel's escape through this place of death. With regard to Christ, only He could die to sin. We cannot, though some try. When Christ died God saw us identified with Him in His death. That is a death which to us is past. Today we are alive because He has taken us through that place of death. This was His work. We must now allow the Holy Spirit to apply that truth to our lives. We are to reckon ourselves dead to sin according to Romans 6:11, but at the same time we are to reckon ourselves alive unto God. In doing this we give ourselves to obedience, not letting sin reign in our mortal bodies (Rom. 6:12).

How can we keep sin from reigning in these bodies of ours? The answer is given in Romans 8:13: "But if ye through the Spirit do mortify the deeds of the body, ye shall live." In other words, when we are tempted by the flesh nature to yield our bodies to work out the evil it prompts us to perform, we are to refuse. We are to call on the Holy Spirit for help, yielding ourselves completely to Him. We can say something like this to the Holy Spirit, "I know I have died to the old flesh and self-life and it has no claim on me, but You must make it effective in my experience. I trust You for it." Thus we mortify the deeds of the flesh by faith. It is not something we can do of ourselves.

We should read Colossians 3 very thoroughly. There are some places where the present tense is used and it should be the past tense. For example, in verse 3 where it says "for ye are dead" the word should read, "for ye have died." But we have also been raised with Christ, so we are to seek those things which are above where our life is hid with Christ in God.

Also in Colossians 3:8 we are told to put off the old things of evil. And in the following verse we are told, "Ye have put off the old man with his deeds." In the one verse we're exhorted to put off these old wicked ways and the next verse tells us we have already put off these things. What is meant here? The truth is that potentially in Christ the old man with his deeds has been put off, but now by an act of faith, by appropriating the new life in Christ, we are to reach the decision of putting off the old man with his deeds.

The same truth is seen where we read in verse 10 that we have put on the new man and yet in verse 12 we are told to put on the evidences of the new life which are the result of the new man being in us. One speaks of what has taken place in our position before God, the other tells us what we are to do now in our daily experience. The tenses here are very instructive. What we receive potentially the moment we trust Christ, we are to make actual through acts of faith.

Joshua also raised the memorial at Gilgal made of 12 stones. Gilgal speaks of resurrection, so that these two memorials, the one in the river speaking of death and the one in Gilgal speaking of life, remind us that both are true for us in Christ. The moment we trust in Christ, that is the very moment we are born again, we have new life. Then we are to appropriate the fact of our resurrection with Christ in our daily experience. The Holy Spirit must make this effective in us. Sin shall not reign over us according to Romans 6:14, but only the Spirit of God is able to make this true in our lives.

Sin shall not have dominion over us because we are not under the law, we are told, but under grace. The law forbade our sinning and then when we did sin, condemned us to death. But grace comes in and pays the penalty of the broken law and provides new life. God provides us grace to live a life of godliness so that sin does not reign in our lives. This calls on us for continuous walking with God. The stones in Gilgal, put on the victory side, mark this truth of new life.

Just as Gilgal became a place of refreshment and a rallying point after either victory or defeat, so we are to daily meet with the Lord denying ourselves and taking up our crosses daily and following Him (Luke 9:23). It is as we maintain a quiet time with the Lord that we can call up this truth of having died with the Lord and of now looking to the Holy Spirit to make effective in our lives the resurrection life of Christ.

The priests stood in the river channel with the Ark until every Israelite was safely across and the memorial was raised to that safe passage through the Jordan. So what we have in Christ is all based on His finished work. Everything we need has been provided through Him. When we meet with failure as Joshua did at Ai, we may wonder if we have really come out of the desert and crossed the Jordan into Canaan. With such failures to humble us we may wonder if we have died to self and are alive to God. Let us remind ourselves of these memorials and their significance: the one that says Jesus died and I died with Him, and the other that says He arose and I arose with Him.

We do not die again. We must reaffirm our position in Christ. We know each day that we have already died in Christ and so we deny self, daily taking up our cross and following Him.

All the 12 tribes were represented in the matter of the memorial stones since one man was selected from each tribe. This meant that all the Israelites shared in this memorial. In contrast to the older generation who had died, the new generation entering Canaan was a believing one.

To go back to the original provision made through Christ, we find that all of us are represented in His finished work. He did not die for a few; He did not die for some special group; He died for all men. We all like sheep have gone astray and we have turned everyone to his own way and God laid on Christ the iniquity of us all. Righteousness and power, however, are not ours automatically just because we are members of the human race. They are available only to those who believe in Christ. We read in Romans 3:22 concerning the righteousness of God: "Even the righteousness of God which is by faith of Jesus Christ unto all and upon all them that believe: for there is no difference."

With reference to the power of God which is available to the believer for the demonstration of the Christian life, Ephesians 1:19 speaks of "the exceeding greatness of his power to us-ward who believe."

The cross does not fail any of us, but we must place the emphasis on faith with regard to its benefits in our individual lives.

We should also see that there was no provision made for retreat after the Jordan River was crossed. Once its waters rolled behind the Israelites on the Canaan side of the river, there was no turning back. To have left a way open would have been an invitation to retreat.

In the spiritual sense we can always go back to Gilgal but not to Egypt. We can go back to the cross for refreshment but not to begin life all over again. The Israelites could return to Gilgal for refreshment but not to Egypt. Hebrews says in this connection, "But we are not of them who draw back unto perdition; but of them that believe to the saving of the soul" (10:39). We do not go back to Egypt and start all over again. If we have failure, we do not begin again with a new birth. Instead, we go back to where we started out on the victory side of the Jordan River, to our spiritual Gilgal. There is no need to question our salvation simply because we see failure at times in our Christian lives. We do not need to ask if we have really died to sin. We have, but we must reckon on this fact constantly in our experience.

Gilgal, a Place of Spiritual Resurrection

Gilgal also marks the place of spiritual resurrection. Christ not only died, but He was buried and rose again and then ascended to the right hand of the Father. Very little is said in many Christian circles these days concerning the resurrection life and practically nothing at all about the life of ascension. But we find in the Bible that these are spoken of very clearly. We read in Joshua 4:19,20 that the people came up out of Jordan, and camped in Gilgal and the 12 stones which they took out of the river were piled together in Gilgal by Joshua.

The Jordan River speaks of the place of death and Gilgal the place of life. We repeat this because we need to remember it. The corresponding New Testament truth is found in Ephesians 2:5,6 and is very important for our learning and growth. Even when we were dead in sins God quickened us together in Christ and raised us up together and made us sit together in heavenly places in Christ. This is our ascension not for the future, but for the present. There is a time in the future when He will come and resurrect these bodies of our humiliation and give us resurrection bodies. But even now in our spiritual life we have already been raised together with Him and seated with Him in the heavenlies. In our position before God we are not only delivered from the self and sin life, but we are identified with Christ in His new life.

In Romans 7 we have a record of a defeated Christian life. There Paul tells how he consented that the law was good; and yet the good things he wanted to do he couldn't do, and evil things he didn't want to do he did do. This is where some Christians still are. Is this your condition?

We should be enjoying the freedom of the Spirit in Christ

Jesus: "For the law of the Spirit of life in Christ Jesus [the principle of life in Christ Jesus] hath made me free from the law of sin and death" (Rom. 8:2). Do we believe this? Do we trust Him?

Paul says in I Corinthians 9:26,27: "I therefore so run, not as uncertainly; so fight I, not as one that beateth the air: but I keep UNDER my body, and bring it into subjection: lest that by any means, when I have preached to others, I myself should be a castaway." The word "castaway" is a poor translation here. The word in the original means "disapproved" or "disqualified."

Paul said he kept his body under. This was done by the power of the indwelling Spirit. This is God's method, and is what Paul referred to in Philippians 3:10-14: "That I may know him, and the power of his resurrection, and the fellowship of his sufferings, being made conformable unto his death; if by any means I might attain unto the resurrection of the dead. Not as though I had already attained, either were already perfect: but I follow after, if that I may apprehend that for which also I am apprehended of Christ Jesus. Brethren, I count not myself to have apprehended: but this one thing I do, forgetting those things which are behind, and reaching forth unto those things which are before, I press toward the mark for the prize of the high calling of God in Christ Jesus."

In our natural spiritual condition we would be bound by Satan. His tools and his temptations would produce failures of all kinds. He goes about as a roaring lion seeking whom he may devour. But we are more than conquerors through Christ. We have been delivered by Him from Satan's power. It is the strategy of our enemy to harass and taunt us if he has any idea that we are aware that Christ has really conquered him. But we have been delivered and are seated together with Christ in heavenly places.

In this connection the Apostle makes a very important statement in I Corinthians 10:13: "There hath no temptation taken you but such as is common to man: but God is faithful [mark this—God is faithful], who will not suffer [permit] you to be tempted above that ye are able; but will with the temptation also make a way to escape, that ye may be able to bear it."

Peter wrote that we should receive "the end of your faith, even the salvation of your souls." This does not mean deliverance from hell only, but victory over trials and tests and all that life holds.

This is why we must humble ourselves before the Lord. God gives more grace and resists the proud, but gives grace to the humble. For this reason we are to submit ourselves "to God. Resist the devil, and he will flee from you" (James 4:7). Any Christian who by faith takes his position on victory ground is invincible. The believer who steps in by faith and claims that life which is above all principalities and powers, is beyond and out of the reach of the Devil.

But this is something we must accept by faith daily and walk in constantly. Gilgal is the place of resurrection. It is the springboard to victory. We must refresh ourselves there often. Concerning this, Dr. Alan Redpath wrote: "Gilgal is a place of resurrection, but it is resurrection only in the measure in which it is remembrance. It is life only in the measure in which it is death. It is victory only in the measure in which I have been humbled. It is triumph only in the measure in which I have gone down with the Lord Jesus to the grave." Only to the extent that we by faith accept our place, and in humbleness before God go down to the grave with the Lord Jesus by faith, and then accept the complete resurrection life—only to that extent do we have victory. But it is right here that the effect on an unbelieving world is tremendous when they see the works of God in us.

This was what the spies found when they entered Jericho. Rahab, having seen what God was doing for Israel, said that there was no strength left in the Canaanites because of the fear that had come upon them. The life of victory is a reality, and it can even make the demons to tremble.

Chapter Eleven

FURTHER PREPARATIONS IN FAITH
(Joshua 5)

From every human point of view the time to strike at the strongholds of the Canaanites was right after Israel crossed the Jordan. Those idolatrous peoples were demoralized. They were terribly afraid. Not only had the Red Sea incident 40 years before filled them with dread, but they had also heard and seen what had happened to the kings on the east side of Jordan. Then came the Jordan crossing and panic spread throughout Canaan. Surely such would be the time for Israel to launch an all-out offensive. This is the way mere human strategy would plan; but God is not confined to man's methods, nor is God ever in a hurry. Neither is He behind time. He knows just when to strike.

We might well beware when we are pressured to act immediately in some situation without having had time to consult the Lord about it. He does not put pressure on us to reach decisions without giving us opportunity for reflection and prayer.

This kind of pressure of which we speak comes from Satan. If he cannot stop us from doing God's will, he will try to get us to push ahead of God's will. He will put pressure on us to do something drastic, because we feel that the time to strike is when the iron is hot. There is a certain amount of truth in this; but we must be careful in this area.

There are times when possibly we should act faster than we do. As far as I'm personally concerned, I'm inclined to be a little bit slow on such decisions, for I want to be sure I am in the will of God. God knows my heart in these matters, and He knows that my personal desire is to be in His perfect will. So I'm sure that God, knowing the purpose and desire and motives of my heart, will not permit an opportunity to slip

154

out of my hands if it is His will for me to take hold of it. He will allow the time necessary for me to reach a decision that I believe is according to His mind.

So it was in the case of the people of Israel just after they crossed Jordan. Some of them might have been in a hurry but God was not. Delay was in order for them. Sometimes we miss God's best by being in a hurry to do things when there should be more emphasis on the condition of our hearts. Doing should come from being. We must take time to fellowship with God in order that our conduct will please Him.

My heart goes out to missionaries and pastors. They are pressed into various avenues of activity to such a degree that time to be alone with God becomes hard to find. Yet such time must be found if God's servants are to be what they ought to be.

It was just as necessary for the Israelites to take time for God's instructions, before He could lead them to final victory.

Gilgal, a Place of Repudiation

The beachhead at Gilgal became a place where Israel repudiated the old life that was still left over from Egypt. The second verse of Joshua 5 tells the story: "At that time the Lord said unto Joshua, Make thee sharp knives, and circumcise again the children of Israel the second time." Joshua did as God directed so that Gilgal in a new way meant the rolling away of reproach, in this case the reproach of Egypt.

Circumcision had long been neglected by the Israelites. The rite had not been practiced during the desert wanderings. Yet this was a significant sign which God had given to His people. The Scofield note on this is revealing: "Circumcision is the 'sign' of the Abrahamic Covenant (Gen. 17:7-14; Rom. 4:11). 'The reproach of Egypt' was that, during the later years of the Egyptian bondage, this separating sign had been neglected (cf. Ex. 4:24-26), and this neglect had continued during the wilderness wanderings. The N. T. analogue is world conformity; the failure openly to take a believer's place with Christ in death and resurrection (Rom. 6:2-11; Gal. 6:14-16). Spiritually it is mortifying the deeds of the body through the Spirit (Rom. 8:13; Gal. 5:16,17; Col. 2:11,12; 3:5-10)."

Paul said according to Galatians 6:14: "But God forbid that I should glory, save in the cross of our Lord Jesus Christ, by whom the world is crucified unto me, and I unto the world." We see from this that the cross of Jesus Christ is the dividing place between the Christian and the world. When a person is hung on a cross he is inactive concerning the things of the world. Furthermore, the world cannot do anything more to him. This was the attitude Paul took with regard to the cross of Christ. And he went on in this same passage to say, "For in Christ Jesus neither circumcision availeth any thing, nor uncircumcision, but a new creature. And as many as walk according to this rule, peace be on them, and mercy, and upon the Israel of God" (vv. 15,16).

Thus the New Testament significance of circumcision is that we have been separated through the cross. This is to be made a reality in our spiritual experience. The application is very clear, for we read in Romans 8:13: "For if ye live after the flesh, ye shall die: but if ye through the Spirit do mortify the deeds of the body, ye shall live." Just as circumcision was a sign of separation, even so the Christian is, through the Holy Spirit, to live a separated life and by the Spirit mortify the deeds of the body. It is only then that we can live in the spiritual sense.

This is what Paul referred to in Galatians 5:16,17: "This I say then, Walk in the Spirit, and ye shall not fulfil the lust of the flesh. For the flesh lusteth against the Spirit, and the Spirit against the flesh: and these are contrary the one to the other: so that ye cannot do the things that ye would."

We have been separated by the cross in our position before God. We must make this a reality in our condition before men. As the Apostle Paul wrote in another place, "And ye are complete in him . . . In whom also ye are circumcised with the circumcision made without hands, in putting off the body of the sins of the flesh by the circumcision of Christ." It is Christ who separates us from sin in our lives.

So far as Israel was concerned there was no inheritance possible to them until they were circumcised. This was clearly stated in the seventeenth chapter of Genesis where the covenant concerning the land was given. So now, as the nation stood at the edge of Canaan, it was necessary that they follow through on the sign of separation which for them was circumcision. This was the sign God made with Abraham and was to be continued by his posterity.

Circumcision pictures the putting off of the flesh nature. This we learn in Colossians 3:3 where we learn we have been raised with Christ, so we are to set our affection on things above and not on things on the earth. We have died and our life is hid with Christ in God. For this reason we are exhorted to mortify our members which are upon the earth. The word "mortify" means "put to death." The flesh nature has been rendered impotent through Christ's death on the cross, but we must make this a reality in our everyday lives by a faith action. We must always distinguish between what we are in Christ by virtue of His death and resurrection, and what we experimentally are or should be by faith. It is when we reckon on this fact through faith that the work of the Holy Spirit becomes effective in our lives.

There is a great difference between our spiritual standing and our spiritual state. The one is our position before God and the other is our experience on earth. It is God's purpose that we become in our experience what we are before Him in our position. It is here that we find the whole basis of the true Christian life. We should die because we have died. We should live because we are alive. We should conquer because we have already won. All of this is by faith in Jesus Christ. We should recognize what we are in our position, and then this recognition should lead us to an act.

Weakness of the Flesh

The rite of circumcision was also a testimony to the weakness of the flesh. Instead of conquering on the momentum of the Jordan experience, the Israelites became weak for at least three days following the renewal of the circumcision practice. This placed the nation in a vulnerable position so far as the enemy was concerned; but God saw to it that their foes had no knowledge of the situation. The practical lesson we learn from this is that we cannot be strong in God until we are weak in ourselves. Paul confessed in Romans 7:18,19: "For I know that in me (that is, in my flesh,) dwelleth no good thing: for to will is present with me; but how to perform that which is good I find not. For the good that I would I do not: but the evil which I would not, that I do."

Paul also recognized according to Romans 8:2 that the law or the principle of the Spirit of life in Christ Jesus has made us free from the principle of sin and death. That is something God has already wrought through Christ.

On another occasion when Paul had asked the Lord to remove a thorn in the flesh, God did not do as the Apostle requested. Three times Paul made the plea and then God said, "My grace is sufficient for thee: for my strength is made perfect in weakness" (II Cor. 12:9). Realizing what God was doing for him and gladly submitting to God's will, Paul said, "Most gladly therefore will I rather glory in mine infirmities, that the power of Christ may rest upon me. Therefore I take pleasure in infirmities, in reproaches, in necessities, in persecutions, in distresses for Christ's sake: for when I am weak, [the personal I] then I [the person in union with Christ] am strong." Until we recognize this fact God cannot work, but when we do, He begins to work. In ourselves we are weak, but our strength lies in Christ.

What our Saviour said in John 15:2,3 brings this out beautifully: "Every branch in me that beareth not fruit he taketh away: and every branch that beareth fruit, he purgeth it, that it may bring forth more fruit. Now ye are clean through the word which I have spoken unto you." It is by the Spirit of God that we must cut off the things that hinder us. According to Romans 8:13 we are to mortify the deeds of the flesh by the Holy Spirit. The doctrinal basis for this, as we have pointed out before, is that we are to reckon ourselves dead indeed unto sin but alive unto God through Jesus Christ our Lord (Rom. 6:11).

The appetites of the flesh nature are to be cut off by the Holy Spirit: self-indulgence, the pride of the flesh, secret pride, secret ambitions, self-assumptions, not only those that are obvious but those that are hidden. If we check our own hearts, we will often find that the reason we get our feelings hurt is due to secret pride or ambition that has not been fed by praise from someone. Self-confidence that displaces confidence in God also needs to be dealt with. Our feelings of superiority with regard to others are all part of the flesh-life. Perhaps we think we are more intellectual than others. All such things will hinder our spiritual life so they need to be mortified or put to death by the Spirit.

There needs to be a separation from these things just as there was when Joshua was told by the Lord after the Israelites were circumcised: "This day have I rolled away the reproach of Egypt from off you" (Josh. 5:9).

Gilgal, A Place of Renewal

Gilgal was not only a place of repudiation of the flesh or separation from it, it was also a place of renewal. We read in 5:10: "And the children of Israel encamped in Gilgal, and kept the passover on the fourteenth day of the month at even in the plains of Jericho." They landed on the Jericho side of the river on the tenth day of the first month. Immediately afterwards there was the time of circumcision and then a wait of three days. This was followed on the fourth day by the keeping of the Passover.

This is very important. Only twice before had they remembered the Passover. The first time was in Egypt itself when lambs were slain and blood sprinkled on the doorposts.

The record is in Exodus 12. The second time the people kept the Passover was at Mount Sinai according to Numbers 9:5. This special feast was to have been remembered regularly as a reminder that their emancipation from Egypt was entirely God's doing. Yet they had neglected the Passover for years.

Israel also needed to remember that they were God's firstborn who owed their very life to Him. The firstborn of Israel had been spared in Egypt because of the slain lamb, yet all the nation owed its life to God. This is true of us also. If it had not been for the grace of God which made possible our redemption, we would be hell bound and dead in trespasses and sins. Our life is in Christ who, as our sacrifice, was also our substitute for judgment. He died in our place.

Gilgal, as we have before noticed, was located between the River Jordan and the city of Jericho. Consequently, when the Israelites celebrated the Passover they did so right under the noses of their enemies. Satan was looking on; but he was looking on with trembling. Think of this in connection with Psalm 23. There we read, "Yea, though I walk through the valley of the shadow of death"—the very position the Israelites were in at that time. They were facing death on every side. They had already faced it and passed through the Jordan, coming out alive because God had opened a way for them. Now they were facing the enemy, but as the Psalmist said, "I will fear no evil: for thou art with me; thy rod and thy staff they comfort me." Thus Israel found her comfort and deliverance in God.

How applicable are the words of the next verse which say, "Thou preparest a table before me in the presence of mine enemies." Israel feasted, honoring God in the Passover while their enemies looked on from the walls of Jericho. Israel rejoiced in what she had in the Lord and the enemy could do nothing to stop her.

As we go forth to conquer, to be spiritual warriors for the Saviour, we must remind ourselves of what we have in Christ Jesus. Right in the thick of the fight, right under the nose of the Devil, so to speak, we can prove by our remembrance of Christ and His death and resurrection that Jesus is the

Conqueror. This is something we should remember at the Lord's Table where we show the Lord's death until He comes. It speaks of our victory and of Satan's defeat. So let us submit ourselves to God, resist the Devil, and he will flee from us.

Gilgal, A Place of New Food

Still another very important matter associated with Gilgal was Israel's change of food. Before they entered into a full-scale conquest of the land their desert menu was changed. We read in Joshua 5:11,12: "And they did eat of the old corn of the land on the morrow after the passover, unleavened cakes, and parched corn in the selfsame day. And the manna ceased on the morrow after they had eaten of the old corn of the land; neither had the children of Israel manna any more; but they did eat of the fruit of the land of Canaan that year." This change of food was an essential change as we see in examining the matter closely.

The people renewed their separation through circumcision and also renewed their relationship by celebrating the Passover. Egypt with its bondage was behind them; the desert wanderings were over; Jordan, the place of decision, was crossed; and the nation was now ready to conquer Canaan.

A new kind of food was necessary as Israel went against her enemies and took possession of the country. As Paul said later, they were forgetting those things that were behind and reaching forth to the things that were before. There was a prize, something ahead, but they needed a change of diet to make them strong for the battles. In the language of the New Testament with regard to Christians, they were passing from the milk stage to the meat stage. They were passing from the child stage to the mature stage. Their wilderness journey was over and with it the wilderness provision ceased.

Manna was a constant miracle, provided for the sustenance of God's people day after day. But there came a time when it ceased. Manna is a type of Christ in His humiliation, as He gave Himself so that the believer might have life. There are many Christians who can give clear-cut testimonies of salvation, yet they never get beyond the manna or the milk stage. All of their testimonies relate to the first phase of salvation. It is wonderful, to be sure, but it is not all of the Christian life. If I were to be constantly saying that the most wonderful day in my life was the day of my birth, you would think there was something wrong with me. You would wonder why I was still concerned about the baby stage in life. Alas, there are many baby Christians who never grow beyond this point.

Redemption is foundational. And it is necessary that there be the manna or the milk stage in the Christian life. But it was not necessary that the children of Israel eat manna 40 years. They did this because of their disobedience and the consequent lack of growth. It is surely unfortunate that many believers live on the milk of the Word from year to year for the same reason.

In speaking to His disciples, the Lord Jesus said, "I am that bread of life. Your fathers did eat manna in the wilderness, and are dead. This is the bread which cometh down from heaven, that a man may eat thereof, and not die" (John 6:48-50). Eating of the manna is equivalent to knowing Christ only after the flesh. Knowing that He walked on this earth and died for our sins is essential, but there is more to total redemption than this. To dwell on this part of His life and work is the milk diet.

The Apostle Paul, inspired of God, would not have us to remain at this point. He says, "Wherefore henceforth know we no man after the flesh: yea, though we have known Christ after the flesh, yet now henceforth know we him no more [after the flesh]" (II Cor. 5:16). In other words, we are not now dealing with a Christ who was here in weakness and died, but rather as II Corinthians 13:4 says, "For though he was crucified through weakness, yet he liveth by the power of God." This is how we, too, are to live—by the power of God.

In Hebrews 5 beginning with verse 11 we read: "Of

whom [Christ] we have many things to say, and hard to be
uttered, seeing ye are dull of hearing. For when for the time
ye ought to be teachers, ye have need that one teach you
again which be the first principles of the oracles of God; and
are become such as have need of milk, and not of strong
meat. For every one that useth milk is unskilful in the word
of righteousness: for he is a babe. But strong meat belongeth
to them that are of full age [spiritually mature], even those
who by reason of use have their senses exercised to discern
both good and evil."

In writing to the Corinthians Paul had this to say: "And
I, brethren, could not speak unto you as unto spiritual, but as
unto carnal, even as unto babes in Christ. I have fed you with
milk, and not with meat: for hitherto ye were not able to
bear it, neither yet now are ye able. For ye are yet carnal: for
whereas there is among you envying, and strife, and divisions,
are ye not carnal and walk as men?" (I Cor. 3:1-3). It is time
all of God's people get off the milk ration, the baby food
ration, and began to eat the spiritual meat of the Word.

The morning after Israel had partaken of the Passover and
were ready to go into battle, they ate of the corn of the land.
The manna ceased the next day. The manna came down, but
corn came up. Manna came down from heaven, speaking of
Christ in His incarnation coming down from heaven. The
corn came up out of the ground after the kernel of corn was
dead, the new corn speaking of the risen Christ. Remember
our Lord said that except a grain of wheat die it abides alone.
Jesus had died and was raised again and we have died with
Him, so the second aspect of His work is now the risen,
victorious Christ; and we, as we learn to know Him in this
position, go on from victory to victory. The corn of the land
is Christ apprehended not only as having died, which is past
and foundational, but Christ apprehended as risen, glorified
and seated in the heavenlies. He is the victorious, living Christ
today.

To be occupied with Christ living on the earth, crucified
in weakness tends to keep us in a wilderness experience. It
produces the experience Paul spoke of in Romans 7. We want

to do good and can't do it. We don't want to do evil but we
do it. The reason is that we are attempting to imitate Christ
as He walked on the earth, instead of allowing Him as the
One who was crucified and raised again to indwell us and live
His life in us.

Are we having trouble with our prayer life? He did not
have trouble with it, and He is in us to work out this prayer
life in us. Do we have trouble with other things? This living
Christ is in us to help us meet the plans and purposes of God
for us.

The conflict ahead of the people of Israel called for food
with a germ of life in it. This the manna did not have, for it
spoke only of the great preliminaries, the death of Christ, the
taking away of our sins. But there is more to the Christian
life than this. Manna was heavenly food fitted for a people in
the wilderness; but the corn of the land speaks of the risen
Christ, the living bread for the life of victory.

Is this line of truth understandable to you? Even the
disciples found difficulty at first. In this same chapter in
John's Gospel, the Saviour said, "I am the living bread which
came down from heaven: if any man eat of this bread, he
shall live for ever: and the bread that I will give is my flesh,
which I will give for the life of the world" (v. 51). He was not
only going to give His life for the remission of sin, but, as
believers are united with Him, they would find Him as the
living One. In verse 53 the Saviour added: "Verily, verily, I
say unto you, Except ye eat the flesh of the Son of man, and
drink his blood, ye have no life in you."

Failure to understand the figurative language the Saviour
is using has caused some to stumble. He continues in the
same vein in verse 56: "He that eateth my flesh, and drinketh
my blood, dwelleth in me, and I in him. As the living Father
hath sent me, and I live by the Father: so he that eateth me,
even he shall live by me. This is that bread which came down
from heaven: not as your fathers did eat manna, and are
dead: he that eateth of this bread shall live for ever" (vv.
56-58).

How can we possibly eat His flesh and drink His blood?

As we have indicated, the Saviour was using figurative language. Just as we take food physically into our bodies, we are to partake of Christ's life by faith. The Lord gave us the solution to this whole matter when He said in verse 63: "It is the spirit that quickeneth; the flesh profiteth nothing: the words that I speak unto you, they are spirit, and they are life." It was unfortunate that because of this many decided not to follow Him anymore. These things were not palatable to them.

We as believers need to apprehend Christ as risen and glorified. We must grasp the power of His resurrection. This is why Paul said that he wanted to know Christ and the power of His resurrection. This is why such passages as Ephesians 1:15-23 should not only be read but meditated upon for hours so that the Spirit of God can begin to unfold their truths to us.

Returning again to the Book of Hebrews, this time to the first part of the sixth chapter, we find information to help us at this point. In the fifth chapter Paul spoke of the Hebrew believers as living on milk instead of the strong meat of the Word. But in the sixth chapter he exhorted them to leave the doctrines of Christ—not to forget them but to go on from them and to go on to perfection or maturity. They were not to keep on laying the foundation, but to build on the foundation. As Paul wrote to the Corinthians: "Other foundation can no man lay than that is laid, which is Jesus Christ. Now if any man build upon this foundation gold, silver, precious stones, wood, hay, stubble; Every man's work shall be made manifest." Our responsibility as believers is to build on the foundation. We go from the kindergarten of the spiritual life on to maturity in spiritual things. It is from crucifixion to resurrection and ascension.

While we are in this world, we are to be strangers and pilgrims. But we should cease to be simply wanderers as were the people in the desert. Too many Christians struggle and work to make their salvation sure. Paul could say he was forgetting those things that were in the past, because he had trusted Christ and was reaching forward to the things which lay ahead (Phil. 3:13,14). So we must have a proper perspective of Christ's work. In the first place He gave His life for our sins. In the second place He gave His life to us. The spiritual warfare that lies ahead in the Christian life calls for far more than human strategy. It demands divine wisdom and power.

This is the testimony of Proverbs 3:5-7 where we read: "Trust in the Lord with all thine heart; and lean not unto thine own understanding. In all thy ways acknowledge him, and he shall direct thy paths. Be not wise in thine own eyes: fear the Lord, and depart from evil." In the New Testament the Apostle wrote, "Be strong in the Lord, and in the power of his might" (Eph. 6:10).

Another passage of Scripture that is rich in its message to us is II Corinthians 10:3-5: "For though we walk in the flesh, we do not war after the flesh: (For the weapons of our warfare are not carnal, but mighty through God to the pulling down of strong holds;) Casting down imaginations . . . and bringing into captivity every thought to the obedience of Christ." There are new weapons designed for our spiritual victory just as there must be strong spiritual food to strengthen us. The strategy followed may seem foolish to the world, but God has chosen what the world calls foolish to confound the wisdom of the wise. Manna, which is the milk stage, was enough to preserve life. But corn, which is the meat stage, is necessary for those going on into spiritual battle.

Where do you stand now? Are you in the desert of defeat or are you in the land of victory and progress? Test yourself by the (spiritual) food you are mostly eating.

Chapter Twelve

FURTHER PREPARATIONS IN FAITH
(Joshua 5) (Continued)

Captain of God's Hosts

Joshua was a man of courage, the kind of man God wanted him to be. He walked away from the camp of Israel in order to view the military situation concerning Jericho. The Israelites could not turn back. They had to go forward. Behind them were Egypt, the Red Sea, the desert and now Jordan. To retreat was impossible. They must go forward, but standing in their way was Jericho, one of the great fortresses of Canaan. According to some authorities the walls of the city were 90 feet high and 30 feet thick. It was not as large as some of the cities of antiquity, being possibly two and a half or three miles in circumference, small enough at least for the Israelites to march around seven times in one day. Yet it blocked Israel's path. It stood in the way of their advance. So Joshua, as soldier and strategist, left the camp in order to view the situation and consider what needed to be done. He was alone, meditating upon God's purpose and will, seeking divine wisdom for the next step.

Then it was that Gilgal became the place of the revelation of the Captain of God's hosts. We read: "And it came to pass, when Joshua was by Jericho, that he lifted up his eyes and looked, and, behold, there stood a man over against him with his sword drawn in his hand: and Joshua went unto him, and said unto him, Art thou for us, or for our adversaries? And he said, Nay; but as captain of the host of the Lord am I now come. And Joshua fell on his face to the earth, and did worship, and said unto him, What saith my lord unto his servant? And the captain of the Lord's host said unto Joshua,

167

Loose thy shoe from off thy foot; for the place whereon thou standest is holy. And Joshua did so" (Josh. 5:13-15).

In our own spiritual warfare we will find that when proper steps of faith have been taken and we have accepted the challenge of spiritual warfare, then God will reveal to us the secret of His might. This is necessary for us.

Nature of the Revelation

Let us now consider the nature of this revelation given Joshua. He was alone, contemplating the next move, undoubtedly feeling the pressure of his responsibilities. Suddenly he was confronted by a man with a drawn sword. This man could be either a foe or a friend. Joshua lost no time in finding out where this person stood.

We have issues in our day which can be settled only by recourse to the Word of God. Yet there are some Christians who use men as the standard, asking if we are against this one or that one. They gauge our spiritual progress or our allegiance to the Lord on human basis instead of on our relationship and standing with the Lord.

In Joshua's case, he simply asked this stranger, "Art thou for us, or for our adversaries?"

On the surface it looked as though Joshua's advance was being challenged, but he fearlessly questioned this person as to where he stood. It was the very thing God expected Joshua to do. After all, the warfare Joshua was involved in had its human aspects. It also had its supernatural aspects.

Concerning our spiritual warfare we read in II Corinthians 11:14: "And no marvel; for Satan himself is transformed into an angel of light." Joshua was face to face with a person who was either a friend or a foe. Israel's leader had to find out. We, too, are to try the spirits according to I John 4:1: "Beloved, believe not every spirit, but try the spirits whether they are of God: because many false prophets are gone out into the world."

So far as Joshua was concerned there were only two sides. There was God's side with the Israelites or there was the enemy's side. A neutral position was impossible. This is something many Christians have not learned. There are issues today of such magnitude that no neutral stand is possible.

At one time our Saviour was accused of being empowered by Satan. Our Lord challenged His critics with these words: "If Satan cast out Satan, he is divided against himself; how shall then his kingdom stand? And if I by Beelzebub cast out devils, by whom do your children cast them out? therefore they shall be your judges. But if I cast out devils by the Spirit of God, then the kingdom of God is come unto you. Or else how can one enter into a strong man's house, and spoil his goods, except he first bind the strong man? and then he will spoil his house. He that is not with me [gathereth with me] is against me; and he that gathereth not with me scattereth abroad" (Matt. 12:26-30). The strong man spoken of here is Satan, and he has many evil beings under his control.

No neutral stand, however, can be taken with regard to Christ. Either we are for Him in spiritual warfare or against Him. He has already overcome Satan and all his forces and asks us to join Him in continuing to overcome the works of evil. Furthermore, we are either gathering souls with Christ or we are scattering them by our so-called neutrality.

Joshua soon discovered that he was face to face with the Captain of the Lord's hosts, the commander of the Lord's armies. Here was the Warrior and Leader coming not to help but to take charge.

This is a lesson we need to learn for ourselves. Too many of us are satisfied to ask God for help in our battles. Yet God does not come to help us in this warfare, for we are too weak in ourselves to even begin it. The Lord takes over in the spiritual life to direct our every aspect of that life and service.

The Captain of the Lord's hosts came not only to direct the armies of Israel, but also to fight for Israel and with Israel and through Israel. This is the same truth as is taught in Ephesians 6:10 where we are told to "be strong in the Lord, and in the power of his might."

This great Captain came with an unseen army. It was an army that surrounds the throne of God and is ready to obey the commands of God at any moment. It is this army that conducts battles in heavenly places against Satanic foes and forces and is eternally ranged on the side of God's people.

Israel was not only facing flesh and blood foes such as the Canaanites, but the evil forces under the prince of the power of the air. Satan was going to oppose the advance of the Israelites with all of his strength and cunning. So it was necessary that Joshua have more than mere human power with which to win in the conquest of Canaan.

Wars among the nations of the earth are fought merely on the human plane. This is why one war is fought, treaties signed, and then another war is begun. But when God fights, He does it in the places that harm the evil forces to the greatest degree. The evil powers of Satan arraigned against us are invisible and the armies of God are invisible, but both are very real. In Ephesians 6:12 we read: "For we wrestle not against flesh and blood, but against principalities, against powers, against the rulers of the darkness of this world, against spiritual wickedness in high places."

Jacob saw the armies of God in his day.

The servant of Elisha had his eyes opened to see the armies of heaven when the soldiers of Syria surrounded Dothan with orders to capture Elisha. The Prophet had spoiled the plans of the Syrian leader by telling the king of Israel what the Syrians intended to do. The king of Syria learned that Elisha was the one who disclosed his schemes, and so he sent a large army to surround Dothan and make a prisoner of God's prophet.

When Elisha's servant went out in the morning, he saw this huge army surrounding the city. He was terrified and told his master about it. Elisha simply prayed that the Lord would open the young man's eyes so that he could see that the forces of God were greater than the forces of Syria. The servant looked again and saw that surrounding the city in far greater numbers than the Syrian army were the chariots of God. These are forces that are still in existence and always will be. Our Lord reminded His disciples that if He had needed help while on the cross or deliverance from the cross,

He could have called on 12 legions of angels and had their immediate help.

This great army of heaven will be with the Lord Jesus Christ at the Battle of Armageddon. Read the description of that great event in Revelation 19. The man Joshua saw was the Captain of the hosts of the Lord, the same One who will lead the armies of heaven at the Battle of Armageddon.

This Captain has appeared to others in different forms. He appeared to Jacob as a wrestler. He appeared to Moses in the flame of fire at the burning bush. There Moses learned that he was to be the human instrument through whom God would release the children of Israel, but over him would be the Captain of the hosts of the Lord.

Isaiah saw this same great Person high and lifted up, occupying the throne of God, and this fact completely changed Isaiah's life.

Joshua saw him as the Captain of the hosts of the Lord and was warned to take the shoes from off his feet for he stood on holy ground. Undoubtedly this was Christ Himself whom Joshua fell down and worshipped.

Job saw Him as a mighty conqueror and said, "I have heard of thee by the hearing of the ear; but now mine eye seeth thee. Wherefore I abhor myself, and repent in dust and ashes" (Job 42:5,6).

According to the record in Jeremiah 1, Jeremiah the prophet saw the same Person as the powerful Living Word of God.

Daniel saw Him as the Ancient of Days and the Answerer of His people's prayers.

John the beloved disciple saw Him in Revelation as the One standing in the midst of the candlesticks and the churches. The Apostle saw Him as Conqueror over death and the Source of all light and life. No wonder John fell at His feet as though he were dead. Yet this same Person laid His hand on John and said, "Fear not; I am the first and the last: I am he that liveth, and was dead; and, behold, I am alive for evermore, Amen; and have the keys of hell and of death" (Rev. 1:17,18).

He is described in the 19th chapter of Revelation in the following words: "And I saw heaven opened, and behold a white horse; and he that sat upon him was called Faithful and True, and in righteousness he doth judge and make war" (v. 11).

We cannot be neutral with regard to Christ in our day. We must choose with regard to Him. We must acknowledge Him as Lord and obey His every command. The most significant moment in any man's life is when God reveals Himself to that man in Jesus Christ. This is not done by a vision, but through the Word of God and the illumination of the Spirit of God. And the Lord will always lead us on to recognize our Saviour as the Captain of the hosts of the Lord. May we cry out like Paul that we might know Him and the power of His resurrection!

As our spiritual Captain He leads us in spiritual warfare, giving us the power to pull down strongholds and cast down imaginations and every high thing that exalts itself against the knowledge of God.

The Effect of the Revelation

The effect of the revelation upon Joshua was very beneficial to him. At first he was somewhat anxious but he did not lose his courage. Then he became a worshipper and accorded implicit obedience to his Leader. It was this last phase of his attitude that was so essential to future accomplishment and blessing. Joshua accepted the leadership of his Captain and put himself absolutely under His control.

One big reason we do not see more taking place in the midst of God's people today is due to the lack of obedience. We make our plans, then invite God to help us fulfil these plans instead of falling in line with His plans. He has spiritual power and the heavenly army to enable us to do His will and be what we should be.

Joshua realized as he stood in the presence of his Captain that the battle was no longer his, but the Lord's. Moses understood this clearly in his day. When 40 years of age, he presented himself to the people of Israel as their deliverer. He had the background of knowledge and training, but he was not ready because he did not know his God. He knew about Him, but did not know Him personally. What a difference the experience at the burning bush made. There he met God face to face and realized that freeing Israel was God's undertaking.

Joshua learned this lesson early in his development as a minister of Moses. When Amalek came against Israel, Joshua led the army of the Israelites against the wicked foe; but it was through Moses' intercession on the mountain that Israel became victor. The battle was fought in the heavenlies as well as on the earth. It was through Moses' intercession that the spiritual power needed for Israel was supplied.

The battle for Canaan was a holy one. It could not be fought merely on the human level. Joshua, like us, needed to learn to submit himself to God and then resist the Devil and he would flee. To be strong in the Lord and in the power of His might was as needful for Joshua as it is for us. It is through taking the sword of the Spirit and the whole armor of God that we are able to advance.

Our battle is a holy battle, just as Israel's was for Canaan. According to Ephesians 6 we must first put on, as we have indicated, the armor God has provided. But that whole section is climaxed by the verse which tells us to pray with all prayer and supplication in the Spirit. This is authoritative praying. This is something we as Christians need to learn.

Behind the vast powers of ungodly Communism which has enslaved some 40 percent of the world's population, lies the power of Satan. It is this power that has so hardened the hearts of many against God's truth. Back of the indifference of men to the gospel of Christ is the god of this evil world. Concerning this the Scripture says: "But if our gospel be hid, it is hid to them that are lost: In whom the god of this world hath blinded the minds of them which believe not, lest the light of the glorious gospel of Christ, who is the image of God, should shine unto them" (II Cor. 4:3,4).

It is evident from this that more than good preaching or

persuasive preaching and fine illustrations are needed to win men to Christ. The power of God itself needs to be in the messages that are preached in order to reach the hearts of men. This calls for prayer in the Spirit. This is where the battle lies. Behind the divided home and the broken hearts and the dissolute lives and shattered testimonies lies Satan. Behind the rapidly closing doors of missionary service, or the broken bodies of faithful men and women who have given themselves to the service of the Lord on foreign soil, lies the attack of the evil one. The shortage of money to keep God's work going stems from the efforts of Satan to keep closed the hearts and pocketbooks of God's people. What is the answer to it? It is not that of mere strategy, different methods, attractive advertising or exciting prizes, but the power of God operating through His people.

First of all, we need to know our Captain. Some will say, "Yes, we know Jesus Christ. He is our Saviour." Granted that this is true. But do we know Him as the Captain of the host of the Lord? Do we know Him as the One who indwells us and who does the spiritual battling through us?

In the second place, do we know our weapons? We have repeatedly considered II Corinthians 10:3-5, for it is a key passage in this area. Our weapons are not fleshly but mighty through God. We are not to fight flesh and blood men, but depend on God to cast down imaginations and every high thing that exalts itself against Him. He will bring into captivity every thought to the obedience of Christ. In short, Christ Jesus is our weapon. If we give obedience to Him it will make no difference what the obstructions are, He will brush them aside and carry us through to victory.

Joshua and the people he led were going to have their faith tested time and again. They discovered, however, that every time they gave implicit obedience to God, He worked on their behalf and they were victorious.

None of us are without testing. Our Lord was tested. He encountered the same enemy we do and met him and conquered him with the Word of God. Satan sought the Lord's life prematurely in Gethsemane and used taunts to try to get Him to come down from the cross. These attacks of the enemy failed. The Lord Jesus had as His resources the same that we have, namely the Holy Spirit and prayer.

Our Lord triumphed over His enemies and ascended through their ranks as He entered into heaven. The power that raised Christ from the dead and set Him at the right hand of the Father in heavenly places far above all principalities and power and might and dominion and every name that is named in this universe is the same power that God will place at our disposal when we obey Him.

When Jesus Christ ascended from earth to heaven, He had to go through the sphere of Satan's influence in the heavenlies. Satan has done all he could to keep men out of heaven, but Christ came here to earth; and then on His return to glory passed in triumph through the hosts of Satan. And He will return again in triumph.

We learn from the Book of Daniel that when Daniel prayed, an angel came to answer his prayer but was held up for three weeks by an evil angel under Satan. Then Michael the archangel came to the first angel's aid and he was able to deliver the message God had given him for Daniel. This is a clear picture of what Jesus has done in conquering for us. He went through the hosts of Satan and took us with Him to sit in heavenly places with Him. We are in the area of victory. He has put all foes under His feet and we share in His conquest.

It was on this personal crisis faced by Joshua that the whole conflict in Canaan hinged. He came to view the place of battle so that he might put in motion plans for conquest. Instead, he met the Lord face to face. Before Joshua could face the foe he had to stand before the Lord.

The same is true for us in the overcoming life. Before we can face the foe we must stand before the Lord. This is not a matter of seeing Him in a vision, but rather allowing the Holy Spirit to reveal Him to our hearts through the Word. It is through this that the power of the living Christ will fill us and work through us.

Chapter Thirteen

JERICHO CONQUERED BY OBEDIENCE TO FAITH
(Joshua 6)

Everything was in readiness for the siege of Jericho. Joshua had met the Captain of the hosts of the Lord and merely awaited His instructions. Chapter six begins with these words: "Now Jericho was straitly shut up because of the children of Israel: none went out, and none came in. And the Lord said unto Joshua, See, I have given into thine hand Jericho, and the king thereof, and the mighty men of valour."

This was to be a land of rest for Israel, but at the same time it was a land of conflict. This is true also in our spiritual lives. Our spiritual rest results from spiritual conflict. This is paradoxical but it is true.

A brief review of the three stages in the Christian life will help us prepare for the studies ahead. First of all, there is the Christian in the world as Israel was in Egypt. The enemy in that situation is the world and this may result in conflict at times. In the second place there is the self-life, the life that lacks surrender which is analogous to the people in the desert. In this situation the enemy is self. There is a constant inner struggle against the self which wants to be exalted. The third stage, the important one we are discussing in these messages, is the useful, productive, victorious life pictured in the people of Israel conquering and possessing the land of Canaan. There the great enemy is no one else but Satan. Conflict in this case is unavoidable. But we need not be discouraged; even our Lord found opposition but was victorious. If and when we move ahead in our spiritual Canaan, we find opposition. There are many forces that will oppose us in any direction we wish to go.

The Lord Jesus said to the religious leaders of His day:

176

"The world cannot hate you; but me it hateth, because I testify of it, that the works thereof are evil" (John 7:7). The world doesn't hate its own and Satan does not hate his own, but both the world and Satan hate Christ because He is against the evil in them.

Jesus said in John 15:18,19 concerning His disciples: "If the world hate you, ye know that it hated me before it hated you. If ye were of the world, the world would love his own; but because ye are not of the world, but I have chosen you out of the world, therefore the world hateth you." The same truth is given in John 17:14: "I [Jesus] have given them thy word; and the world hath hated them, because they are not of the world, even as I am not of the world."

Over against this we have these glorious assurances: "These things I have spoken unto you, that in me ye might have peace" (John 16:33). Our rest and our peace are in Christ. The Lord Jesus went on to say, "In the world ye shall have tribulation; but be of good cheer; I have overcome the world." So then, in spite of the fact that we are in the world, in the place of turmoil and conflict, we can have rest and peace.

This is further borne out by our Saviour's promise in John 14:27: "Peace I leave with you; my peace I give unto you; not as the world giveth, give I unto you. Let not your heart be troubled, neither let it be afraid." So then, the life of rest is a life of conflict. Though this may seem paradoxical, we find rest in the conflict depending on whom we trust and whether or not we are looking away unto Jesus. In Christ we are overcomers. Remember, Christianity is far more than a mere ticket to heaven.

The situation confronting the Israelites was not that of a mere battle shaping up, but the beginning of a great campaign. A battle is a single engagement, but a campaign is a series of concerted operations directed toward a single objective. It is this spiritual campaign that gives unity to all the events and experiences of our lives. This is borne out by a passage well known to most of us. Some of us may have memorized it, but the question is, do we believe it? Verses 28 and 29 of Romans 8 must be taken together. Paul begins the passage by saying, "We know that all things work together for good." This means that the defeats, the heartaches, the controversies, the disappointments and the victories fit in here. They "work together for good to them that love God, to them that are the called according to his purpose. For whom he did foreknow, he also did predestinate to be conformed to the image of his Son, that he might be the firstborn among many brethren."

The purpose of all these things in our lives, whether we think of them as negatives or positives, is all for our good because God knows what our needs are. But this involves a campaign, not a single battle. It would be too bad if life's issues were to be determined by a single fight that we might lose. Rather, it is a campaign where there may be some losses but where there will also be a preponderance of victories.

Jericho might have been a discouraging sight to the Israelites. It was completely closed to any entering or any leaving. Its walls may have seemed impassable. Yet God assured His people that He had given it to them.

The victorious life is exactly the same. We can be assured of victory because our Captain, Jesus Christ, has already won the battle, defeated the enemy, and thus assures us of victory. Our Lord in His death overcame Satan; and in His resurrection and ascension He broke through the territory which Satan controls in the air around us. Then Christ entered into heaven itself, having conquered all foes.

This means we are not on the losing side when we are on the same side as our Lord. We are more than conquerors. We cannot be suddenly attacked without warning. God alerts us. We are to take the initiative in the campaign, then we will see victory as the result of our faith in Christ Jesus.

Israel was assured of victory over Jericho. It was the key city to the whole campaign in Canaan. Once that obstacle was removed the armies of Israel could spread out in all directions. So it is no wonder that we find in this incident of history an abundance of spiritual lessons.

Israel herself could not retreat, as we have seen. They had

no alternative except to go forward in victory or suffer death. The death the Israelites might have suffered would have been that of dying at the hands of their foes. In the spiritual realm our danger is in succumbing to the enemy because we do not apply the victory.

Humanly speaking, Jericho was so strongly fortified as to be almost incapable of being taken. It guarded all the passes to the interior of the land of Canaan. Consequently, so long as Jericho held out, the land was safe from invasion.

We find that the same experience meets us once we choose to go on in Christian warfare. Invisible forces rise up to try to stop us and will succeed unless we follow our Captain implicitly. The enemy, Satan, will get us to consider our weaknesses such as temperament or lack of ability or self-control, but these are the very things over which the Lord will give us victory.

There were treasures locked up inside the city of Jericho. But Jericho could be opened and its treasures used for God's glory. Perhaps we will be discouraged from going ahead in some phase of service for the Lord for lack of funds. It may seem, for example, as though doors are closed to missions; but the Lord has promised that the gates of hell shall not prevail against His Church. We have weapons which are not carnal but mighty through God to the pulling down of strongholds. So when we remember that we are not wrestling against flesh and blood, and wisely put on the whole armor of God, the result will be victory for the Lord and His cause.

Any opposition to the plans of God must be demolished by Christians who are aware that they are not fighting flesh and blood individuals or organizations, but the very Devil himself. Our battle is fought as a battle of prayer and a battle of obedience. It is then that we find the weapons of our warfare are mighty through God to the pulling down of strongholds that stand in our way. According to Ephesians 1:22 all enemies of Christ have been placed under our feet, as well as under His feet. Nothing but self can stop us. So far as the Israelites were concerned they left the self-life behind when they crossed the Jordan. Have we made that decision?

The Secret of Victory

The secret of victory for Israel lies in Joshua 6:2 where the Lord promises, "I have given into thine hand Jericho, and the king thereof, and the mighty men of valour." The conquest of Jericho was God's undertaking. So is our spiritual life God's undertaking. We have this promise in Philippians 1:6: "Being confident of this very thing, that he which hath begun a good work in you will perform it until the day of Jesus Christ." Whether it is something within or something without, our sufficiency is in Christ, for we also have this promise: "I can do all things through Christ which strengtheneth me."

Similar truth is taught to us in the parable of the vine and the branches. In John 15:5 the Saviour said, "I am the vine, ye are the branches: He that abideth in me, and I in him, the same bringeth forth much fruit: for without me ye can do nothing."

The marching orders for Jericho's defeat are given in verses 3-5 of Joshua 6. "And ye shall compass the city, all ye men of war, and go round about the city once. Thus shalt thou do six days. And seven priests shall bear before the ark seven trumpets of rams' horns: and the seventh day ye shall compass the city seven times, and the priests shall blow with the trumpets. And it shall come to pass, that when they make a long blast with the ram's horn, and when ye hear the sound of the trumpet, all the people shall shout with a great shout; and the wall of the city shall fall down flat, and the people shall ascend up every man straight before him."

From this we gather that the people were to march in the following order. First of all there were the armed forces of Israel. Then seven priests with rams' horns followed with the Ark just behind them. Bringing up the rear were the people of Israel. These were all to march around the city once each day for six days; then on the seventh day they were to march around it seven times. There was to be no noise made by the marchers except for the sound of the rams' horns. Each trip from Gilgal around Jericho and back took two hours.

One can imagine the jeers of the Canaanites on the walls, but it is not hard to imagine also their fears and panic-stricken condition.

Doing God's Work His Way

The tactics employed by the Israelites must have seemed stupid and ridiculous beyond words to the people of Jericho. The silence itself must have been almost unbearable. Ordinarily when men went into battle they would make a great noise with the hope of unnerving the foe. But there was just this silent march of the soldiers and the priests with the Ark of the Covenant and the people following behind. The sound of the marchers was broken only by the raucous blaring of seven rams' horns.

At the end of each march the walls of Jericho looked the same as they had when the march began. The same was true on the seventh day after the city had been encircled seven times. But a remarkable change was about to take place. Let us trace the various steps as indicated in the Scriptures.

In Joshua 6:12 we read: "And Joshua rose early in the morning, and the priests took up the ark of the Lord." Early rising on the part of Joshua was important. There was need for strength. An early meeting with the Lord was essential. Even in the wilderness the people had learned that in order to gather manna they had to do it early in the morning. This is a very practical lesson for us with regard to spiritual warfare. We need to put on the whole armor of God each day before we enter into the daily conflict. We must read the Scriptures carefully before we go into battle, using Ephesians 6:10 and the verses following as a guide in these matters.

It is always well to remember that we must do God's work each day in the way God intends us to. Instruction in this realm is found in Proverbs 3:5-7. The passage says, "Trust in the Lord with all thine heart; and lean not unto thine own understanding. In all thy ways acknowledge him, and he shall direct thy paths. Be not wise in thine own eyes: fear the Lord, and depart from evil." We need this type of heart attitude just as Joshua needed it in considering the taking of Jericho. God had a particular method for the Israelites to follow, so implicit obedience to His instructions was essential.

The Conquest of Faith

The city of Jericho was to fall as the result of a *conquest of faith*. We learn in Hebrews 11:30: "By faith the walls of Jericho fell down, after they were compassed about seven days." All the battles Israel fought were to be fought by faith, just as all our spiritual battles are to be fought and won by faith. Without faith, we learn, it is impossible to please God. This we find in Hebrews 11: "But without faith it is impossible to please him: for he that cometh to God must believe that he is, and that he is a rewarder of them that diligently seek him" (v. 6).

In the 11th chapter of Hebrews the expression "by faith" runs like a refrain all the way through. We find "by faith Enoch," "by faith Noah," "by faith Abraham," "by faith Sarah," "by faith Isaac," "by faith Joseph," and so all through the chapter. Faith is a working principle of life for the believer. Faith is reliance upon Almighty God.

It was said about Abraham in Romans 4:20,21: "He staggered not at the promise of God through unbelief; but was strong in faith, giving glory to God; and being fully persuaded that, what he had promised, he was able also to perform." The world cannot understand this, consequently to worldlings faith is foolishness. In their view faith is folly, and those who exercise it are sometimes regarded as fools. Undoubtedly this was the way the people of Jericho looked on the Israelites as they marched around the city.

The whole work of God in taking the land of Canaan, symbolic of our spiritual warfare, is a conquest of faith not arms. It is true that the Israelites used weapons, but it was always faith that won the victory for them.

This was true with regard to Jericho. There is no natural explanation for the collapse of its walls. No weapons were used, no undermining, no assault. The walls fell because of God's power. In this connection it is well for us to read again II Corinthians 10:3-5. No better illustration of what God does for us in a spiritual way is to be found than the taking of the great fortress of Jericho.

In the second place, the conquest of Jericho was an *adventure of faith* involving a stupendous risk on the faithfulness of God. The Israelites had no fortresses to which they could retreat. They had lived in tents, not in houses. They staked everything on the trustworthiness of God. The Jordan River made retreat impossible. They had no place to which they could flee. They were shut up to total trust in God.

We, too, need to come to this place where it is either God or nothing. Our personal victories over sin are all won on the basis of faith and that alone. This was the principle our Saviour emphasized when He said in Mark 11:22-24: "And Jesus answering saith unto them, Have faith in God. For verily I say unto you, That whosoever shall say unto this mountain, Be thou removed, and be thou cast into the sea; and shall not doubt in his heart, but shall believe that those things which he saith shall come to pass; he shall have whatsoever he saith. Therefore I say unto you, What things soever ye desire, when ye pray, believe that ye receive them, and ye shall have them."

In the third place, the conquest of Jericho demanded the *obedience of faith.* It must be an obedience without any questioning. God rarely interprets His commands in advance. He simply asks us to believe Him. If He always gave us an explanation ahead of time as to what He was going to do, that would rob faith of its opportunity. Our Lord said to His disciples in one place, "What I do now thou knowest not; but thou shalt know hereafter."

Men are always seeking new methods in their attempts to overcome Satan. It is not new methods that are needed but obedient men. Some Christian workers argue that people do not want Christianity, so these workers bring in Hollywood methods. But such methods will not convict men of their sins and bring them to a faith in Christ by which they are regenerated. They may be attracted by glamorous methods, but such methods of themselves will never break down the walls of a Jericho. Essential to our purpose are the weapons described in II Corinthians 10:3-5.

It may be that some of these methods designed to attract people may win some, but they will leave them in the desert of Christian experience, weak and powerless. And this, sad to say, is where I believe, multitudes of Christians are today, simply because they have depended upon things instead of depending upon God.

Israel was to obey God. They were not told why the plan to be followed was good, nor what the consequences would be. Joshua knew, but the people as a whole did not.

We may be inclined to say how absurd such a method is. But never let us be guilty of saying that when God tells us to follow certain procedures. When God says do a thing a certain way, let us do it. To the worldling this is irrational and unbelievable. But to the true believer in God there is no alternative to obedience. Christian obedience is not based on knowledge of what is going to happen or why such and such a method is the best one to follow. We trust what God says and that is sufficient. Salvation itself is based entirely on faith. Our sanctification is based on faith. Our growth in grace follows in obedience to faith.

In the fourth place, we find the *discipline of faith.* Here was a nation notorious for its complaining spirit and its criticism of God's ways. For 40 years this had characterized them in the desert. Of course, the nation that had crossed Jordan was the new generation. They had heard their parents criticizing and complaining concerning the ways of God. Now this generation was disciplined to absolute silence. Joshua had commanded them saying, "Ye shall not shout, nor make any noise with your voice, neither shall any word proceed out of your mouth, until the day I bid you shout; then shall ye shout" (Josh. 6:10). What an order! Yet imagine the confusion if everyone had been free to express his views on the strategy being followed. Criticism and doubts would soon have paralyzed their faith. They would have talked themselves out of faith before they had completed the first circuit of the city. According to God's instructions, 13 such journeys had to be made.

To my way of thinking, the Christian's greatest difficulty today is to keep silent and let God work. We seem to think we have to complain.

The central feature of the procession was the Ark of the Covenant of the Lord. It is mentioned 11 times in chapter six of Joshua. God was with His people—in the very midst of them. They did not have to know what He was doing. All that was necessary was for them to recognize His presence among them. He walked with them. We learn from verse 11 in chapter 6 the Ark of the Lord "compassed the city, going about it once: and they came into the camp, and lodged in the camp." The passage does not say that the Israelites took the Ark, but that the Ark of the Lord was there when they went around the city. This emphasizes the presence of the Lord with them in their circuit of the fortress.

There is a lack of the supernatural in many churches today. God's people do not keep silent and let God work. So they have to shout. They must line up with the world about us using loud advertising and other worldly methods to attract people's attention. We seem to think that the person who shouts the loudest gets the people inside the churches. But the conquest of our Jerichos will not be won in this manner. Such conquests are won on our knees.

This does not mean inactivity or passivity. It is recognizing ourselves as weak and helpless, but depending on our omnipotent God. I have been considered old-fashioned on several occasions because I do not go in for certain gaudy advertising schemes with regard to Back to the Bible. If this work is not God's work, and it cannot be done in God's way, then I want nothing of it. We do let God's people know what is going on, but we depend upon God to work in their hearts and to reach out to win the lost and build up the saved.

In the fifth place, there was the *patience of faith*. The Israelites encircled the city 13 times in seven days. Yet at the

end of each circuit the walls were just as stout and forbidding
as ever. There was not the slightest evidence the eye could see
that a collapse of the walls was imminent. Even at the end of
the 13th circuit, just a few seconds away from the climax,
the walls stood completely intact.

Perhaps some of our prayers have not been answered
simply because we have not completed enough circuits in our
personal prayer life. An old gospel song brings this clearly
before us. The third verse is as follows:

    Unanswered yet? Nay, do not say ungranted;
    Perhaps your part is not yet wholly done;
    The work began when first your prayer was uttered,
    And God will finish what He has begun.
    If you will keep the incense burning there,
    His glory shall you see, sometime, somewhere.

The Israelites evaluated the whole situation 13 times.
Each time they were convinced they were powerless to do
anything by themselves to conquer Jericho. Only God could
remove the obstacles before them. Like Paul we must learn
that when we are weak, we are strong in the Lord. We can do
all things through Christ who strengthens us. We must come
to the place of hopelessness in self, before God can and will
give the victory.

Paul saw his own hopeless condition in overcoming sin in
his life and cried, "O wretched man that I am! who shall
deliver me from the body of this death?" (Rom. 7:24). Then
realizing where victory lay, he said, "I thank God through
Jesus Christ our Lord."

Long centuries before this the patriarch Job had a similar
experience. He passed through trials and heartaches that
brought him to the end of himself, and he cried to the Lord:
"I have heard of thee by the hearing of the ear: but now
mine eye seeth thee. Wherefore I abhor myself, and repent in
dust and ashes" (Job 42:5,6).

Isaiah had to be brought to the end of himself before he
could be a man God could use. The record of the wonderful
change that took place in his life is given in the sixth chapter
of his prophecy. He cried: "Woe is me! for I am undone;

because I am a man of unclean lips, and I dwell in the midst of a people of unclean lips." Then it was that the Lord came and touched him.

Jeremiah was another prophet who had to be brought to the end of himself before God could use him. The Prophet said, "Ah, Lord God! behold, I cannot speak: for I am a child." Then it was that the Lord put forth his hand and touched Jeremiah's mouth and said to the Prophet, "Behold, I have put my words in thy mouth" (Jer. 1:4-9).

Moses thought he was ready to be used of God when he was 40 years of age. He had been well educated and trained for leadership, but he was too big for God to use. God took him down to the desert for 40 years and there had him labor as a shepherd. Moses was whittled down in his own eyes, but built up in the Spirit. At the age of 80 when commissioned by God to emancipate the Israelites, Moses said he could not do the work. It was then that God showed him He would be with him and use him as a victorious servant.

There is also the illustration of Gideon who gathered 32,000 men to fight the Midianites who had an army of 120,000. This gave the enemy an advantage of four to one. When Gideon went to the Lord about it, the Lord did not add to Gideon's army but told him he had too many men. He showed him how to cut them down until there were only 300 left; and it was with this group that God gave Gideon the victory.

We need to recognize that in our flesh dwells no good thing (Rom. 7:18). God will test our faith to see whether or not we will trust Him. We are assured, however, that the trial of our faith "being much more precious than of gold that perisheth, though it be tried with fire, might be found unto praise and honour and glory at the appearing of Jesus Christ" (I Pet. 1:7).

The method God prescribed for the downfall of Jericho gave no room for human boasting but every room for the exercise of faith. The Israelites were to march around the city 13 times in all. It took at least two hours for them to leave the camp, walk around the city and get back to their camp.

Why should they have to do this so many times? The reason, I believe, was to impress on them how utterly impossible it was for them to capture Jericho. God would have to do the job or it could not be done. Thirteen long looks at the enemy and their high walls convinced the Israelites. They died to every hope of conquest unless God undertook for them.

Potentially they had died to self in the Jordan, but now it began to be practiced in their experience. Could they really say experientially, "I am dead to self?" This was necessary. We find it difficult to admit our problems are too big for us. We struggle on and on trying to accomplish our goals for service and trying to conquer sin but get nowhere. The power of the enemy is exceeded only by the power of God. The power of Satan is far too great for us. But when we recognize that it is God who is working on our behalf, things happen. If our Jerichos are to fall, God must bring them down. However, before God will entrust any of His people with a real measure of spiritual power leading to victory, He must bring them to the place where they have surveyed their Jericho so long that they see the case for self-help is absolutely hopeless. We all have Jerichos. How do we face them?

A little later we will see that Israel failed at Ai. But failure was to be expected when the Israelites went forth in their own power and strength. Nothing but failure can be expected from us under the same circumstances. So long as we want to do something alone or even any part of it, the omnipotent resources in Christ who is a risen and exalted Lord cannot help us.

Victory Is a Gift to Us

Everything we have of blessing and power is in Christ Jesus. It is ours to take. It is a gift, but we must take it. God had promised that Israel would be given every bit of land they walked on. But they had to walk on it before it became theirs.

So it is in the spiritual life. God will give to us the victory we need when we admit in His presence that we are utterly unable to win the battle for ourselves. So we must stop trying to scale the walls of our Jerichos with man-made plans. We must look to the Lord for His help and presence.

The final step of faith with regard to the taking of Jericho was the *shout of faith*. This came at the very close of the last encirclement of the city. The seven priests bearing the seven trumpets of rams' horns went before the Ark of the Lord blowing the trumpets, and the armed men went before them. But during none of this procedure did the walls begin to crumble. Yet every step around Jericho was a step of the appropriation of faith. The city had to be encircled the 13 times before the shout of victory was given. This shout was the outward expression of the Israelites' inward confidence in their omnipotent God. The shout of faith was given while the walls were still intact. Once again God's people risked everything on the faithfulness of God. The 16th verse tells us: "And it came to pass at the seventh time, when the priests blew with the trumpets, Joshua said unto the people, Shout; for the Lord hath given you the city." "So," according to verse 20, "the people shouted when the priests blew with the trumpets: and it came to pass, when the people heard the sound of the trumpet, and the people shouted with a great shout, that the wall fell down flat, so that the people went up into the city, every man straight before him, and they took the city. And they utterly destroyed all that was in the city, both man and woman, young and old, and ox, and sheep, and ass, with the edge of the sword."

According to Hebrews 11:30 the walls of Jericho fell down by faith. Some persons want to attribute the collapse of the walls to an earthquake. It makes no difference to us what means God used. Whatever He did was timed so that after Israel had passed around the city the 13th time, and when the trumpets blew and the shout was made, then the walls fell. It took place just when God said it would.

God will speak again and this time to the whole world. Just as the shout of the Israelites preceded the judgment on Jericho, just so will the Lord Jesus come for His saints descending from heaven with a shout and with the voice of the archangel and the trump of God and the dead in Christ shall rise first (I Thess. 4:16). Then will follow the Great Tribulation time, the time of awful judgment for the earth.

Hebrews 12:26 prophesies of this when it says of God: "Whose voice then shook the earth: but now he hath promised, saying, Yet once more I shake not the earth only, but also heaven." Peter describes it in the third chapter of his Second Letter in these words: "But the day of the Lord will come as a thief in the night; in the which the heavens will pass away with a great noise, and the elements shall melt with fervent heat, the earth also and the works that are therein shall be burned up" (v. 10).

The fall of the walls of Jericho was the end of the road for the people there. But for Israel it was the beginning of conquest.

For us who know the Lord there is a glorious prospect ahead. Where do you who read these words stand? We read in Revelation 21:1-4: "And I saw a new heaven and a new earth: for the first heaven and the first earth were passed away; and there was no more sea. And I John saw the holy city, new Jerusalem, coming down from God out of heaven, prepared as a bride adorned for her husband. And I heard a great voice out of heaven saying, Behold, the tabernacle of God is with men, and he will dwell with them, and they shall be his people, and God himself shall be with them, and be their God. And God shall wipe away all tears from their eyes; and there shall be no more death, neither sorrow, nor crying, neither shall there be any more pain: for the former things are passed away."

There was an exception to the judgment of the people of Jericho. Rahab and her family were spared as was promised by the spies whom she hid when the king of Jericho sought their lives. The portion of the wall where Rahab lived stood and Joshua said "unto the two men that had spied out the country, Go into the harlot's house, and bring out thence the woman, and all that she hath, as ye sware unto her. And the young men that were spies went in, and brought out Rahab, and her father, and her mother, and her brethren, and all that she had; and they brought out all her kindred, and left them without the camp of Israel" (6:22,23).

This is one of the most beautiful illustrations of household salvation in the Scriptures. Rahab believed God at the time when the spies came to her house. She believed not only for herself but for her family also and persuaded them to stay with her during the siege of the city. Then when God spoke, they were saved. We read in Hebrews 11:31: "By faith the harlot Rahab perished not with them that believed not, when she had received the spies with peace."

When judgment strikes in the Tribulation days that are ahead, when our Lord comes at the climax of that period, remarkable things will take place. We read in Matthew 24: "Then shall two be in the field; the one shall be taken, and the other left. Two women shall be grinding at the mill; the one shall be taken, and the other left. Watch therefore: for ye know not what hour your Lord doth come" (vv. 40-42).

There is a remarkable difference between this passage in Matthew 24 and I Thessalonians 4. The people taken out of the world according to I Thessalonians 4 are the children of God. They are caught up into His presence. But in Matthew 24, at the end of the Tribulation, those who are taken out will be taken out for judgment. Those who will be left will go on into the millennial kingdom. So God is going to speak again. He knows those who are His. The foundations of God stand sure; so let everyone of us who know the name of Christ depart from iniquity. Do you belong to Him?

The city of Jericho was demolished. There was also a curse placed upon it. Speaking through Joshua, God said, "Cursed be the man before the Lord, that riseth up and buildeth this city Jericho: he shall lay the foundation thereof in his firstborn, and in his youngest son shall he set up the gates of it" (6:26).

The fulfillment of this is seen in I Kings 16:34 where we read: "In his days did Hiel the Bethelite build Jericho: he laid the foundation thereof in Abiram his firstborn, and set up the gates thereof in his youngest son Segub, according to the word of the Lord, which he spake by Joshua the son of Nun.''

Several important objectives were accomplished in Jericho's downfall. First of all, it inspired Israel's confidence and enthusiasm as they faced the great tasks which lay ahead. This is true also in our own lives. When given our first great victory, we are encouraged to go on and on. Sometimes we are discouraged by failure, but a few victories bring new assurance.

Israel's conquest of Jericho also brought fresh terror to the hearts of the Canaanites. This helped condition them for the defeats they suffered in the weeks, months and years that lay ahead. For the first time after crossing the Jordan, Israel had defeated one of their enemies. There were many others they had to face and many difficulties they had to overcome, but this was the first victory in their conquest of Canaan after having crossed the Jordan.

The Lord's Portion

Another matter of great importance is that God had assigned a certain portion of Jericho's treasures for Himself. He had made this very clear to Israel. This also became a test both of their faith and of their obedience. The Lord said, "And ye, in any wise keep yourselves from the accursed thing, lest ye make yourselves accursed, when ye take of the accursed thing, and make the camp of Israel a curse, and trouble it. But all the silver, and gold, and vessels of brass and iron, are consecrated unto the Lord: they shall come into the treasury of the Lord" (6:19,20).

We learn in verse 24 that the Israelites burned Jericho with fire and all that was in it. However, they put the silver and the gold and the vessels of brass and iron into the treasury of the Lord's house. In this way God's special portion was preserved for Him.

God was with His people all through the conquest of Canaan, as far as they went, but they had no conquest quite like the one over Jericho. It was God who brought down

Jericho's defenses and made it possible for the Israelites to get into the city. It was surely fitting that the treasuries of the city should belong to the Lord as His portion. This is a principle that should be emphasized more among us. The first portion of that which we receive by way of material blessing belongs to the Lord. We hurt our own lives and the cause of the Lord when we neglect this. The 7th chapter of Joshua brings the subject very vividly before us.

We should recognize in passing that though the city was burned with fire, the precious metals would pass through the fire without harm. Gold, silver and other metals would even be purified by the intense heat and be of more value as a result.

Chapter Fourteen

SIN-THE DEFEAT OF FAITH
(Joshua 7)

Chapter six ends with a glorious note of victory. It says, "So the Lord was with Joshua; and his fame was noised throughout all the country."

But there is a marked change in the beginning of the seventh chapter. It begins with the little word "but." It introduces a marked contrast from the victory of the one chapter to the tragedy of the other. We read: "But the children of Israel committed a trespass in the accursed thing." The nation had to share in the blame of a certain man's sin. This man took what belonged to the Lord and the whole nation suffered. The passage goes on to say: "for Achan . . . took of the accursed thing: and the anger of the Lord was kindled against the children of Israel" (Josh. 7:1).

It is no light matter to steal God's portion. Some may wonder what that is. Yet anyone familiar with his Bible would know that a certain part of our income belongs to the Lord. Some people say it is the tithe. Others say that it is more than the tithe. In Old Testament times it was the tithe, and in certain instances God asked for more than one tithe from the Israelites. Actually, we have no New Testament passage that confines us to the tithe. Yet we owe the Lord a portion. We cannot improve on God's method of setting aside a tithe for His work though that is the least any believer of this age should give. And it should not be given as a legal obligation but as a happy gift to the Lord. But more than the tithe is intended. Believers of this age are to give proportionately. As a man purposeth in his heart so he is to give. This is the Lord's portion and this is what we should set aside first of anything we receive (I Cor. 16:1,2).

The conflict with Ai was only the second battle the

194

Israelites had fought since crossing the Jordan. It proved, however, to be a sad defeat for them.

Joshua sent men from Jericho to Ai and they brought back the advice that only a small group, possibly two or three thousand men, was all that was needed to take Ai. So about 3000 Israelites attempted to take the city but were soundly defeated. "The men of Ai smote of them about thirty and six men: for they chased them from before the gate even unto Shebarim, and smote them in the going down: wherefore the hearts of the people melted, and became as water" (Josh. 7:5). This was only the second battle for the Israelites and was a minor one as compared to Jericho, but it was a terrible defeat for them.

This defeat for Israel followed hard upon their great victory. But this is the greatest danger time for any of us. Satan is always quick to take advantage of us when we have triumphed. Then is the time for us to be alert against his stratagems by studying the Word and watching through prayer.

Joshua did not know what the matter was, so he took it to the Lord in prayer. We read: "And Joshua rent his clothes, and fell to the earth upon his face before the ark of the Lord until the eventide, he and the elders of Israel, and put dust upon their heads. And Joshua said, Alas, O Lord God, wherefore hast thou at all brought this people over Jordan, to deliver us into the hand of the Amorites, to destroy us? would to God we had been content, and dwelt on the other side Jordan! O Lord, what shall I say, when Israel turneth their backs before their enemies! For the Canaanites and all the inhabitants of the land shall hear of it, and shall environ us round, and cut off our name from the earth: and what wilt thou do unto thy great name?" (vv. 6-9).

Joshua fell on his face before the Lord. He was completely dismayed. We might wonder if God had deserted the Israelites or if He was unable to cope with the powerful enemy? Then what would happen to the great Name of the Lord in the eyes of the Canaanites?

It is God's intent that His children should live a life of

unbroken victory. There was no need for the defeat at Ai. God does not make it impossible for men to sin, but He always makes it possible for them not to sin. He does not eradicate the old nature so that if a person wanted to sin he could not. But on the other hand, He always makes it possible for us not to sin.

In I Corinthians 10:13 we learn: "There hath no temptation taken you but such as is common to man: but God is faithful, who will not suffer you to be tempted above that ye are able; but will with the temptation also make a way of escape, that ye may be able to bear it." God assures us that with the temptation which He allows He will make a way of escape for us so that we can bear it. He does not promise to take away the temptation, but He does promise to provide a way of escape.

Defeat may happen to any of us but it is not necessary. According to I John 2:1: "My little children, these things write I unto you, that ye sin not. And if any man sin, we have an advocate with the Father, Jesus Christ the righteous."

The child of God who is determined to live in the center of God's will, will be exposed to the attacks of the enemy. But there is no reason for despair, because as David said, the Lord is our High Tower. He is our Protector and Deliverer. This is true regardless of what methods Satan may use against us.

What caused Israel's defeat at Ai? First of all, there was self-confidence or presumption. We learn in verse 2 of chapter 7 of Joshua that Joshua "sent men from Jericho to Ai [not from Gilgal, but from Jericho], which is beside Bethaven, on the east side of Bethel, and spake unto them, saying, Go up and view the country. And the men went up and viewed Ai. And they returned to Joshua, and said unto him, Let not all the people go up; but let about two or three thousand men go up and smite Ai; and make not all the people to labour thither; for they are but few." So, as we have seen before, there went up "thither of the people about three thousand men: and they fled before the men of Ai."

Presumption is a form of pride. And it was this pride that the men of Israel fell into when they considered Ai to be just a small place and counseled the sending of only a small portion of the army. Apparently they thought that they had taken care of Jericho very adequately and were quite able to take care of Ai by themselves.

Fear and pride can do different things to us, and either one brings defeat. Fear is like a magnifying glass which makes the enemy appear greater than he really is. This was the problem with the Israelites 38 years before when they stood at Kadesh-barnea and got the report from the ten spies concerning the land. These men said, "The land, through which we have gone to search it, is a land that eateth up the inhabitants thereof; and all the people that we saw in it are men of a great stature. And there we saw the giants, the sons of Anak, which come of the giants: and we were in our own sight as grasshoppers, and so we were in their sight" (Num. 13:32,33). Fear magnifies the enemy.

On the other hand, pride will blind us. It can cause us to think the enemy is much smaller than he really is. Peter warns us in his First Epistle that our adversary goes about as a roaring lion. The Israelites had to learn that their real battle was not against flesh and blood men but against spiritual evil forces. The enemy was far greater than the flesh and blood beings the Israelites saw with their eyes. The Devil and his forces were at hand to aid the people of Ai in their opposition to the Israelites.

This we must constantly remind ourselves of with regard to our spiritual warfare. Our wrestling is not against flesh and blood foes but against spiritual powers in high places. However, we are not without resources. In fact, we have the highest resources, for "greater is he that is in you, than he that is in the world."

We read nothing in the first battle for Ai of the Ark being taken along. Neither do we find that the Israelites had gone back to Gilgal, which was the place of refreshment. That was the place where they received orders from God. They went instead from Jericho, the place of their last victory.

One gets the impression that the Israelites thought they had captured the city of Jericho. This was not the case. God did it. Jericho's defeat was not a testimony or witness to Israel's strength but to the strength of God.

It is remarkable how some people, even God's people, want to look for some secret method or approach to the continuance of the work of Back to the Bible Broadcast. They speak of it as being successful and want to know what the secret of that success is. But the truth of the matter is that what success we have is God's doings and not ours.

Some Christians also seem to have the idea that each victory a man has in the Lord adds strength for the next battle. But this is not so. Further victories are won in the strength of the risen Lord, not in the accumulation of victories behind us. So we do not receive any praise for what God has done. Our strength lies in Him. When we are weak, then are we strong in His strength.

Another point of failure on the part of the Israelites at this time was that they did not consult the Commander-in-Chief concerning Ai. They underestimated the enemies strength and sent only a small army. The center of gravity had shifted from God to their own reasoning. It had shifted from spiritual might to fleshly mathematics. They forgot that our weapons are not carnal but mighty through God. They also forgot that the real enemy is unseen and has power beyond man's power to overthrow.

No work of God is easy when we consider the enemy that must be defeated. But with God all things are possible. Our Lord reminded us that without Him we can do nothing. Paul came through with a note of triumph to the effect that in Christ he could do all things.

Prayerlessness

A second reason for failure was prayerlessness. We might be inclined to dispute this point at first. Do we not read how Joshua rent his clothes and fell on his face before the Lord, he and the elders of Israel? (Josh. 7:6). This was a good indication of repentance on their part. But other things were not right. See now how Joshua prayed: "And Joshua said, Alas, O Lord God, wherefore hast thou at all brought this people over Jordan, to deliver us into the hand of the Amorites, to destroy us? would to God we had been content, and dwelt on the other side Jordan!" (7:7). This does not sound like Joshua; it is more like the people of Israel in the desert. What we must remember is that the old man or old nature was still in Joshua's life and won the ascendency at this place. Joshua failed the Lord in that particular moment.

The Lord answered Joshua right to the point. We read in verses 10 and 11: "And the Lord said unto Joshua, Get thee up; wherefore liest thou thus upon thy face? Israel hath sinned, and they have also transgressed my covenant which I commanded them: for they have even taken of the accursed thing, and have also stolen, and dissembled also, and they have put it even among their own stuff."

There was prayer on the part of Joshua, but it was at the wrong time. He prayed after the defeat at Ai instead of praying before he ever sent the soldiers.

It is a wonderful thing when we are in trouble to go to the Lord. This we should do. At the same time, however, if we would make proper preparations ahead of time in prayer, there are many mistakes we would not fall into. Had Joshua made preparations for the taking of Ai as he had for Jericho, God would have revealed to him that there was sin in Israel. This would have meant that the soldiers would not have been sent until the sinful cause had been removed.

Perhaps the greatest temptation to neglect prayer comes after a God-given victory. There is always a certain amount of hidden pride within us. We are not always aware of it, but it is there nevertheless. However, if we will come humbly before God, whether before or after such conditions, He will give us grace. This is the promise in James 4:6,7. God gives more grace, for He resists the proud but gives grace to the humble. So when we submit ourselves to God and resist the Devil, the evil one flees from us. It is good that we can go to

God at any time; but we should remember to go to Him first regardless of what is facing us.

A failure to pray always makes us insensitive to sin. If we do not take time to pray, we will often not recognize sin for what it is. When we pray in the time of victory, we will not have to plead in the time of defeat.

When Joshua bowed his head in prayer following Israel's defeat, the Lord told him to get up and do something. This may sound like a contradiction to all the teaching we have had on prayer, but it is not. God was simply telling Joshua that that was not the time to pray in the way he was praying. Israel had sinned; it was Joshua's responsibility as leader to erase this sin from Israel's life. The fault for this military reverse did not lie with God but with Israel.

How often we, like Joshua and the elders of Israel, are inclined to blame God when things go wrong. We sometimes say when reverses come that God has forsaken us. Some persons harden their hearts against God and blame Him for things not going as they thought they should go. Yet had these individuals gone to God in the first place, they would have been directed in the proper way. God knows from the very beginning what He is doing and why He is doing it. He knows all the underlying causes that are related to all the incidents in our lives. There is nothing hidden from Him.

Disobedience

The Lord also used this occasion to point out a third reason for Israel's defeat. It was due to disobedience concerning God's portion of the treasures of Jericho. Covetousness had entered Achan's heart and led to his disobeying God's instructions. Achan actually stole from God, a sin not uncommon among Christians today.

Achan had taken the accursed thing. It was accursed in the sense that it was devoted to God and for a man to use it for himself was evil.

We read of just such a sin in Acts 5. "A certain man named Ananias, with Sapphira his wife, sold a possession, and kept back part of the price, his wife also being privy to it, and brought a certain part, and laid it at the apostles' feet" (Acts 5:1,2). There was no reason for them not keeping back part of it if they so wished. Their sin lay in professing to be giving all of the money they had made from the sale of their land. This was pretense and hypocrisy; in this way they actually stole from God. They kept something for themselves that they said they had given to God.

Let us all remember that "all things are naked and open unto the eyes of him with whom we have to do" (Heb. 4:13). One of the greatest sins a believer can possibly commit is the sin of stealing from God. This is clear from Joshua 6:18,19: "And ye, in any wise keep yourselves from the accursed thing, lest ye make yourselves accursed, when ye take of the accursed thing, and make the camp of Israel a curse, and trouble it. But all the silver, and gold, and vessels of brass and iron, are consecrated unto the Lord: they shall come into the treasury of the Lord."

After Jericho, the Lord allowed the Israelites to keep the spoils for themselves, but those from the city of Jericho were set aside for the Lord.

Not only had Achan sinned but God also said that Israel had sinned. One man fails, and the whole army is defeated. There is really no such thing as a private sin. We are all members one of another. So far as believers today are concerned, we are all members of the Body of Christ. We know that so far as our physical body is concerned, when any part of it is hurt the whole body feels it. The same is true with regard to the Body of Jesus Christ: "And whether one member suffer, all the members suffer with it; or one member be honoured, all the members rejoice with it" (I Cor. 12:26). It is also for the sake of the Body of Christ that we are to reject sin. Ephesians 4:25 says, "Wherefore putting away lying, speak every man truth with his neighbour: for we are members one of another." Thirty-six men in Israel lost their lives because of Achan's sin.

I often pray to the Lord to give me a vision of what would happen if I failed Him. Such a failure would not only

202 JOSHUA—VICTORIOUS BY FAITH

hurt me but many others also. Even secret sins will affect others. If a drop of poison is taken, it does not remain at the point where it has been injected into the body but affects the whole body. The venom from a snake's bite enters the body at one point but gradually spreads throughout the body.

Achan was given many chances to confess his sin and repudiate it. His conscience must have troubled him when he saw 36 lives lost, and he knew he was the cause of it all. He should have confessed then.

Later when lots were cast, they did not point immediately to Achan. First the tribe of Judah was taken which was the tribe to which Achan belonged. He should have confessed then. He had the opportunity to come clean, but he did not.

Then the casting of the lots led to the family of Achan, naming his great-grandfather, then grandfather and finally, of course, it came to Achan's household and Achan himself was taken.

As we study the Scriptures we cannot help but see the progress of sin. It acts with all as it did with Achan. In the case of the first sin committed, Eve first looked, then desired, then she took of the fruit, ate it and finally gave it to her husband. It was the same in Achan's case. He saw the treasure and coveted it. Then he took it and hid it. The Bible says concerning temptation that "every man is tempted, when he is drawn away of his own lust, and enticed. Then when lust hath conceived, it bringeth forth sin: and sin, when it is finished, bringeth forth death." It is not sin to be tempted. The sin lies in giving way to the evil suggestion and thus letting the sin nature reign in our mortal bodies.

God's Cure for Sin

Sin must be thoroughly judged before there can be victory over it. This, of course, is a message for those who have trusted in Christ. So far as an unsaved person is concerned, he must first be born again through faith in Christ before he can enjoy God-given victory over sin.

There are some Christians who believe that their old nature has been eradicated and that they do not sin anymore. But this is not according to the teaching of the Word. In our position before God we are dead to the fallen nature, but in our daily practice we must reckon on this fact in order to make it a reality in our experience.

Once Achan was identified as the thief and had confessed his sin and told where he had concealed the treasure, Joshua sent young men to investigate and found Achan's confession was true. Then we read beginning with verse 23: "And they took them [the Babylonish garment, the silver and gold] out of the midst of the tent, and brought them unto Joshua, and unto all the children of Israel, and laid them out before the Lord. And Joshua, and all Israel with him, took Achan the son of Zerah, and the silver, and the garment, and the wedge of gold, and his sons, and his daughters, and his oxen, and his asses, and his sheep, and his tent, and all that he had: and they brought them unto the valley of Achor. And Joshua said, Why hast thou troubled us? the Lord shall trouble thee this day. And all Israel stoned him with stones, and burned them with fire, after they had stoned them with stones. And they raised over him a great heap of stones unto this day. So the Lord turned from the fierceness of his anger. Wherefore the name of that place was called, The valley of Achor, unto this day" (vv. 23-26).

Several steps were involved in this which are a guide with regard to the handling of sin and the cure of it in the believer's life. First of all, the stolen goods were brought out from hiding. Sin, whatever its nature, has to be brought into the open. The person who attempts to hide his sin cannot prosper. In the second place, they brought him to Joshua, who in this case stands in the position of Christ. Our Lord is both the Saviour from sin and the Judge of sin. In the third place, this sin of Achan's was laid before the Lord, for all sin is directed against Him. If in the process of our sin we have affected others, then they, too, should hear our confession. Public sin should be publicly confessed. It was only after this that Achan and his family were taken and stoned to death, then their bodies and possessions were burned. It is clear from this that the family was party to the father's sin, not innocent victims of it.

God's way of curing sin among believers in our day is given in I John 1:9. There we read: "If we confess our sins, he is faithful and just to forgive us our sins, and to cleanse us from all unrighteousness." The word "confess" means to "bring out into the open." We lay our sins out before the Lord and agree with Him concerning them. So we lay our sin out before the Lord completely and judge it. Thus the word "confess" also means "I agree with the Lord in this matter." We admit to the Lord that He has a right to judge us. We agree that the sin is terrible. Therefore we confess it. An Old Testament passage which serves as a commentary on this whole transaction is Proverbs 28:13; "He that covereth his sins shall not prosper: but whoso confesseth and forsaketh them shall have mercy."

Sin must be completely judged. There is no alternative to this. God is not a hard taskmaster, but is holy, sinless, undefiled and cannot tolerate sin. Neither can He lead His people when there is sin in their midst. He cannot provide them with victory when they have unconfessed sin among them. God and sin cannot coexist. There is no need to argue that God is hard. We must recognize the fact that He is holy and looks for holiness in us. When we do wrong, we cannot appease Him by thinking we'll do something extra for Him. Sin must be judged. It was not until Achan and his family had been stoned and thus sin had been put out of Israel that the Lord turned from the fierceness of His anger.

God's anger is not to be thought of as anger in men. The word "anger" as used of God speaks of His holy indignation against sin. God cannot tolerate or condone sin in any way. We must put all evil beneath our feet if we are to expect God's blessing on our lives and labors.

In the instance already referred to concerning Ananias and Sapphira, they apparently had been able to deceive a number of people, but not Peter and certainly not God. Peter said to them, "Why did you lie against the Holy Spirit?" Sin cannot be hid from God; and for it to be gotten rid of it must be brought out into the open and judged.

Chapter Fifteen

RESTORATION TO FAITH
(Joshua 8)

With sin judged in Israel the Lord was ready to lead His people out into further triumphs. He said to Joshua, "Fear not, neither be thou dismayed: take all the people of war with thee, and arise, go up to Ai: see, I have given into thy hand the king of Ai, and his people, and his city, and his land" (Josh. 8:1). The Israelites had lost a battle, but they did not need to stay on the losing side. They were assured of conquest as long as they obeyed the Lord. Here again it was God who made the plans and gave the orders.

We have repeatedly emphasized the fact that Ephesians is the New Testament counterpart of the Book of Joshua. In chapter 6, verses 11 and 13 we are told to put on the whole armor of God in order to withstand Satan. There can be no victory without obedience to God in this matter. Not partial armor but the whole armor. This is what Israel needed to overcome the people of Ai.

No Christian need be overcome with the spirit of defeatism or frustration or despondency. If we put sin in its proper place and judge it and get right with God and then go on and trust in God, we will be victorious. David reminds us that God's "mercy endureth forever." The psalmist cast himself continuously upon the wonderful mercies of God. No wonder David was called a man after the heart of God. He was given that description because he did the will of God. Part of that will is to cast ourselves upon the mercies of God.

Many times I speak to God about my weaknesses. God knows them, and because of them I cast myself on God's mercies. I know the truth of what David says, "Behold, thou desirest truth in the inward parts: and in the hidden part thou shalt make me to know wisdom" (Ps. 51:6). Once a conviction of this nature burns into our beings we will be less likely to trust ourselves and will trust God more.

The whole matter of victory in the Christian life is God's doing. The triumphant life in us is God's undertaking. Just so, Israel's conquering of Canaan was God's undertaking. For them as for us, all things work together for good. But this means the judgments, the punishments, the trials, the testings, the defeats—everything that goes to make up life works together for good. In our case it is in order that we may be conformed to the image of God's Son.

When sin is confessed, judged and forsaken, God is able to work. We see this over and over again in David's life. We see it in Peter's life. He denied the Lord, but when he came clean with God, he became a leader among the early disciples. John Mark forsook Paul and Silas but later on he got right with God. Then Paul urged that Mark be brought along and used in the cause of Christ.

Failure in the past should teach us valuable lessons but not halt our ministry. We must not let past failures paralyze our present or mortgage our future. Let us get right with God and then go on. Paul's admonition fits in here where he told us to forget the things that are behind and to press forward to the goal before us.

New Orders and Methods

With regard to the continuing effort to subdue Ai, Joshua received new orders. He was to follow a different method than what was used to bring Jericho down. The Lord does not always do things the same way. The method followed for Jericho's capture was not repeated for any other city or fortress in Canaan. So for Ai there was a new plan. God never changes in His character, but He does not necessarily follow the same plans in everything He does.

In our own personal lives God has made it plain that He is not stereotyped in the way He does things. We are told in I Corinthians 12 that God has diversities of operations. The passage reads: "Now there are diversities of gifts, but the same Spirit. And there are differences of administrations, but the same Lord. And there are diversities of operations, but it is the same God which worketh all in all." There is but one Holy Spirit and He guides and plans in your life and mine and in the work of God today. The glory belongs to the Lord and not to us. It is God who gives the strategy to retake what has been lost in our lives just as He formulated a new strategy for the capture of Ai.

The way back may seem to be hard at times. We don't like to travel that road. We don't like to face our sins. The Devil makes us ashamed, but God says the only way is to go back as He has planned the way for us, and in that way only. In our work for the Lord we seem to want to imitate others who are successful, follow their methods, and do pretty much as they do. Yet God may have an entirely different method for us to follow. He has plans and orders for each one of us. I am sure that is true with regard to Back to the Bible Broadcast. During that first year in which the Broadcast was begun, I read a book on the life of George Mueller. It told how he received finances from God though he did not tell any human being his needs, but simply prayed about them. This did not work so far as I was concerned, so one day I asked the Lord about it. I wanted to know, if that was the method to follow why was it not working for me? The Lord just as good as told me, "I made only one George Mueller and you are not he. Follow My orders, not the instructions I gave someone else."

After the victory at Ai the Israelites sidetracked for some 30 miles to Mount Ebal and Mount Gerizim. There they were taught how they would be blessed if they were obedient and how they would be cursed or judgment would fall upon them if they were disobedient. There was no alternative. It was either life or death depending on their obedience to God.

So we too must go back to Ephesians 6:10-18 and do it often. There we see the balance between the Word of God (v. 17) and the prayer life under the Holy Spirit (v. 18). Both are needed. One without the other would be impractical and ineffective.

Chapter Sixteen

PRESUMPTUOUS FAITH
(Joshua 9)

Subtlety of the Enemy

The ninth chapter of Joshua relates how Joshua and the other leaders in Israel were deceived by a group of Canaanites. This serves as an illustration to us of the subtlety of Satan who, if he can't overthrow our plans with one method, will try another. This is why we read in Ephesians 6:11: "Put on the whole armour of God, that ye may be able to stand against the wiles of the devil."

Satan will disguise himself as an angel of light in order to further his ends. We must be on the alert lest he "get an advantage of us: for we are not ignorant of his devices" (II Cor. 2:11). At times he comes as a roaring lion (I Peter 5:8). But at other times he comes as subtle as a snake. This was how he appeared to our first parents: "Now the serpent was more subtil than any beast of the field which the Lord God had made. And he said unto the woman, Yea, hath God said, Ye shall not eat of every tree of the garden?" (Gen. 3:1). The roar of a lion may give us speedier warning than the hiss of a serpent.

Jericho had fallen, and after Israel had gotten right with God, Ai was captured and destroyed. Each victory, however, seemed to be a fresh invitation for an attack by the foe. This was true in Israel's experience in Canaan, and it is also true in our spiritual experience as we move out into the life of conquest prescribed for us by God and provided for us in Christ. As we appropriate the life of Christ for moment-by-moment victory, Satan will do everything he can to thwart God's purposes through us. Even though Satan's power has been broken, he is not idle. The wing feathers of an eagle may be clipped so that he cannot fly, but he is still dangerous. So it is with Satan. Though his power was annulled through Christ's death and resurrection, Satan can still act against us if we provide him with the opportunity.

To be attacked by Satan and have struggles and conflicts is not something that should depress us. These are an indication that we are on the offensive, not merely on the defensive.

If on the other hand we are like the Canaanites, concerned with our tribal quarrels, our petty squabbles, bogged down with minor problems, Satan will leave us alone. We are out of the will of God in any case under such circumstances.

There came a day, however, when the Canaanites realized that they had a common enemy in Israel. These pagan tribes temporarily played down their petty squabbles and hatreds and decided to join forces against the common enemy: "And it came to pass, when all the kings which were on this side Jordan, in the hills, and in the valleys, and in all the coasts of the great sea over against Lebanon, the Hittite, and the Amorite, the Canaanite, the Perizzite, the Hivite, and the Jebusite, heard thereof; That they gathered themselves together, to fight with Joshua and with Israel, with one accord" (Josh. 9:1,2).

There are times when the world unites. Nations will forget their differences and unite to repel a common enemy or to grab more land and power for themselves. The Devil is so subtle that he can unite certain portions of the visible church to fight the true church and to oppose the things of God. A present-day illustration of that is the ecumenical movement.

Satan's greatest wrath is exhibited when he realizes God is getting the upper hand in your life or mine. It is then that he will gather all his forces; but our Lord can easily dissipate the power of these evil beings.

One tribe did not join with the others in their battle plans against Israel. They decided to use guile. "And when the inhabitants of Gibeon heard what Joshua had done unto Jericho and to Ai, They did work wilily, and went and made as if they had been ambassadors, and took old sacks upon their asses, and wine bottles, old, and rent, and bound up" (9:3,4). They disguised themselves as though they had come from a long distance. Their garments were old and even their bread was moldy. They came to Joshua at Gilgal and duped him and the Israelites.

The Gibeonites said, "We be come from a far country: now therefore make ye a league with us" (9:6). Israel at this time was in the right place, but once again there seemed to have been prayerlessness on their part. And prayerlessness always destroys the spirit of discernment. It is as we pray that God gives us wisdom. Remember James 1:5 says, "If any of you lack wisdom, let him ask of God, that giveth to all men liberally, and upbraideth not; and it shall be given him."

As we follow the story in Joshua nine we find that the Gibeonites claimed to come from a distant country, having heard of the fame of God and what He did for Israel in Egypt. Then they also said that they had learned how the two kings of the Amorites on the other side of Jordan had been destroyed by Israel whose God was invincible. They called attention to their torn and travel-stained clothing and what was left of the food supplies. The bottles of wine, they said, were filled when they left their homeland, but now they were empty and the wine bags torn and dilapidated. They said they began with good shoes for their feet, but the shoes were now practically worn out.

The Gibeonites wanted Israel to make a league with them, which was contrary to God's instructions. God had said all the Canaanites were to be destroyed. Unfortunately, the leaders of Israel believed the lying Gibeonites and did as they suggested.

We are no match in ourselves for Satan's subtle ways. We can defeat him only as we remember the admonition of Proverbs 3:5-7 to trust in the Lord with all our hearts and to lean not on our own understanding. We are to acknowledge

God in all our ways and He will direct our paths. It is when we turn to Him that He gives us wisdom.

Israel's problem was that they were presumptuous, acting on the basis of their own wisdom. In our case Christ has been made unto us wisdom, but we must watch.

Be especially careful of decisions that have to be made under pressure. This is an area I have been careful about with regard to my own life, and it has paid off. When someone comes along and tells me that I have to make a decision right now because the opportunity might be gone by tomorrow, then I am even more on the alert. That kind of argument, particularly with spiritual things involved, could be Satan's subtle way of deception. Many persons have been led from the work of the Lord into side issues because they made decisions suddenly without consulting God.

I have found it wise to stand and wait. God will never let an opportunity go by that He wants us to have. Even if we are late, and it is God's desire for us to have what He has planned, we will receive it. Israel was 40 years behind, but the opportunity to conquer the land came again. God did not forget His promises, but waited for His people to be ready to accept it.

I would rather wait on the Lord and even have Him wait on me than to be too quick in a decision, only to be left with a feeling of indecision and not knowing for sure that what I had decided was the will of God. Those who wait on the Lord shall never be ashamed.

Israel's response is given in verses 14 and 15. The words are, "And the men took of their victuals and asked not counsel at the mouth of the Lord. And Joshua made peace with them, and made a league with them, to let them live: and the princes of the congregation sware unto them." The Israelites took the evidence of the victuals instead of asking counsel of the Lord. This was their great mistake. Satan is more dangerous in his wiles than in his open assaults.

The Church flourished under the persecutions of Nero and other Roman emperors, but it succumbed to the flatteries of Constantine. In the times of persecution God's people waited on Him, but when Christianity became popular and fashionable, its spirituality was corrupted.

The Israelites discovered too late the deception that had been practiced on them. They thought they had made a league with a people who lived outside of Canaan, but "it came to pass at the end of three days after they had made a league with them, that they heard that they were their neighbours, and that they dwelt among them" (9:16).

The Israelites were incensed against their leaders for having made a treaty with the Gibeonites. Since, however, an oath had been taken in the name of God to spare that pagan people, the princes of Israel stood firm in their promise.

Joshua called the Gibeonites to him and asked why they had deceived the Israelites in this way. Then he passed the judgment on them that had been decided by the Israelites: "Now therefore ye are cursed, and there shall none of you be freed from being bondmen, and hewers of wood and drawers of water for the house of my God" (v. 23). He made them slaves, but the real damage had been done. Satan's strategy of coexistence had been successful. The enemy had by deception accomplished his purpose.

The modern Gibeons in the political world are the Communists. They operate through deceit. But there are Gibeonites in the religious realm, in the church also. They are the non-surrendered elements, the persons who do not walk with God. They bear watching. They are not to be trusted.

Once the league was made by Israel and the Gibeonites, God held Israel to it. He would not let them destroy the cities or the people.

God works on this principle in other areas in our lives today. Even when we make mistakes, we are still under obligation to carry through our part of the transactions we have entered into. Where we involve ourselves and God's word in our testimony, we have to stick by the promise made. Take for example the subject of marriage. Paul says in I Corinthians 7:12: "But to the rest speak I, not the Lord: If any brother hath a wife that believeth not, and she be pleased to dwell with him, let him not put her away." If a mistake has been made in marriage by a believer marrying an unsaved person, the Christian is to make the best of it and trust God for the rest. If the unsaved partner wants to continue on in the marriage, the marriage must not be broken up. This does not result in God's first choice or best. It is His second best, but this is His method or way.

Israel and Joshua had made a mistake. They were not to make any alliance with any nation in Canaan. But they did, and what was the result in their own future conduct? This mistake drove the Israelites to prayer. The presence of the Gibeonites among them was a constant reminder of the mistake made. Israel learned to watch but they learned it the hard way. The mistakes at Ai and Gibeon were not made again during Joshua's lifetime.

Satan was not able to discourage the Israelites from going on in their conquest of Canaan. Neither should a mistake we have made cause us to give up. Let us confess it to God, forsake it and go ahead.

Chapter Seventeen

THE ULTIMATE OF FAITH
(Joshua 10)

The Greatest Battle of All

In the tenth chapter of Joshua is recorded one of the most remarkable battles of all time. It shows how God works with men when they dare to trust Him fully.

The events leading up to this particular battle are as follows.

By deceiving the Israelites into making a covenant with them, the Gibeonites thought they had avoided any threat to their future existence as a people. Their pagan neighbors, however, were incensed against them. Five of the Amorite kings came together to destroy Gibeon and its people. These kings looked on the Gibeonites as traitors to their cause and decided to wipe them out.

The Gibeonites learned of this plot against them and sent word to Joshua concerning their plight. So, when the kings of the South attacked Gibeon, Joshua and his army came to the rescue.

The Scriptures tell us, "So Joshua ascended from Gilgal, he, and all the people of war with him, and all the mighty men of valour" (10:7). We have called attention previously to the importance of Gilgal which was the first beachhead made by the Israelites on the Canaan side of Jordan. It was the place to which they returned again and again after victory or defeat. It was there they replenished themselves physically, but even more so, spiritually. It was there they went to receive orders from Almighty God. This was where Joshua was located when he received word of the impending attack on Gibeon.

215

Gilgal is mentioned five times in chapter 10 of Joshua. It was, indeed, an important place to the Israelites. Its importance reminds us that in every move we make in our spiritual lives we must go to our Gilgal. It is our place of communion with God and the place where we find out His will for us.

As Joshua considered his responsibility to go against the five kings in order to fulfill his obligations to Gibeon, the Lord spoke to him. He said, "Fear them not: for I have delivered them into thine hand; there shall not a man of them stand before thee" (v.8). What a wonderful assurance that was!

Just such an assurance is given to us as Christians in our spiritual battles. Regardless of how much force Satan with his angelic hosts can muster against us, he will fail if we will put on the whole armor of God (Eph. 6:10-18). This armor, though largely defensive, is at the same time offensive because there is the sword of the Spirit and the "all prayer"—the two basic offensive spiritual weapons. When we put them on, we can say with Paul as he did in I Corinthians 15:57: "But thanks be to God, which giveth us the victory through our Lord Jesus Christ." He stated the same glorious truth in another way in II Corinthians 2:14: "Now thanks be unto God, which always causeth us to triumph in Christ" against the enemy. This triumph, of course, lies in Christ Jesus. With Him controlling us and fighting our battles through us we cannot fail.

God intervened in a very specific way in the battle against the five Amorite kings. This God always does for us when we are on His side and obeying His instructions. He will allow nothing to stop His children when they are ready to obey Him and go forth in faith.

We read: "And the Lord discomfited them before Israel, and slew them with a great slaughter at Gibeon, and chased them along the way that goeth up to Beth-horon, and smote them to Azekah, and unto Makkedah." The Lord, however, did not leave it to the Israelites to do all the fighting. He bombarded the Amorites from the heavens with huge hailstones. "And it came to pass, as they [the five kings] fled from before Israel, and were in the going down to Beth-horon, that the Lord cast down great stones from heaven upon them unto Azekah, and they died: they were more which died with hailstones than they whom the children of Israel slew with the sword" (v. 11). The Lord is ever nearby to aid those who are doing His work in His way.

The fight lasted all day as we have previously noted. Yet it was far from over by the time night was approaching. The darkness would allow the enemy to escape to oppose the Israelites at a later time. For this reason Joshua began to pray, apparently not only for the safety of Israel but for the honor of his God. Joshua then spoke words which initiated one of the greatest miracles God ever wrought on behalf of men working together with Him. "Then spake Joshua to the Lord in the day when the Lord delivered up the Amorites before the children of Israel, and he said in the sight of Israel, Sun, stand thou still upon Gibeon; and thou, Moon, in the valley of Ajalon" (v. 12).

Joshua spoke first to the Lord. Israel's leader did not speak to the heavenly bodies on his own initiative. He waited upon God. He sought God's will especially with a view to God's honor, for it was at stake at this time. Then, with God's consent that he should ask for the lengthening of the day, Joshua spoke in the sight of all Israel. There was no secret here. This was a step of faith, but faith is not a hidden thing. It must be out in the open. If we trust God for something but keep it secret, our purpose may be to avoid embarrassment if what we are looking for does not take place. Joshua was not only a man who sought the will of God and believed God, but he had permission to speak to the sun and tell it to stand still. Joshua spoke the words that brought on the miracle. Praying is not always asking, it is sometimes saying.

We read in Matthew 7:7 to "ASK, and it shall be given you; seek, and ye shall find; knock, and it shall be opened unto you." But in Mark 11:23 the Lord said, "Whosoever shall SAY unto this mountain, Be thou removed," showing that prayer sometimes moves out of the realm of our asking and leads us to saying under the direction of God. The prayer of faith will also say, "I have witnessed this experience in my own life numerous times, for which I thank God."

Joshua spoke out in front of all Israel. They all heard what he said. If he was going to be embarrassed this would be the time. But God will not embarrass a man who has been with Him, received His instructions, and then openly stated them. In this case something was to take place that was absolutely out of this world. It had never been done before, but it was done then, and the next verse says, "And the sun stood still, and the moon stayed, until the people had avenged themselves upon their enemies. Is not this written in the book of Jasher? So the sun stood still in the midst of heaven, and hasted not to go down about a whole day" (v. 13).

Whatever God did either to the sun or the earth or whatever else was involved, the result was that there was light for a period extending about the length of another day. One scientist who went into the subject in considerable detail figured that the day was lengthened 23 hours and 20 minutes. God who is the God of the impossible aided the Israelites by prolonging the daylight and by showering hailstones upon the Amorites. Concerning that day the 14th verse of Joshua 10 says, "And there was no day like that before it or after it, that the Lord hearkened unto the voice of a man: for the Lord fought for Israel."

Joshua knew his God. He had become acquainted with Him personally. This was especially true at the time he met the Lord as the Captain of the Lord's hosts. Joshua's knowledge of the Lord, however, must have begun with his years in Egypt, then increased in the 40 years he spent under the tutorship of Moses in the desert. Serving as Moses' minister, Joshua saw the mighty miracles of God and was introduced to some of the more personal aspects of God's dealing with Moses and his people. Joshua was one of the two men who dared to believe God the first time the spies were sent into Canaan. He knew that God was sovereign and accepted God's sovereignty for his own life.

When reading in the prophets for my devotions I am constantly impressed by the presentation of God's sovereignty, His limitless might and the finality of His Word. What He says He will do, He does. Time in no way limits Him. Do you know this God as the Bible presents Him?

God is great. There is none to compare to Him. No wonder we who know Him love to sing "How Great Thou Art."

Paul's doxology in Romans 11:33-36 as translated by Williams is moving and inspiring: "How fathomless the depths of God's resources, wisdom, and knowledge! How unsearchable His decisions, and how mysterious His methods! For who has ever understood the thoughts of the Lord, or has ever been His adviser? Or who has ever advanced God anything to have Him pay him back? For from Him everything comes, through Him everything lives, and for Him everything exists. Glory to Him forever! Amen."

Faith in cooperation with God is invincible. Nothing is impossible to Him. The person who is obedient to God can say as did Paul, "I can do all things through Christ which strengtheneth me." Do we believe this? Let us put it into practice.

How often we have interpreted Philippians 4:19 to mean only finances. The passage says, "But my God shall supply all your need according to his riches in glory by Christ Jesus." But ALL needs are involved. There are physical needs, spiritual needs, need for strength and grace to successfully oppose the evil one—all are supplied through Christ.

We love to repeat Psalm 23:1: "The Lord is my shepherd; I shall not want." This means we lack nothing when He is our Shepherd. And this is what God emphasizes in II Chronicles 16:9: "For the eyes of the Lord run to and fro throughout the whole earth, to show himself strong in the behalf of them whose heart is perfect toward him." The heart that is perfect toward God is the heart that is wholeheartedly surrendered to Him.

Following the great victory during which God had extended the day to enable the Israelites to thoroughly defeat the forces of the five kings, Joshua returned with Israel to Gilgal (Josh. 10:15). It was an important move for them. Joshua brought all his forces back to the place of refreshment, for he had well learned the great lesson that after victory one needs to get back to close fellowship with the Lord. Only He can keep us humble so that pride does not arise in us when we go forth again in the Lord's battles. Twice before Joshua had made a mistake in this connection but now his lesson was learned.

Thorough Victory Over Sin

We read in verse 16: "But these five kings fled, and hid themselves in a cave." This is characteristic of the enemy when he is defeated. Hidden enemies, however, can be very dangerous. When we expose Satan, he runs but very often hidden sins remain and lie dormant and will show up when opportunity comes.

There is a very important lesson in connection with these five kings. It is a spiritual truth that has been of great help to me personally since it illustrates how to properly deal with sin in our lives.

Why did not God leave the five kings alone after they had hidden themselves? The answer is given in Deuteronomy 7. After naming the different nations of Canaan, all of which were greater and mightier than Israel, God said these nations were to be cast out. He promised to deliver them into Israel's hands and Israel was to "utterly destroy them" and in nowise make a covenant with them. The account continues: "Neither shalt thou make marriages with them; thy daughter thou shalt not give unto his son, nor his daughter shalt thou take unto thy son. For they will turn away thy son from following me, that they may serve other gods: so will the anger of the Lord be kindled against you, and destroy thee suddenly. But thus shall ye deal with them; ye shall destroy their altars, and break down their images, and cut down their groves, and burn their graven images with fire. For thou art an holy people unto the Lord thy God: the Lord thy God hath chosen thee to be a special people unto himself, above all people that are upon the face of the earth" (vv. 3-6).

In Deuteronomy 9:3,4 we are given further information: "Understand therefore this day, that the Lord thy God is he which goeth over before thee; as a consuming fire he shall destroy them, and he shall bring them down before thy face: so shalt thou drive them out, and destroy them quickly, as the Lord hath said unto thee. Speak not thou in thine heart, after that the Lord thy God hath cast them out from before thee, saying, For my righteousness the Lord hath brought me in to possess this land: but for the wickedness of these nations the Lord doth drive them out from before thee."

There is no room for guesswork as to why Israel was to destroy these nations. Their cup of sin was full. Their day of reckoning had come. The Lord had given them opportunity to change their ways, but they persisted in sin. Let us remember that this is God's way of dealing with nations and with individuals. The nations of our day are ripening for judgment. Communism will not go on forever, nor will some of the other "isms" without meeting judgment. In our own country where we speak of God and in some ways try to honor Him yet reject Christ, serving not God but ourselves, we, too, will fill our cup of iniquity and reap the consequences. Individual or nation, this is the program. God does show mercy to the sinner who repents, but God shows no mercy to sin.

There are several ways of handling sin in our lives, two of them we will seek to illustrate from this section of Joshua we are now studying.

First of all there are sins which I call "open" sins. These are sins that others can see. This was true of Achan's sin when it was exposed to all the people. Judgment on such in Israel was public punishment. In the case of Achan it was death by stoning. Achan's sins, for they were many, included covetousness, theft and deceit.

There are other sins such as immorality, greed, envy,

quarreling, gossip, slander, boastfulness, unchastity, impurity, lewdness, idolatry, animosity, jealousy, bad temper, dissension, factional spirit, drunkenness, and carousing. These are all sins that are more or less exposed openly and need to be dealt with openly. The judgment of death should be put on each one of them. This is how we as believers are to rid them from our lives.

Colossians 3:3 reads: "For ye are dead [have died]." Then in verse 5 the Apostle says, "Mortify therefore your members." Put off or put in the place of death such evils as fornication, uncleanness and covetousness. In Christ Jesus we have died to sin, but if we let it creep back into our lives again, we must do something about it. We must take our position before God as dead to such things. At the same time we are to be alive unto Him.

There is a second class of sins that is harder to deal with, more difficult to find and expose. I call them the sins of the heart (hidden sins). These, too, must be dealt with vigorously.

They are in the category of secret sins. They are not out in view where others can see them readily. Such sins as impatience, pride, selfishness, and evil thoughts are in this group. It is not easy for someone else to know if we have evil thoughts concerning another person. Bitterness of heart towards another or worldly thinking or impure thoughts can be present with us and yet be well hidden. Self-pity, hypocrisy, faithlessness—these and many others can all be part of secret sins. Nevertheless, God has a marvelous provision for dealing with them.

We learn in Romans 6 that "our old man is crucified with him [Christ], that the body of sin might be destroyed, that henceforth we should not serve sin" (v. 6). This is illustrated for us in Joshua 10 with regard to these five kings. We find, first of all, that the five kings hid themselves just as hidden sins are put out of sight but still exist. Now, Joshua said what was to happen to the five kings: "Open the mouth of the cave, and bring out those five kings unto me out of the cave" (v. 22).

The lesson for us here is not to try to hide secret sins even though only we and God may know them. It could be that some of our closest friends do not suspect such sins are present, but we will not prosper if we hide such evil. This does not mean we are to expose them to the eyes of other people, but they must be confessed before Christ. Sin must be brought out into the open before God.

Many years ago an incident occurred in my life that taught me a good lesson in this connection. We were having some difficult internal problems in our work, yet could not put the finger on them. This continued for some time.

Early one morning a dear saint of God came to see me. He was one who knew how to contact the Lord and had made a 100-mile trip to talk with me.

He said to me, "Brother Epp, I have come to see you because you have some inner problems."

I replied, "How do you know that?"

"Ah," he said, "I've been talking with God. He sent me to you." Then he added, "If you will tell me what they are, we'll pray about them."

I said, "I can't tell you that for I cannot put my finger on them."

He replied, "All right, the Devil is hiding, but there is a way to get him out. We will pray together, claiming the promise where two of you agree as touching anything. We will thus have God expose the Devil, and when he is exposed he'll flee."

So it was on that basis that we prayed together. Within a week everything was laid out into the open. God brought it out so that we knew what it was. We knew how to deal with it. With God's grace the slate was cleared and the problems eliminated.

A good Psalm to read in this connection is Psalm 139. It tells us how God knows everything about us. There is not a thing we can hide from Him. All our deeds are exposed to His view and our innermost thoughts are open to Him. The psalmist said, "Search me, O God, and know my heart: try me, and know my thoughts: And see if there be any wicked way in me, and lead me in the way everlasting." In this connection ask God to bring out into the open the evil that is in us. This is very necessary. It must not be overlooked.

But something more must be done. In Joshua 10:24 we learn that Joshua told the leaders to "come near, put your feet upon the necks of these kings. And they came near, and put their feet upon the necks of them."

It was the custom in those days for the person defeated in battle, regardless of his station in life, to prostrate himself before the victor who would put his foot upon the vanquished person's neck. This was an act symbolizing the submission of the one and the victory of the other.

With regard to sin in our lives, God will reveal it if we ask Him, then we must take a stand similar to the above with regard to it. In Ephesians 1:21-23 we learn that God has put everything under Christ's feet, for He is Victor. Then the promise is made in Romans 16:20: "The God of peace shall bruise Satan under your feet shortly." These are truths we can apply to our lives even now.

First of all, there must be a determination on our part that we want the secret sin in our lives dealt with one way or another. In the second place, we must take our position as victors because we are victors through Christ. We do not have to be subject to these sins. Satan will seek to tempt us with them again and again, but we can put our foot on them, figuratively speaking, again and again.

The foes were publicly humiliated before Israel when they lay prostrate on the ground with the victor's feet upon their necks. This was done to show that the Lord had wrought a great victory. Joshua used this as a means of encouraging the Israelites, saying to them: "Fear not, nor be dismayed, be strong and of good courage [put your foot upon their necks]: for thus shall the Lord do to all your enemies against whom ye fight."

God's promise is for complete victory. We dare not allow sins to lurk unjudged within the hidden recesses of our hearts. We must bring these sins out into the open before God and take a determined stand against them.

This is something I do in my own life whenever the Lord reveals to me that there is a sin there that needs to be judged. I say something to this effect: "Lord, we must take this thing and conquer it once for all. I am putting my foot down upon it."

Not only were these kings brought out from the cave and put in the place of defeated foes, they were also slain. We read that Joshua "smote them, and slew them" (v. 26).

Joshua, who is a type of Christ in this illustration, was the executioner of these kings. So Christ is the executioner of the sins in our lives. He has already overcome them through His death. The benefits of His work for us must be applied through faith. Paul said in Galatians 6:14: "But God forbid that I should glory, save in the cross of our Lord Jesus Christ, by whom the world is crucified unto me, and I unto the world." So the work for our release from sin has already been accomplished. It is for us to take our stand upon the fact, to reckon upon it thus making it real in our daily experience.

We must put our feet upon the neck of our jealousy, pride, critical spirit, harsh tongue and all the other things that are part of the old life. We must pronounce ourselves to be victors in Christ Jesus; and when we do, we must trust Him to be the Executioner of our sins.

In Joshua 10:27,28 we read: "And it came to pass at the time of the going down of the sun, that Joshua commanded, and they took them down off the trees, and cast them into the cave wherein they had been hid, and laid great stones in the cave's mouth, which remain until this very day."

According to the law, by hanging these men upon a tree, they were put in a place where they were cursed. This is where sin belongs. But we must remember that for our salvation it was Christ who was cursed for us by being hanged upon a tree. Our sins, both our secret sins and our open sins, were judged there. Let us accept our position with Him and let sin be literally cursed.

The record also tells us that the bodies of these five kings were returned to the cave and stones used to seal up the mouth of it. They were hid away once for all as it were. It is following this that we have the next note of victory: "And that day Joshua took Makkedah, and smote it with the edge of the sword, and the king thereof he utterly destroyed, them, and all the souls that were therein; he let none remain: and he did to the king of Makkedah as he did unto the king of Jericho." This was treating the cities and their sinful inhabitants according to God's instructions.

Sin to which we do not apply death can become the means of our own downfall. It was a sad thing in Israel's experience that they did not completely possess the land. They did conquer but did not dispossess the enemy so that they themselves could possess their inheritance. More on this in the next chapter.

Sins may be forgiven, but God wants to see us conquer them. He wants us to dispossess them, and in their place He wants to put the fruit of the Spirit.

The people of Israel became a source of fear to all the Canaanites in the land. These pagans began to have respect for God's people and for their God. According to Joshua 10:21: "None moved his tongue against any of the children of Israel." This is a remarkable statement concerning the power God was manifesting through Israel. We might well ask ourselves why it is there is no such power being manifested through the Church as a whole today. We can thank God for individual churches of power, but the vast majority are powerless. We like to sing "How Great Thou Art," but so few appropriate His greatness. Our lives and testimonies are weak for lack of the presence of supernatural power among us.

The people of God should always be on the offensive. Their experience should be that of Canaan, not of the desert. We should launch full scale offensives in the Name of the Lord Jesus against the powers of evil instead of running and hiding from them. The following stanzas from Monsell's hymn should encourage us in this direction.

> Fight the good fight with all thy might!
> Christ is thy strength, and Christ thy right;
> Lay hold on life, and it shall be
> Thy joy and crown eternally.

Faint not nor fear, His arms are near,
He changeth not, and thou art dear;
Only believe, and thou shalt see
That Christ is all in all to thee.

Chapter Eighteen

INHERITANCE AND POSSESSION BY FAITH
(Joshua 11-18)

The third division of the Book of Joshua is concerned with Israel possessing the conquered territories. The spiritual application to us is our need to possess our possessions in Christ.

The first section of the Book emphasized the entrance into the land. Great decisions had to be made, decisions of faith, and this led to God working miracles of such a nature that the Canaanites were terrified in heart at the presence of the Israelites in their midst (chapters 1-5).

Then there was the section of the Book dealing with the actual conquests of Israel. This section covering chapters six through twelve gives an account of what was done to take the various areas in Canaan. First a few cities were taken, then five kings from the south, finally 31 kings from the north. One after another, these foes were conquered.

Joshua's success as a leader in this enterprise is expressed in Joshua 11:15: "As the Lord commanded Moses his servant, so did Moses command Joshua, and so did Joshua; he left nothing undone of all that the Lord commanded Moses." This was true obedience and is the reason why God could bless His servant as He did.

We read in Joshua 11:23: "So Joshua took the whole land, according to all that the Lord said unto Moses; and Joshua gave it for an inheritance unto Israel according to their divisions by their tribes. And the land rested from war." It is very likely that five years elapsed before peace came. It was a long campaign but a successful one.

The extent of the conquest is given in verse 16: "So Joshua took all that land, the hills, and all the south country,

228

and all the land of Goshen, and the valley, and the plain, and the mountain of Israel, and the valley of the same."

Then we learn beginning with verse 18 that the Israelites had to fight for every inch of territory. "Joshua made war a long time with all those kings. There was not a city that made peace with the children of Israel, save the Hivites the inhabitants of Gibeon: all other they took in battle. For it was of the Lord to harden their hearts, that they should come against Israel in battle, that he might destroy them utterly, and that they might have no favour, but that he might destroy them, as the Lord commanded Moses. And at that time came Joshua, and cut off the Anakims from the mountains, from Hebron, from Debir, from Anab, and from all the mountains of Judah, and from all the mountains of Israel: Joshua destroyed them utterly with their cities" (11:18-21).

In order to benefit from these things we must remember that Canaan was an inheritance to Israel just as Christ is our inheritance.

We read in Hebrews 1:3 concerning Christ that He by Himself purged our sins and then sat down at the right hand of God. He finished His work on earth, something He emphasized in His high priestly prayer and also reiterated on the cross itself. It was following this that He sat down at the right hand of the Majesty on High, for it was there that He was to continue His work on our behalf in and through us by the Holy Spirit.

We as God's people have a rest that remains to us according to Hebrews 4:9. This is not physical rest, but a rest of soul which comes from placing total confidence in Christ. This relieves us of turmoil of mind and of heart, of our being constantly upset through trials and troubles. It is a rest from frustration and discouragement. Come what may, we find our rest in Him. The passage continues: "For he that is entered into his rest, he also hath ceased from his own works, as God did from his." This kind of rest means that we have ceased trying to do what only God can do. We depend on His strength and not our own. We have learned what it means to relax in Christ and see Him win the victories through us. This is the rest that God has for us and this is why we have the following exhortation: "Let us labour therefore [give diligence] to enter into that rest, lest any man fall after the same example of unbelief" (v. 11). The unbelief spoken of here has to do with the Israelites who failed to find Canaan rest because of their lack of trust in God. They tried in their own strength but because of unbelief, they did not go in and take what God had provided for them. Learning not to do as they did we find our rest comes as the result of our trust or belief in Christ.

Difference Between Inheritance and Possession

Turning back now to Joshua, we find quite a marked contrast in the last verse of Joshua 11 and the first verse of chapter 13. Chapter 12 is merely a roster of the kings of Canaan; but there is a marked contrast between the end of the narrative in Joshua 11 and its beginning in chapter 13.

We read in 11:23: "So Joshua took the whole land, according to all that the Lord said unto Moses; and Joshua gave it for an inheritance unto Israel according to their divisions by their tribes. And the land rested from war." The important word in this is "inheritance." Joshua gave Israel the land for an inheritance. But in chapter 13 we read: "Now Joshua was old and stricken in years; and the Lord said unto him, Thou art old and stricken in years, and there remaineth yet very much land to be possessed." This appears on the surface to be a contradiction with what chapter 11 says. In chapter 11 they were told that the land was given for an inheritance and also that the land rested from war. In chapter 13 the Lord says, "There remaineth yet very much land to be possessed." In reality there is no contradiction when we understand what is meant by inheritance and what is meant by possessing the land.

God had given all the land to Israel but they were responsible to go in and possess it. They were promised according to Joshua 1:3: "Every place that the soul of your

feet shall tread upon, that have I given unto you." We also
know now that God gave them the land for an inheritance. It
was divided among the tribes as is outlined for us in the third
section of the Book of Joshua. Nevertheless, each tribe had
to go in and possess the land in order to enjoy its benefits.

This meant that they had to oust the former inhabitants.
They had to be dispossessed before Israel could possess their
inheritance. This was the responsibility facing each tribe.
There was no other way to get control of the land and live in
it. Joshua and his armies had conquered great kings and
subdued many areas, but there were still pockets of land
where Canaanites lived and resisted any effort to dispossess
them.

So is it with our possessions in Christ. These must be
appropriated on an individual basis. The Church on a whole is
blessed only as we as individuals possess what is ours in
Christ. Our inheritance is in Him. In fact He is our
inheritance.

It is not a matter of us wanting a part of Him but rather
that Christ is all in all to us. The Apostle Paul wrote in
Colossians 2:10: "And ye are complete in him, which is the
head of all principality and power." In Ephesians 1:23 we
learn that He permeates everything in the world and the
universe including the body of Jesus Christ, the Church. So
He today is our inheritance.

We make a distinction between an inheritance and a
possession. An inheritance is something that God provides for
us. A possession, on the other hand, is something that we
take when God offers it to us. There is a world of difference
between the two. The inheritance for Israel was a whole
geographical area as promised to Abraham: "In the same day
the Lord made a covenant with Abram, saying, Unto thy seed
have I given this land, from the river of Egypt unto the great
river, the river Euphrates" (Gen. 15:18). The land was
promised Abraham, but it was necessary at a later time for
his posterity to go in and possess it, to live in it and enjoy its
fruits.

Possession is that part of the land which has been

entered, conquered, dispossessed and then lived in by Israel. That is, they enjoyed the fruit thereof.

Canaan was entered at the River Jordan crossing. In the second place Canaan was conquered through war. In the third place it was to be dispossessed as the inhabitants were either driven out or destroyed.

Our spiritual inheritance is all that God has given us in Christ. Everything we have is found in Him. It is Christ Himself. Possession, on the other hand, is that much of what we have in Christ that we have appropriated by faith. We must dispossess before we can possess. We must conquer, subdue and then take possession.

What are we to dispossess in our lives? We have considered a number of things. There are such things as sins and shortcomings, all of which must be dispossessed before what we have in Christ can be possessed.

There were first of all five kings in Canaan that had to be conquered and later on thirty-one. In the spiritual aspect of these things there is much in our lives to be overcome for Christ, dispossessed of that which is evil, and possessed of that which is righteous. Let us search our Bibles to see how many things there are we have not yet possessed in Christ. Then let us go ahead by the grace of God to possess them by an act of faith.

Three Important Words

There are three important words that relate to Christian experience. The first is *surrender.* It speaks of the fact that we must be under total submission to Christ. Our wills must be His. He must be the Lord of our lives. Everything relating to us must be utterly surrendered to His control and direction.

The second word is *consecration.* The verb "to consecrate" simply means to "set apart." Everything we have is to be set apart for His use. Regardless of what our talents or abilities may be, all are to be used for His glory. It is not just a matter of laying them at His feet but of giving back to

Him for His use that which belongs to Him, since He first gave them to us.

I recall one time talking to a man about his soul. He said to me, "I don't mix my religion with my business." It happened that we were talking together in his business establishment. It was apparent that business was one thing to him and religion was another. It is quite clear that he did not know our Christ.

The third very important word in our Christian experience is *appropriation*. By faith all that Christ is and has is ours if we will, by faith, take it. First of all, He must possess us. We have been purchased by Him, for He paid the price of our redemption. And because we have trusted in Him, the Spirit of God has taken up residence in our bodies which belong to Him: "Know ye not that your body is the temple of the Holy Ghost which is in you . . . and ye are not your own? . . . Ye are bought with a price" (I Cor. 6:19,20). But He must possess us. Everything we have and are must be handed over to Him. He must first conquer our wills, then it is that we are in a position to possess our possessions in Him.

In Ephesians 1:18 we learn that He has His inheritance in the saints. Since we are united with Him, we inherit everything from Him. But His inheritance is the Body, the Church, His own Bride.

An experience of Abraham furnishes us a good illustration of how God must first conquer our wills and our minds in order to possess us. There was a time when Abraham had a problem with Lot. Friction arose between their herdsmen and the only solution was for the two groups to separate. Abraham, knowing God and wanting only His will, told Lot to choose whatever part of the land he wanted. Abraham did not make the first choice but left it to God to make the provision for him.

What was the result? God gave Abraham the title deed to all the land. Lot, on the other hand, lost everything. He was not possessed of the Lord. He had not turned his will over to the Lord. He chose what looked good to him, acting on self-will and not surrender. Let us be sure to allow God to choose our part in the inheritance for us.

In dividing the land of Canaan, the decision was based on the casting of lots. This was not gambling, but a method ordained of God whereby His will was made known to those involved. God chose the inheritance for each tribe and group and His decision was the best one for the parties involved. Let us with equal confidence surrender ourselves to the Lord so that He might choose to give us what is His for us in Christ.

The Lord does not equip us all alike for service. Some have one gift and some another. Here in our organization at Back to the Bible Broadcast, some persons are good musicians. There are others who are not talented in this line but in other lines. Their talent is just as much God-given as is the musicians'. So let us allow God to give us what He wants and by faith claim it, appropriating it through the Holy Spirit.

The Israelites were reminded that there was "yet very much land to be possessed." Even after years of hard fighting and with Joshua's ministry drawing to a close, the Israelites still had not possessed all that God had for them.

The initial victories concerning the conquering of the land had already been won. We have seen how Israel's deliverance at the Red Sea was not only the mark of their release from the Egyptian army, but the beginning of their conquering of Canaan. The Canaanites were filled with dread when they learned how God had delivered His people Israel from the Egyptians. Then when the Israelites passed over Jordan and entered Canaan, the people of the land were terrified. The hearts of their leaders melted with fear. There was no spirit left in them. There was no question concerning the outcome of the conquest of Canaan. The problem lay with Israel and their slowness to possess what was already theirs.

We, too, face the same problem with regard to our inheritance in Christ as believers. We need to be reminded again and again that the enemy has already been conquered by Christ. Our inheritance has been set out for us and we need only to appropriate it. Our Lord finished His work on Calvary, then was raised from the grave and ascended on high to sit down at the right hand of the Father. We are told we are seated with Him in heavenly places and so can claim what He has already conquered for us. We have an enthroned position with Him in the heavenlies, and in order to possess that which belongs to us even now as believers, we are to appropriate it by faith through prayer. We are to put on the whole armor of God and to pray with all perseverance and supplication in the Holy Spirit.

We have conquered sin because of Christ's death and now possess His life. It is our responsibility to conquer sin in our daily experience and to lay hold of the spiritual blessings that are ours in Christ.

The Israelites conquered the nations of Canaan, but they had to dispossess the land of them before they could possess the land themselves. And so, as we have pointed out, we too in Christ Jesus, since we have been identified in His death, have the privilege of conquering over sin and also possessing His life. When we do, the fruit of His indwelling will be seen.

The Lord Jesus could not do many great works in Galilee because of the unbelief of the people. It is this same sin that keeps us who are Christians from possessing our possessions in Christ. There is a difference between unbelief and disbelief. Christians who know the truth but do not appropriate it show unbelief. They do not deny the fact but they fail to make it real in their experience. Disbelief on the other hand is a rejection of the truth altogether.

It is not our intention to cover all of the Book of Joshua in these studies. We will take up some of the important principles laid down and analyze them and apply them.

Possession Versus Coexistence

Some of the tribes failed to fully possess what was theirs. We read in Joshua 16:9,10: "And the separate cities for the children of Ephraim were among the inheritance of the children of Manasseh, all the cities with their villages. And they drave not out the Canaanites that dwelt in Gezer: but the Canaanites dwell among the Ephraimites unto this day, and serve under tribute." This was coexistence. The Israelites lived side by side with the people of Canaan. They had conquered them and put them under tribute—but had not destroyed them so they could possess their land. In this way these tribes failed to possess their inheritance. They allowed their enemies to live among them.

The same truth is seen in Joshua 17:13. This was not according to God's program. Israel went as far as conquering the foe but not dispossessing their enemies.

In the same chapter in the section following, we read how the children of Joseph wanted more land and Joshua told them they could get it if they would go ahead and conquer it as they were instructed to. Joshua reminded them, "Thou art a great people, and hast great power: thou shalt not have one lot only: But the mountain shall be thine . . . drive out the Canaanites, though they have iron chariots and though they be strong." The Israelites did go ahead and conquer that area but there is no record that they drove out the inhabitants.

The same is true of many of God's children today. Some of us claim to have come a long way in our Christian lives, giving as evidence the fact that there are many things we don't do now that we used to do. Possibly we can point to sins that are no longer committed by us. But are we living in His power? Is the Holy Spirit's power in our lives evident for total victory so that the world can see what things are really taking place in our lives?

Seven Tribes That Failed

Joshua 18 starts on a sad note. We read in verse 1: "And the whole congregation of the children of Israel assembled together in Shiloh, and set up the tabernacle of the congregation there. And the land was subdued before them." The land was conquered. The hard battle for it was over. Yet we learn, "And there remained among the children of Israel

seven tribes, which had not yet received their inheritance."
That means they had not gone into the land to possess it. It
had been given to them but they had not gone in to receive
it. No wonder Joshua admonished them saying, "How long
are ye slack to go to possess the land, which the Lord God of
your fathers hath given you?"

Another translation puts it this way: "What? Still hanging
back, when the land promised by the Lord God of your
fathers waits for you to occupy it?" The land was waiting for
them. Yet they failed to occupy it.

In Joshua 21:43 we read: "And the Lord gave unto Israel
all the land which he sware to give unto their fathers; and
they possessed it, and dwelt therein." The thought is that
they had a home in which they could settle. The Lord gave
them rest round about from their enemies and, "There failed
not ought of any good thing which the Lord had spoken unto
the house of Israel; all came to pass" (21:45). But they did
not go in to possess it. They subdued the people and made
them pay tribute. This was coexistence, not dispossession.
This program was a fruitful source of trouble for Israel. It is
also a dangerous one for us to follow with regard to sin and
the failure to possess our possessions in Christ.

Chapter Nineteen

THE FAITHFULNESS OF GOD
(Joshua 23)

Joshua's Wise Counsel

Some 25 years after Joshua took over the leadership of Israel he realized that his days of ministry were drawing to a close. He called the people and their elders together and God through him imparted some wise counsel to the nation. The scripture source for this is Joshua 23. First we are told how the inheritance was secured. This is given in verse 3: "And ye have seen all that the Lord your God hath done unto all these nations because of you; for the Lord your God is he that hath fought for you." Joshua reminded the Israelites that the record of the conquest was the record of what God had wrought on their behalf. They had been taken from Egypt, the house of bondage, to the place of a separate nation honored in God's sight in the land of Canaan.

We, too, have been taken from a place of sin and condemnation and put in a place of blessing and victory. We read in II Corinthians 5:17: "If any man be in Christ, he is a new creature; old things are passed away; behold, all things are become new." We, too, have a deliverance from day to day as Israel had deliverance from its enemies in Canaan. It is the Lord's battle still, for the enemies that are ranged against us—the world, the flesh and the Devil—are too much for us in ourselves. Our power is insufficient. But with God on our side our power is unlimited. This is what Israel found on entering Canaan and is true in our individual spiritual experiences as we follow Christ from victory to victory.

238

Three Steps

The first step in securing the inheritance is given in verses 4,5: "Behold, I have divided unto you by lot these nations that remain, to be an inheritance for your tribes, from Jordan, with all the nations that I have cut off, even unto the great sea westward. And the Lord your God, he shall expel them from before you, and drive them from out of your sight; and ye shall possess their land, as the Lord your God hath promised unto you." This tells us of a work that God had done. He had divided the nations that had been cut off. The land they had controlled was now the inheritance of the Israelites who were to go in and possess it. Furthermore, the Lord promised that He had divided all the land of the nations that still remained. So far as He was concerned the work was done. Yet, He promised the Israelites that He would expel even those Canaanites who remained, for God had no intention of stopping short of complete victory. This was prophetic and was an encouragement for the Israelites to venture by faith in possessing the rest of the land.

The application to our own spiritual lives is clear. God has begun a good work in us and will perform it until the day of Jesus Christ. What He began He will continue and He will finish. There is nothing impossible with Him. God's promise to us is to remove any mountain that may stand in the way (Mark 11:23).

It was a sad commentary on Israel that after God had wrought victory for them all through Canaan, seven tribes failed to possess their inheritance.

The record continues in Joshua 23:6: "Be ye therefore very courageous to keep and to do all that is written in the book of the law of Moses, that ye turn not aside therefrom to the right hand or to the left." To be courageous in the face of dangers confronting them was not only God's will but His command. This is equally true with regard to us today. We are to be courageous in godly living as we seek to live according to the Word of God. All three members of the

Trinity are working in our behalf so that all we have to do is by faith accept and appropriate what has been provided.

We may face defeat at times, but we are not to dwell upon our defeat. We are to return to the Lord, confess our wrongdoing, forsake it and go on with Him. We are to forget those things which are behind. There is more land to be possessed.

A negative admonition follows. Joshua said, "That ye come not among these nations, these that remain among you." There were still many of the pagan peoples remaining in Canaan but Israel was not to have fellowship with them. God's people were not to copy the heathen forms of worship, but to be completely separated from them. There was to be no coexistence with the enemy.

This is also the Christian life. There is to be a putting off of what is evil and a putting on of the armor of God. The Israelites were to cleave to the Lord their God and put off the ways and beliefs of the Canaanites.

We learn in verses 9 and 10 that nothing can stand before the man who will dare to trust God. "For the Lord hath driven out from before you great nations and strong; but as for you, no man hath been able to stand before you unto this day. One man of you shall chase a thousand: for the Lord your God, he it is that fighteth for you, as he hath promised you." Everything is in the favor of those who trust God. With God on their side, total victory is assured.

This is true with regard to us in our spiritual warfare. The enemies are great and more powerful than we, but they are helpless when we go in the strength of the Lord Jesus Christ.

Admonition is added to these assurances as Joshua speaks to the people. He warned them that they must be careful how they conducted themselves and that they, above all, must love the Lord. This positive and then negative approach would serve to alert Israel to their blessings and also to their dangers.

Joshua continued in verse 12, warning that if the Israelites went among the people and went back from following the Lord and cleaved "unto the remnant of these nations, even these that remain among you, and shall make marriages with them, and go in unto them, and they to you: Know for a certainty that the Lord your God will no more drive out any of these nations from before you; but they shall be snares and traps unto you, and scourges in your sides, and thorns in your eyes, until ye perish from off this good land which the Lord your God hath given you" (vv. 12,13).

We too have been warned not to seek to coexist with sin. We are not to make any covenant whatsoever with our spiritual enemies. In II Corinthians 6:14-17 we read: "Be ye not unequally yoked together with unbelievers: for what fellowship hath righteousness with unrighteousness? and what communion hath light with darkness? And what concord hath Christ with Belial? or what part hath he that believeth with an infidel? And what agreement hath the temple of God with idols? for ye are the temple of the living God; as God hath said, I will dwell in them, and walk in them; and I will be their God, and they shall be my people. Wherefore come out from among them, and be ye separate, saith the Lord, and touch not the unclean thing; and I will receive you." The application is not hard to follow. Just as the Israelites could not hope to improve the Canaanites, neither can we hope to improve the flesh nature. That old nature is unchangeably evil and will only bring us misery. To suggest that we become more like the worldlings around us in order to win them is a doctrine of demons and not wisdom from God.

The admonition in verse 11 already alluded to says, "Take good heed therefore unto yourselves, that ye love the Lord your God." The word for "love" here is not mere human love but a God-given love. It is not a love that is divided in its affections, but is centered wholly on the Lord.

Lot's wife was a person whose heart was divided. She knew the will of the Lord, but her heart yearned for some of the things of Sodom.

Joshua admonished the Israelites not to go back but to keep on going forward. All evil things were to be driven out from before them so that the Israelites would not be ensnared by them.

The same applies to us. We must not turn back in defeat but go forward in Christian victory. There are evil things that will entangle us and ensnare us, so we must get rid of them. These may be but little things in our lives, but it is the little foxes that spoil the vines. The little things can destroy us.

We are warned in Hebrews 12:1 to "lay aside every weight, and the sin which doth so easily beset us, and let us run with patience the race that is set before us." Nothing is to be allowed to hinder us. The weights spoken of in this passage may not be sins, but they could lead to sin or at least they could hinder us. There is a danger of losing what we have gained. We can be sure of this: our sin will find us out.

Three Possible Losses

Three losses are possible for the believer as they were possible for Israel. Joshua warned that the Lord would not drive out the nations before Israel unless Israel went on in faith. So first there would be the *loss of power.* God removes His power when He is not honored and when His child is out of the will and plan He has ordained. Samson is a good example of this. When he turned aside to follow his own will, he lost his power.

We read in John 15 that if we do not continue in union with Christ we *shall not be able to bear fruit.* Separation from the Vine separates us from victory. And such separation grieves the Holy Spirit. To turn from light is to turn toward darkness. There is no neutral ground.

The passage goes on to point out that there will also be a *loss of comfort.* The enemies would ensnare Israel, trap them, scourge them, put thorns in their paths until they perished from off the land.

What a calamity when the soul runs from God and remains comfortable. This was why God warned He would take away His comfort from Israel.

I believe that the greatest mercy God can show any of His

children is to awaken our conscience when we sin. Let us beware when a man is completely comfortable in an evil path. If his conscience does not trouble him he is in an insecure place.

When our consciences bother us, we should come to God and talk to Him about what is troubling us. We must not go back to the world, for that will only lead to further disaster.

In the third place, the Israelites were warned against the complete loss of capacity. They were told they would perish from off the land if they continued to reject the way of God.

Backsliding is progressive. We can see this from Psalm 1 where we are told what the blessed man does not do. He does not walk in the counsel of the ungodly nor stand in the way of sinners, nor sit in the seat of the scornful. This is a progression in evil that the man of God avoids when he walks with the Lord; but this is the very course he will follow if he backslides and persists in it.

Israel was promised that if they were willing and obedient they would eat of the good of the land. But if they refused and rebelled, they would be destroyed with the sword. This principle is ever operative in God's dealing with His people.

Chapter Twenty

THE FINAL CHARGE TO FAITHFULNESS
(Joshua 24)

Recognizing that his death was imminent, Joshua told the Israelites that he was going the way of all the earth and then reminded them, "Ye know in all your hearts and in all your souls, not one thing hath failed of all the good things which the Lord your God spake concerning you; all are come to pass unto you, and not one thing hath failed thereof" (Josh. 23:14). What a faithful God! What He promised He fulfilled.

As I think back over my own life and God's dealing with us at Back to the Bible Broadcast, I, too, have to say that not one thing God has promised has failed. I have failed at times to appropriate what God has for me, but He has never failed. It is this very fact that should cause us to press on with Him. He is faithful and willing, in fact eagerly desirous to see us go on to the end in victory. So why not appropriate all things that God has provided for us?

A serious warning is also given. God was faithful in keeping His promises to the Israelites. He was faithful in blessing. He was equally faithful in judgment when that was necessary. Here is what Joshua said: "Therefore it shall come to pass, that as all good things are come upon you, which the Lord your God promised you; so shall the Lord bring upon you all evil things, until he have destroyed you from off this good land which the Lord your God hath given you. When ye have transgressed the covenant of the Lord your God, which he commanded you, and have gone and served other gods, and bowed yourselves to them; then shall the anger of the Lord be kindled against you, and ye shall perish quickly from off the good land which he hath given unto you" (vv. 15,16).

This message was necessary to Israel. They failed by neglect, carelessness and lack of faith, to appropriate everything that God had given to them for an inheritance.

The same warning is needed by us. God has offered us everything in Christ. He will not fail, but if we go back in our Christian experience we will be the losers. To know truth and not obey it is to retrogress. God wants us to grow in the knowledge of Christ and appropriate by faith all that has been provided for us.

God said to Israel in Psalm 81: "I am the Lord thy God, which brought thee out of the land of Egypt: open thy mouth wide, and I will fill it. But my people would not hearken to my voice; and Israel would none of me. So I gave them up unto their own hearts' lust: and they walked in their own counsels" (vv. 10-12). God's illustrations are graphic. Israel is pictured as a bird in the nest waiting to be fed. Its mouth is wide open to receive whatever the parent bird will bring. But Israel would not obey God. She rejected God's provision and so He had to give the Israelites up to their own desires and counsels and the judgments that followed.

We are reminded in Galatians 6:7 that whatsoever a man sows that shall he also reap. God will not be mocked either by His people Israel or by the people of God today.

Joshua's Charge to Israel

In this final part of his discourse, Joshua rehearsed God's wonderful deliverances of Israel beginning with God's calling of the people in Abraham and His protection and leading of the patriarchs, Isaac and Jacob. Israel's deliverance from Egypt, the opening of the Red Sea and the destruction of Pharaoh's army are briefly retold. God's protection and provision for them in the wilderness, His deliverance of them from the Amorites, from those who would have enslaved them and tried to curse them, and His bringing Israel safely into Canaan, giving them a glorious land as a gift are recounted. Then Joshua added that God did not give them the possessions in Canaan because they deserved them. They

did not merit His gifts. God said, "I have given you the land
for which you did not labour, the cities which you did not
build, you dwelt in them and all of the vineyards and all the
which you did not plant, I have given them to you."

Then Joshua said, "Fear the Lord, and serve him in
sincerity and in truth: and put away the gods which your
fathers served on the other side of the flood, and in Egypt;
and serve ye the Lord. And if it seem evil unto you to serve
the Lord, choose you this day whom ye will serve; whether
the gods which your fathers served that were on the other
side of the flood, or the gods of the Amorites, in whose land
ye dwell: but as for me and my house, we will serve the
Lord" (vv. 14,15).

Joshua admonished the people first of all to fear the
Lord. This does not mean to be afraid of Him but to place
reverential trust in Him. With such trust in the Lord they
would follow Him with confidence. With such fear of the
Lord there would be a hatred for evil. So what he was asking
the Israelites to do was to have an attitude of heart of
complete trust in God. Because of this, then, they would
avoid evil and walk in faith.

The second admonition was to serve the Lord. Israel was
to serve Him in sincerity and in truth. After a proper attitude
of heart comes the activity of the mind and the body. To
serve in truth means to serve in perfection and with stability.
For us this means to serve the Lord now with a perfect heart.
We must put on the whole armor of God so that we can stand
against the wiles of the Devil. We need this in order to fight
the battles of the Lord successfully.

Joshua warned the Israelites, in the third place, to put
away those things which God did not allow. The idolatry so
characteristic of Canaan with all its attendant evil, unbelief,
carelessness and backsliding was to be put away. It was not a
matter of following majority opinion, but finding out what
God wanted and doing it. Joshua made it very plain that the
Israelites had to choose whom they would serve. We, too,
face the same issue.

We cannot be neutral. Many try to be, but they are not

really neutral; instead they are negative. We must choose positively to go on with the Lord.

Perhaps some of these things we have covered in this Book have been hard to understand. It is the meat of the Word and will help us to grow into spiritual maturity. Failure to understand some of these things is not a reason to be discouraged, for we have the promise of spiritual enlightenment if we will press on. Paul said to the Philippians that he was forgetting those things which are behind and reaching forth to the things that were before and pressing toward the mark of the prize of the high calling of God in Christ Jesus (Phil. 3:14). The Apostle then added: "Let us therefore, as many as be perfect [mature], be thus minded: and if in anything ye be otherwise minded, God shall reveal even this unto you." In other words, if there is something that we do not understand, God will reveal it to us if we will give Him time. For this we must wait upon Him, trusting Him to open up our spiritual eyes through the Holy Spirit. We must also be determined to go ahead.

The admonition of Philippians 3:16 also urges us to go ahead: "Nevertheless, whereto we have already attained, let us walk by the same rule, let us mind the same thing." We may not have reached final maturity, none of us have, but let us press on with no thought of going backward at all. Go on from where you are spiritually to attain even higher goals. Joshua's own personal testimony was, "As for me and my house [my family], we will serve the Lord."

How could Joshua be so emphatic with regard to his family? For himself, yes, but what about the others? First of all, he had taught his house well. In the second place, they were no doubt completely committed to the Lord, and Joshua was trusting the Lord to keep them. We have the same promise for us today. It is for our house—for the father and mother to trust the Lord for their children. It is the parents responsibility to seek to lead the children to faith in the Lord, and then they can trust that God will keep these children in the faith. It is God's purpose to bring all of His people to the place of maturity, and we should join Him in this desire and prayer. Let us learn, then, to commit our families to the Lord in this way.

It is true that each one must make a personal choice for himself. Each one must give an account to God. Nevertheless, we can trust God to work in each individual heart. But if we neglect our responsibility to our loved ones and are careless with regard to our own life and become indifferent, we need not expect to see this goal attained. Joshua had taught his family and committed them and knew that God would lead them through.

Each one, as we have noted, must give an account to the Lord. Concerning Christians the Scripture says, "For we must all appear before the judgment seat of Christ; that every one may receive the things done in his body . . . whether it be good or bad" (II Cor. 5:10). The word "bad" in this context means it is not good for anything whatsoever.

The people were decided and definite in their reaction to Joshua's admonition: "And the people answered and said, God forbid that we should forsake the Lord, to serve other gods." Then they continued: "For the Lord our God, he it is that brought us up and our fathers out of the land of Egypt, from the house of bondage, and which did those great signs in our sight, and preserved us in all the way wherein we went, and among all the people through whom we passed." The people responded with a definite decision to follow the Lord.

Warning the people that they were making no light decision, Joshua said to them: "Ye cannot serve the Lord: for he is an holy God; he is a jealous God; he will not forgive your transgressions nor your sins" (v. 19). They needed this reminder. God is holy and cannot coexist with sin. He is a jealous God and will not take a secondary place. We cannot serve God and live in sin.

The lesson for us is inescapable. He indwells us, but for us to have fellowship with Him we must give Him first place. He will not coexist with our self-made ideas.

The Israelites assured Joshua that they would obey the Lord, for they said, "Nay; but we will serve the Lord. And Joshua said unto the people, Ye are witnesses against yourselves that you have chosen you the Lord, to serve him. And they said, We are witnesses."

There was even a covenant made and Joshua took a great stone and placed it under an oak as a witness of the people's intention to serve God.

The generation that made the promise were true to their word. We learn in verse 31: "And Israel served the Lord all the days of Joshua, and all the days of the elders that overlived Joshua, and which had known all the works of the Lord, that he had done for Israel." This was a good beginning, and what a different history we would have had, had each succeeding generation of Israelites reached the same decision and stayed with it.

Chapter Twenty-one

FAILURE TO APPLY TOTAL FAITH
(Judges 1, 2)

The greatest poverty in our day is found among Christians who, though not necessarily materially poor, are spiritually so because of lack of faith. It is no light matter for God's people to turn aside from the provision He has made for them. Israel found this to her sorrow; and we too will find what happens when we do not take possession of that which God has in store for us in Christ Jesus.

We found that after Joshua's last charge to the people of Israel, they responded by promising complete faithfulness to God. All the rest of the days of Joshua and the days of those leaders who outlived him, the Israelites were true to their pledge. But when we turn to the Book of Judges, we find what happened to succeeding generations who did not give God this wholehearted allegiance.

We have seen before that we cannot possess what we do not first dispossess. We cannot possess what someone else has control of. Israel could not possess that portion of Canaan where they coexisted with the Canaanites even though the Canaanites were their slaves. Instead of destroying the Canaanites or driving them out as God had commanded, the Israelites in many areas allowed them to live in their midst. It was not a complete victory for God's people. Time after time we are told how they failed to go all the way to accomplish God's purpose. Passage after passage tells us the same story.

"Neither did Manasseh drive out the inhabitants of Beth-shean" (Judges 1:27).

In verse 28 we learn that when Israel was strong "they put the Canaanites to tribute, and did not utterly drive them out."

250

"Neither did Ephraim drive out the Canaanites that dwelt in Gezer" (v. 29).

"Neither did Zebulun drive out the inhabitants of Kitron" (v. 30).

"Neither did Asher drive out the inhabitants of Accho" (v. 31).

"Neither did Naphtali drive out the inhabitants of Beth-shemesh . . . he dwelt among the Canaanites . . . nevertheless the inhabitants of Beth-shemesh and of Beth-anath became tributaries unto them" (v. 33).

"And the Amorites forced the children of Dan into the mountain: for they would not suffer them to come down to the valley" (v. 34).

"Yet the hand of the house of Joseph prevailed, so that they [Amorites] became tributaries" (v. 35).

This is the story of the seven tribes of Israel that did not completely dispossess the inhabitants and thus possess the land for themselves. God said to drive out these Canaanites, for their cup of sin was full. Israel was to get rid of them and then to dwell where they had dwelt.

There are things that God has told us to get rid of in our lives. And there is no need for us to protest that we cannot, because Christ died and rose again to make it possible for us to do so. Furthermore, we have the Holy Spirit indwelling us so that Christ now indwells us through the Holy Spirit to live out His life in us. Thus day by day we can, by faith, overcome in the spiritual warfare and be victors through Christ.

What follows when we fail to do God's will is pictured for us in Israel's experience. In chapter 2 of Judges we read beginning with verse 11: "And the children of Israel did evil in the sight of the Lord, and served Baalim." The reason was they had allowed the Canaanites to stay among them and were corrupted by their idolatrous living. The Canaanites dragged Israel down to their low level.

Some seem to think we have to meet the world on its level in order to reach its followers for Christ. But they can never be won in this way. Not until they see that we have something they do not have will they begin to respond to the gospel. And it will be only then that the Holy Spirit can give them the desire and longing for the things that we possess.

The people of Israel did what was wrong in the sight of the Lord, and forsook Him who was the God of their fathers. They followed the gods of the heathen around them and thereby provoked the true God to anger.

We read in verses 13,14: "And they forsook the Lord . . . and the anger of the Lord was hot against Israel, and he delivered them into the hands of spoilers that spoiled them, and he sold them into the hands of their enemies round about, so that they could not any longer stand before their enemies." God simply took off His protecting hand from them and as much as said, "All right, you have refused to take what I give you; therefore, I will let you have what you want."

What did they get? They received bondage. They were made to serve the heathen and the Lord let them continue that way. He did not fight their battles for them any longer. Different areas of the country became subject to various heathen kings. But let us never forget that God is still a God of grace and mercy. His longsuffering is amazing. We read in verse 16: "Nevertheless the Lord raised up judges, which delivered them out of the hand of those that spoiled them." This is very much the course of the Book of Judges. Some 14 times God permitted the people of Israel or a part of the nation, at least, to succumb to their enemies. Then, after they cried out in their distress and began to return to the Lord after five, ten, fifteen or even up to forty years, God would send them a judge. He was a leader who in the name of the Lord would claim victory and lead the people to victory. So they would be free for a time until that judge died.

The record says, "And when the Lord raised them up judges, then the Lord was with the judge, and delivered them out of the hand of their enemies all the days of the judge . . . And it came to pass, when the judge was dead, that they [Israel] returned, and corrupted themselves more than their fathers, in following other gods."

Their spiritual condition was up and down, a condition which lasted some 400 years while God dealt with them in grace and mercy. He was longsuffering and sent them judge after judge to deliver them.

Then we have the account in Judges 2:20: "And the anger of the Lord was hot against Israel; and he said, Because that this people hath transgressed my covenant which I commanded their fathers, and have not hearkened unto my voice; I also will not henceforth drive out any from before them of the nations which Joshua left when he died: that through them I may prove Israel, whether they will keep the way of the Lord to walk therein, as their fathers did . . . Therefore the Lord left those nations, without driving them out hastily; neither delivered he them into the hand of Joshua." So this is the sad condition into which the people of Israel were plunged because they would not follow the Lord.

The lesson is obvious for us. If after we know the truth of the victory provided for us in Christ Jesus (for the Lord always causes us to triumph in Christ Jesus), we do not follow, then chastisement must fall. If we do not take a definite stand against sin and the self-life, we must face the consequences. It is this rebellious attitude of mind and heart that is the root cause of much of the useless kind of Christianity we see today. There are Christians who have a ticket to heaven but who are useless to God, failing to accomplish anything for Him.

Chapter Twenty-two

THE CONSEQUENCES OF UNFAITHFULNESS
(I Sam. 15)

One of the grimmest lessons of all in this connection begins back in the seventeenth chapter of Exodus. The first time we met Joshua was as the leader of the forces of Israel against Amalek. Now the Lord gave some very strict instructions to Moses concerning this nation. He said, "Write this for a memorial in a book, and rehearse it in the ears of Joshua: for I will utterly put out the remembrance of Amalek from under heaven" (Ex. 17:14). This was God's decision and promise some 1500 years before Christ. Nearly 500 years after Moses God did something more about this.

Saul was king of Israel at the time God chose to do something more about Amalek. Concerning that heathen people, God said to Israel's king: "I remember that which Amalek did to Israel, how he laid wait for him in the way, when he came up from Egypt. Now go and smite Amalek, and utterly destroy all that they have, and spare them not; but slay both man and woman, infant and suckling, ox and sheep, camel and ass" (I Sam. 15:2,3).

The Amalekites were outstanding transgressors against the Lord. They were unremitting in their opposition to Him and to His people. Even after they had withstood the onward march of Israel under Moses, God gave them another 500 years of opportunity. Yet at the end of that time they were still implacable in their rejection of Him. By the time Saul was made king of Israel the cup of sin of the Amalekites was full.

Amalek was a grandson of Esau, the twin brother of Jacob. Under ordinary circumstances Esau would have had the family birthright. The birthright was not concerned with material things only, but in the case of the birthright through

254

Abraham and Isaac it was mostly spiritual. The man who
inherited the birthright was also responsible to be the
spiritual head of the family. He was to be the priest, in a
sense, to the entire group. He was the one who was to
intercede between them and God. The qualities for this
position were far from being fulfilled by Esau.

We read of him in Hebrews 12:16: "Lest there be a
fornicator, or profane person, as Esau [a profane person is
one of low views, not appreciating the things of God], who
for one morsel of meat sold his birthright. For ye know how
that afterward, when he would have inherited the blessing, he
was rejected: for he found no place for repentance, though
he sought it [the blessing, not repentance] carefully with
tears."

Amalek was definitely a type of the old nature, a picture
of the old flesh. God is not mocked. Whatever a man sows he
will reap. If he sows in the field of his lower nature he will
reap from it a harvest of corruption. If he sows in the field of
the Holy Spirit, the Spirit will bring him a harvest of eternal
life.

There is a battle going on in a believer's heart
continuously. It is a battle between the Spirit and the flesh.
The flesh-life or old nature does not want to take second
place or to be shut out entirely from our lives. It goes on
fighting for recognition. We are told to ignore it completely
and treat it as being non-existent because we have died to it.
Yet it will fight for recognition every step of the way. It will
try to hinder our progress in spiritual life.

The old Adamic nature, the natural fallen tendency in
each one of us, must be put aside. Amalek was as great a
danger to Israel as the fallen nature is to us. This was the
reason God commanded Saul to go and fight against Amalek
and destroy it completely.

How this is done in a spiritual way in our lives is
illustrated for us also in Exodus. This is review once more,
but it is something we easily forget. It was through
intercession by Moses that the battle was won in the valley

by Joshua and his army. It took the prayer life to bring victory on the battlefield.

We have a greater intercessor than Moses. This one who is Christ our High Priest is at the right hand of God the Father, making intercession for us. We have no reason whatever for suffering defeat and giving in to the flesh nature. The Lord Jesus is able to save us to the uttermost seeing He ever lives to make intercession for us. The flesh is as a dead thing if we will take up the battle of faith against it. All the people in Canaan were as good as dead if only Israel had gone in and taken the victory God provided for them. Yet it was 500 years later and God had to say to Saul to go out and get rid of Amalek. Yet once again God was disobeyed. In this case Saul failed Him, because he spared of Amalek what he considered to be the best.

The record is, "And he took Agag the king of the Amalekites alive, and utterly destroyed all the people with the edge of the sword. But Saul and the people spared Agag, and the best of the sheep, and of the oxen, and of the fatlings, and the lambs, and all that was good, and would not utterly destroy them: but every thing that was vile and refuse, that they destroyed utterly" (I Sam. 15:8,9).

Remember, there is no good thing in the flesh. God challenged Saul through Samuel in these words: "And the Lord sent thee on a journey, and said, Go and utterly destroy the sinners the Amalekites, and fight against them until they be consumed. Wherefore then didst thou not obey the voice of the Lord, but didst fly upon the spoil, and didst evil in the sight of the Lord?" (vv. 18,19).

When will we believe God? Paul came to the place where he saw that in his flesh dwelt no good thing. Do we realize that it is true for ourselves and for others also?

Saul shifted the blame from himself to the people when he said, "But the people took of the spoil, sheep and oxen, the chief of the things which should have been utterly destroyed, to sacrifice unto the Lord thy God in Gilgal" (v. 21).

The answer through Samuel left Saul no ground to stand

on: "Hath the Lord as great delight in burnt offerings and sacrifices, as in obeying the voice of the Lord? Behold, to obey is better than sacrifice, and to hearken than the fat of rams" (v. 22). God will not accept any righteousness produced by the flesh. Saul's excuse was that he was afraid of the people. God, however, reminded him that obedience is more important than sacrifice. Saul had been told to get rid of Amalek and had disobeyed. How about us with regard to the flesh and the control of the flesh-nature over us? God tells us to make this matter of our deliverance through Christ a reality in our experience. We are to reckon ourselves dead to sin but alive to God.

So far as Saul is concerned, the matter did not end with his disobedience at that time. Years later, though Saul was still king, he was rejected by God. As he led the Israelites out to fight the Philistines, he found himself in a very deplorable situation. Just before the battle he had gone to a witch to find out the outcome of the fight, for he could not get in contact with God. God was no longer telling Saul what to do or what not to do. It was not that Saul was lost to God; for, to the consternation of the witch, Samuel had briefly appeared to tell Saul that on the morrow he and his sons would be where Samuel was. The former prophet and judge was in the place God provided for the believing dead.

In chapter 31 of I Samuel we learn that the battle went against Saul. He was sorely wounded by archers and fearing lest the Philistines would come upon him and kill him and mutilate his body, Saul asked his armor-bearer to kill him with his sword. This he would not do. "Therefore Saul took a sword, and fell upon it. And when the armourbearer saw that Saul was dead, he fell likewise upon his sword, and died with him."

So Saul attempted to commit suicide because he did not want to fall into the hands of the Philistines. From the human standpoint that was the only thing he could think of that would remedy the situation for him. The armor-bearer, looking upon him, seemingly thought he was dead. But we learn something more from II Samuel.

We learn there in the first chapter the story told David concerning Saul's death. According to a report by a certain young man who claimed to have come upon Saul on Mount Gilboa, Saul was wounded but not dead. The young man said, "He looked behind him, he saw me, and called unto me. And I answered, Here am I . . . he said unto me again, Stand, I pray thee, upon me, and slay me: for anguish is come upon me, because my life is yet whole in me. So I stood upon him, and slew him, because I was sure that he could not live after that he was fallen: and I took the crown that was upon his head, and the bracelet that was on his arm, and have brought them hither unto my lord" (vv. 7-10).

David was saddened at the news of Saul's death and mourned exceedingly. Then David asked the young man, "Whence art thou?" (v. 13). Here was the shocking answer: "I am the son of a stranger, an Amalekite."

Saul, by sparing a few of the Amalekites, had given life to his own slayer. This young man had evidently joined the army of the Philistines and eventually took the life of Saul.

The Amalekite thought he was going to get a reward from David, but David was a righteous man who was angered that anyone would lay his hand on God's anointed. The young Amalekite was slain on the basis of his own confession.

It seems that not only did Saul spare Agag the king of the Amalekites, but apparently his household as well. Another descendant of Agag was a prominent man in the days when the Jews were ruled by the Persians. Haman, the last of the Agagites, almost accomplished his purpose of wiping out the entire Jewish nation. But God stepped in and Haman lost his life instead. We cannot fool God. Whatever a man sows he will reap.

Obedience to God is the way to all blessing from His hand. He has provided all we need to make such obedience a reality. "He that spared not his own Son, but delivered him up for us all, how shall he not with him also freely give us all things?" (Rom. 8:32). Everything is in our favor. There is nothing to stop our growth. Let us heed the admonition of Hebrews 6:1: "Therefore leaving the principles of the doctrine of Christ, let us go on unto perfection (spiritual maturity)."

> Fight the good fight with all thy might!
> Christ is thy strength, and Christ thy right;
> Lay hold on life, and it shall be
> Thy joy and crown eternally.
>
> Run the straight race through God's good grace,
> Lift up thine eyes, and seek His face;
> Life with its way before us lies,
> Christ is the path, and Christ the prize.
>
> Cast care aside, lean on thy Guide,
> His boundless mercy will provide;
> Trust, and thy trusting soul shall prove
> Christ is its life, and Christ its love.
>
> Faint not nor fear, His arms are near,
> He changeth not, and thou art dear;
> Only believe, and thou shalt see
> That Christ is all in all to thee.